BETWEEN THE MENORAH AND THE CROSS

BETWEEN THE MENORAH AND THE CROSS

Jesus, The Jews, and The Battle
for The Early Church

STEPHEN BEEBE

To order additional copies of this book, contact:
Xlibris Corporation
1-888-795-4274
www.Xlibris.com
Orders@Xlibris.com
37255

DEDICATION

This treatise is dedicated to the memory of my grandmother,
Ruth Bovell Beebe, who was my example of faith during my own years of
alienation from religion, and whom I still miss; and to her sister Mabel,
who gave her life in the path of Christian service.

CONTENTS

Acknowledgements ix

Chapter 1: Jacob's pillow: A scientific materialist reconciles with Christianity.... 1

Chapter 2: From Abraham to Jesus: The building blocks of faith................. 10

Chapter 3: Jewish roots and Camelot lost... 25

Chapter 4: The synagogue: Something new under the sun........................... 37

Chapter 5: The Early Church: Two poles of a new faith 51

Chapter 6: Loose canon on deck: Christian Scripture in the early years....... 66

Chapter 7: The kingdom of Christ: Surprise answers to Jewish questions 81

Chapter 8: Resurrection and spirit: Options for the afterlife?...................... 92

Chapter 9: Holy Spirit: A glimpse into the soul of the Prophets 108

Chapter 10: Sin, sacrifice, and redemption: Go and sin no more 121

Chapter 11: Crisis in the church: Caught between two extremes 139

Notes 151

Index 157

Acknowledgements

The author wishes to express his gratitude to Annie Jones for her careful editing of the manuscript; to Kurosh Sadeghian and Diego Bolaños for help with the cover art; to Lynne Yancy for her review of the manuscript; and to Wendy Momen and Lee Minnerly for their encouragement.

CHAPTER 1

JACOB'S PILLOW: A SCIENTIFIC MATERIALIST RECONCILES WITH CHRISTIANITY

The crowd gazes at Jesus. They surround Him on all sides, with different motives and reactions. Their eyes reflect a range of emotions and conflicting attitudes—curiosity, adoration, and hostility—all can be read on their faces. Some respond with their hearts, and their love wells up spontaneously. Others respond with their intellect, and bring their questions; still others look on with suspicion. Who is this Nazarene? Why is He here? What does He want from us? A world of emotions from this microcosm of humanity swells and ebbs as He speaks, teaches, proclaims, instructs, touches, heals, uplifts.

Jesus gazes into the crowd, and while our eyes do not quite meet, I feel a distinct sense of discomfort move within me, anticipating the possibility that He might look directly at me. It is a feeling akin to panic that I least expect, and it catches me by surprise because I did not realize beforehand that I am so ill prepared to respond to Him. I do not find within myself that reaction that leads to immediate acceptance, nor can I walk away as if I had never seen Him. Even if He does not utter a single word, His very presence issues an imperative. By every standard of human action I have to respond to that imperative, and I have to respond to it positively, yet that response sticks in my heart like words that stick in your throat—words that you have every intention of articulating, but that never quite break through into communication. I am trapped in my own ambivalence, capable neither of ignoring Him, nor of facing up to the conclusions that I know to be the truth.

The fact that a distance of two thousand years lies between Jesus and myself does not make that sense of discomfort any less vivid. I am acutely aware that I am before One who towers over me in rank, and I feel thoroughly naked and susceptible, as if my shortcomings are as transparent as glass before Him. So how can I relate to Him?

The adoration of others seems an irritant. How can they approach Him so confidently, while I find myself in a state of limbo, unable either to advance or retreat? Who is this Nazarene? Why is He here? What does He want from me?

The crowd continues to grow and press in upon Him, and I am squeezed back, to the point where He is no longer within sight. I will only be able to see Him through the eyes of those who arrived earlier than I. A handful of witnesses will have to be my eyes—Matthew, Mark, Luke, John, Paul, James, and a few others. And if even they are not firsthand witnesses and their own versions are second- or third-hand testimonies written a generation after the fact, then I will have to content myself with understanding better how they viewed Jesus in their own age at a distance of thirty or forty years. But that will be far better than not understanding anything at all, and seeing Jesus and His Message more clearly through their eyes will serve me to come to terms with Him and with what He expects of me.

I grew up in Iowa in the midst of America's heartland. Iowa is the Corn Belt, not the Bible Belt, but in a sense it is truly the *heart*land, the spiritual heart of the country where Christian fellowship, if not called that explicitly, takes the form of neighborliness and unbounded good will. People here are naïve by others' standards, trusting to a fault, and largely free of malice and ambition. We may be dumb farmers and the butt of jokes for the rest of the country, but to one another we are just neighbors.

In fact the Midwest has some spiritual traditions of its own. The Mormons arrived here from New York and established their center in Illinois for several years until Joseph Smith was assassinated in Carthage in 1844. Nauvoo is still a cultural center for Mormons around the world. The Midwest also gave birth to William Jennings Bryan, the populist firebrand of the turn of the century who took on Darwin in the Scopes trial. He won the battle but lost the war. But Bryan was an exception to the rule. Religion is usually not intense here as it may be elsewhere. Most Midwesterners are not vociferous about religion, to the contrary they are rather shy when it comes to discussing the "R" word, but in their own way they take their religion seriously. A majority are churchgoers, usually raised in some formal belief structure. They graduate from their religious training with an upright character, convinced of their faith, and dedicated in their own low-key way to their Christian duty. They are solid citizens, good Samaritans, and worthy examples of what a Christian upbringing produces.

Not me.

I should have been an upright and respectable Christian like everybody else, or at least I had everything going for me. My upbringing was pretty standard for a farm boy in the 1950s—hard work and an insistence on scrupulous honesty, within that institution called the family farm that died out in the following decades. In virtually every regard I was a docile and obedient child and an exemplary student, and should have accepted religious instruction readily. I was the second of three children, and if psychologists are to be believed about children in the middle, a natural peacemaker. I was even a Libra, and thus supposedly balanced and easygoing.

My parents did not attend church, but my mother had been baptized a Catholic (which was not as odd as one might imagine in eastern Iowa, where several cities and towns enjoy a Catholic majority) and she made every effort in my earliest years to teach me the Lord's Prayer. It was my grandmother, to whom I was especially attached, who kept the religious tradition alive. She was a faithful member of our local church, which at that time had no specific denominational affiliation. The community was rural and small, and had to contract ministers that were willing to make the drive out from town. Thus community members did not have the luxury of committing consistently to one or another doctrinal orientation. They took their preachers where they could find them, and so from year to year the church would swing from fundamentalism to liberal doctrine and back again. Grandma had a college education and did not care for the fundamentalists, and would occasionally come home fuming over some hellfire-and-brimstone sermon on the evils of evolution.

Our family even had a modest religious tradition of its own. Grandma's father was a Baptist minister of the old school who was remembered for his pulpit pounding and howling threats of damnation. Grandma's sister went to China early in the twentieth century to serve in the Missions. That was no mean feat in those days and her diary told of floating down the Yangtze on a raft to escape from local warlords. She died rather young in 1925, but a state history of the Baptists refers to a committee in her name that continued to support the Missions several years after her death.

And me? Did I benefit from this heritage? Did I follow in the footsteps of my forebears in the Christian tradition? Did the nostalgia and inertia of mid-century, heartland America keep me on track? Not quite.

When it came to religion, I was the black sheep, the Esau, the prodigal son, the doubting Thomas. From the very beginning I had problems with religion. My religious training summed to one or two years of Sunday school when my mother would bundle me up in corduroy slacks and ship me off with my grandmother to the local house of worship. For some reason that I do not understand myself, I resisted this ritual vigorously, and would seek any excuse to avoid attendance. I would lurk around corners on Sunday morning hoping that it would escape my mother's attention that it was *that* day of the week until it was too late to get me dressed in the ritual garb. If the fact of it being Sunday had escaped my mother's attention—or if she just did not have the energy for the weekly battle—then I got off the hook. Or if she felt compelled to fulfill her motherly duty and further my moral instruction, then I was stuck.

Sunday school was less than inspiring and consisted of listening to a neighborhood farmwife recite a Bible story that was accompanied by a colored handout picture. After the story we muddled around in Play-Doh for a few minutes until Grandma would reappear to rescue me from spiritual ennui. My shortage of any more significant memories is symptomatic of its lack of influence on me.

Yet one Sunday school lesson did catch my attention and left its mark on me. It was the story of one Hebrew patriarch (I learned later that it was Jacob) who in the course of a journey fell asleep by the side of the road using a rock for a pillow. The image of a stone pillow somehow caught my youthful imagination and was engraved on my memory for all time. A stone for a pillow! What kind of hero sleeps in the rough like that? Even in cowboy movies where ranch hands slept on the ground they had saddles or bedrolls for pillows—not rocks! I was intrigued by the very idea of a stone pillow, and the idea stuck with me. As years passed I thought that such an unlikely scenario must have been a figment of my imagination that I invented in some childish daydream. Thus, it was immensely gratifying while reading the book of Genesis many years later that I found just that story in the history of the patriarchs. It would be overly dramatic to say that I was rediscovering my spiritual roots, but I did experience an unexpected connection to my earliest years to have that one dim and distant childhood memory suddenly confirmed.

Reflecting on this later, I think that Jacob's pillow had more symbolic significance for me than I realized at the time. Although Jacob managed to sleep comfortably and even have a visionary dream out there under the stars, that rock pillow might well have represented something else for me and would have interrupted more sleep than it would have facilitated. The rest and peace that others found in religion was somehow denied me, as if I, too, were sleeping on my own rock pillow, tossing and turning and unable to find that just-right position. My relationship to God was destined to be unsettled for some time to come. And, like Jacob wrestling with the Lord by the river Jabbok, I would wrestle long and hard with God before the day was done.

Besides the story of Jacob's pillow, my other early memory of Judaism took the form of one elderly Jew named Louie Seasons, a short-statured, talkative fellow in a battered hat, who would drive his rusty pickup out to my grandfather's greenhouse every year to buy vegetable plants for spring gardening. Louie's story was curiously intertwined with the family history from many years before, when he had fled Europe on the last boat out of France as World War I was breaking out. My grandmother was studying in Paris at the time and was on that same boat with Louie, a fact that they discovered only years later. Thus, this early firsthand memory of Judaism, trivial as it was, had a familiar Iowa face to it—one that would perhaps make Judaism a naturally friendly topic in future years.

Meanwhile, my relationship with religion was not improving. Apart from the distaste of attending Sunday school, a smoldering doubt made me distrustful of religion, and with time came to be articulated in the following way: "If religion and everything that is associated with it occurred some two to three thousand years ago, and time is destined to advance, then we are all moving away from our religious roots. So how can we know what happened back then, if with every passing minute it is becoming more and more remote from us?" Or, to employ a common metaphor, religious faith is like driving a car by looking in the rearview mirror. How can one derive one's guidance for the future by looking at the past? And the further you drive, the more likely you are to lose sight of your guiding principles altogether.

I do not pretend that this thought is especially novel. Distrust in the distant past with its potential for mythologizing and misinterpretation is by no means uncommon nowadays. For me, it was an instinctive reaction, possibly rooted in a certain linear mentality that eventually led me to study the sciences: A leads to B, which is followed by C and then D, but at some moment knowledge about A is simply irretrievable. We cannot know what really happened in the Big Bang, we cannot know how life really evolved and how dinosaurs disappeared, and we cannot know how Christianity or any other ancient religion really came to be and what its root principles were. Religion is subjective enough as it is, and if the inexorable march of time makes that truth draw further away from us at every moment, then it is all the more suspect.

With the passage of time, that innate distrust of religion grew into adolescent skepticism, which as it became increasingly conscious, was articulated as atheism. And although at that time Marxism was still fashionable in some circles, my disbelief did not share that or any other formal philosophical basis, outside of having adopted a materialistic stance that life was a biological phenomenon and had evolved through natural selection. When I say that I had no philosophical basis for atheism, I mean that I was not moved to atheism by having adopted any philosophical or doctrinal basis. My atheism resulted from simple lack of belief and a vacuum of faith. I thought that biology held sufficient answers about the origins of life, and physics sufficient answers about the origins of the world, to make religious faith superfluous. I was reliving a common materialist experience of the "modern" scientific thinker that flowered in the nineteenth century and that still appears frequently. I simply did not find within me the basis for believing in spiritual reality or a Supreme Being. Jacob's pillow was not getting any softer for me.

I viewed faith as a crutch for those too weak to face life in its stark reality (again, not a very novel idea) and reveled in the imagined heroism of the brave existential soul confronting the meaningless universe. I would have benefited from the playful jabs of one spiritual thinker who said that the cow was the best of materialist philosophers—no agonizing, no rationalizing, just contented peaceful cud chewing in the midst of a materialist reality.

Eventually, when I came full circle and found a door that opened on spiritual transcendence, those childlike questions and distrust of antiquity were no longer an obstacle. My reencounter with religion initiated with the Bahá'í Faith, through which I overcame the one big hurdle of accepting the existence of God. The Bahá'í Faith recognizes the Founders of all great revealed religions as divinely inspired, and so upon becoming a Bahá'í, I was obliged to accept the reality of Christ intellectually. But this was merely the start of a reconciliation that took a long and circuitous route. Although as a Bahá'í I could no longer deny Jesus, neither could I claim to really feel comfortable with Him. Perhaps even worse, in my own immature mindset I now viewed Christianity as a set of doctrines that essentially competed with my own beliefs. This attitude was at odds with the spirit and the letter of the Bahá'í Faith and was a defect to be overcome, and that was only possible by coming to terms with Jesus.

As I said before, the route that I followed was long and circuitous. My road to Christianity started in the Book of Revelation, then doubled back on itself and leapt back to the Old Testament, and finally spiraled in on the Gospels. And at the center of that spiral stood Jesus.

Ironically it was antiquity and, more specifically, a study of Judaism that led me to a fuller reconciliation with Jesus, and permitted me to come to grips with a broader gamut of questions. Nowadays much is said and a lot of energy is spent on studying Judaism, in hopes of finding the historical Jesus and uncovering the real, believable, and factual Central Figure of Christianity that will confirm our faith. Having a historical figure to visualize and cling to, a concrete Being with whom to associate transcendence, is somehow a need felt by many in the modern world. We are familiar with the New Testament accounts and their representation in pictures and movies, but we would like to have some external confirmation for our images of the Son of God on earth, some "scientific" basis drawn from archaeology or historical record. I do not pretend to have discovered "the" historical Jesus any more than the next guy, and that is frankly not my concern. I doubt that we will ever know more than we do now, so the historical Jesus is not the object of this book. My concern is rather with the historical setting in which Jesus lived and moved and taught, and especially in which His followers propagated His Message, because I am convinced that the historical setting has a lot to offer to an understanding of the Message of Christ. And for me it was a study of Judaism that made Jesus and Christianity more coherent. If my foremost memory of Sunday school was of Jacob, then it was Jacob's heritage and descendents who eventually cleared the way to Jesus.

There are at least two reasons for returning to a study of Judaism. First, and quite obviously, Judaism forms the backdrop of Christian doctrine and history. This theme has been central to the scholarly study of the New Testament for all of the twentieth century, and is now frequently finding its way into popular literature as well. When I refer to seeking the Jewish roots of Christian doctrines, I do not mean to imply with this that Christianity simply evolved from previous doctrines in response to historical or political pressures. Nor am I suggesting that Christianity did not represent a quantum shift and a unique event, in relation to Judaism or anything else that preceded it. I am still sufficiently orthodox to believe that the advent of Jesus was a milestone in human history and, even more significantly, an earth-shaking intervention of God in human affairs. However, if we understand better the context in which Jesus lived, spoke, and taught, and in which the Gospel writers set down their testimonies and narratives, this understanding enriches the biblical text as well as revealing intentions and meanings.

The second reason for studying Judaism is, that when we look for historical sources that can complement the New Testament, the historicity of Judaism is firmer than that of Christianity throughout the first century, in spite of being more ancient than Christianity, or rather because of this fact. Extra-biblical sources that describe a primitive Christian community are nearly non-existent, whereas a more ample historical and archaeological record exists (although far from perfect) for Judaism, mainly because, compared to the Christians, the Jews enjoyed the advantage of an established civilization and a widely diffused culture. They were well known to both Greek and Roman conquerors and administrators, and occasionally occupied government posts. Extra-biblical sources that can convey a sense of the general milieu of the New Testament do not refer to Christianity (except in a couple of rare exceptions) but rather to the Greek, Roman, or Jewish context. All of these have relevance for the theological content of the New Testament, but it is the Jewish context that is most important and to which I will refer.

In particular, scholars have three especially important sources on Judaism of the first century that are largely extant. One is the works of Josephus, a Romanized Jewish historian who was an eyewitness to the destruction of Jerusalem. He wrote two especially important volumes, one on the war per se, and the other on the history of the Jews in which he refers to Jesus. The second source is the so-called Dead Sea Scrolls, which describe the doctrine and practices of a sect that had withdrawn to the Judean desert to live a life of ascetic purity. The third source is that of Hellenistic Jewish philosophers and in particular Philo, a Jewish philosopher of Alexandria in Egypt where a huge Jewish colony resided. These have supplied scholars with additional information in the historical record of the first century to complement the New Testament story regarding the Jews and, indirectly, Christianity. Still other sources include so-called apocalyptic writings that describe in visionary fashion the expectations of the authors for a dramatic intervention of God to redeem His faithful and to punish those who oppress His followers.

I want to make just a couple of comments about history. When we say that we will "turn to history," this has a certain ring of authority to it, as if we are putting a stamp of finality on the subject once and for all. When we say that we will recur to history to clarify this or that point, this may sound like we are returning to hard and fast facts of ancient events, but of course it is never that simple. In reality we are dealing with a woefully incomplete picture pieced together by scholars in different disciplines to the best of their ability and with whatever scant evidence is available to them. Any picture so derived will have its flaws, its subjectivity, and the particular "angle" of the author. The reader is encouraged to approach treatises dealing with this topic with certain skepticism, including the present book. And if the reader finds any particular author to be repugnant, s/he has the consolation that some other author will have an opposite viewpoint. Yet with each new viewpoint, we are afforded another vantage from which to approach Jesus, His times, and His Mission.

At the same time, a caveat must be added about the scientific or historical approach to the New Testament. This is a field of study that received great impetus in Protestant Germany in the nineteenth century, eventually penetrating into other countries and continents as well as some circles of the Catholic Church. The scholarly approach has some aspects in common with popular faith, but other points of view differ radically from that of the man on the street. Among believers, I think a natural human impulse is to know exactly what happened to Jesus, to feel closer to His life and times, and to visualize more clearly what He experienced. Scholars dealing with the historical Jesus reveal a wide array of viewpoints ranging from faith to skepticism, and each viewpoint has its respective assumptions.

I think that the most common, subtle, and potentially dangerous assumption associated with a historical approach is to view Jesus as the equivalent of His environment and a product thereof. In other words, by using as a point of departure the fact that Jesus was born a Jew at the opening of the first century, He is often assumed to have been inspired with Jewish motives, Jewish feelings, Jewish allegiances, etc. Within this mindset, Jesus was a Jew who had Jewish aspirations of purifying the Jewish nation. In academic speak, He was an apocalyptic prophet who, like other Jews in that period, arose to proclaim the imminent end of the age and the intervention of God to do away with evil. He was born in the backwoods of Galilee and was moved by the revolutionary fervor that swept through Galilee at that time. He traveled to Jerusalem to further His cause, but met with opposition and was crucified. Period.

There is nothing wrong with discovering the Jewishness of Jesus as a context in which He lived and taught, but the problem arises from equating being Jewish with being simply human, with no transcendence above His surroundings and His historical heritage. The more Jewish we make Jesus, the more we imply that He was therefore a product of the historical processes of the first century and those that preceded it—processes that created the Jewish tradition and that brought it to a point of crisis under Roman domination.

I find this approach of relativizing Jesus to the first century milieu potentially dangerous, as it will essentially make Christianity an accident of the first century, a proposition that I consider to be false (just as it would be false to make Moses and His message a simple product of the second millennium BCE). I want to assure the reader that I do not intend to subvert his/her faith with the approach that I will take; rather I believe that these questions of the context of Jesus have perfectly good answers, which do not lead to rejection, but rather to affirmation of faith. And I can state this because this is what I have derived from this journey that I invite you to share with me.

As we approach the Gospels through a lens of the first century, it is useful to appreciate the import of certain questions: Who was the principal audience of the Gospels? With what issues were they dealing? How was history evolving in that period when Jesus spoke, and later when the Gospels were being written? We might not have all the right answers, and maybe we never will, but it is a big help at least to have some of the right questions—because the right questions alert us to what we need to look for in reading the Gospels. And the context within which to formulate these questions was, not exclusively, but largely, Judaic.

CHAPTER 2

FROM ABRAHAM TO JESUS:
THE BUILDING BLOCKS OF FAITH

The year is 2000 BCE, and the place is Nuzu, an important administrative center of the kingdom of Mitanni in the Tigris valley of Mesopotamia. Nuzu's social relations are regulated by well-established norms, and the scribes of the royal library have a daunting task to record all the legal details, for even minor transactions are registered and filed here. Day in, day out, the scribes hunch over their tables and their writing instruments—soft clay tablets about a hand-span long and half as wide, and small sticks that impress a monotonous string of wedges into the wet clay surface to create the script of cuneiform. The tablets will be kiln-fired to conserve them, thus assuring their ready reference for future generations desiring to consult the legal records. Today the scribe has received a minor legal matter to record and place amongst the many thousands of other tablets in the royal archives. A father has elected to change his rightful heir. His wife had given him no son for several years and he had found it necessary to engender an heir by his wife's maidservant, as is common in this society. Both polygamy and the holding of concubines are widely accepted and practiced, and the legal norms of Nuzu regulate the questions of inheritance that naturally arise among half-siblings.

In the present case, the father at last has an heir by his legal wife who has now borne him a son, and he seeks to establish the rights of primogeniture for his newborn. This he does in accord with the customs of Nuzu and, by submitting his desires to be registered in the archives, he assures his son's rights of inheritance for all time.

Archaeologists have uncovered many thousands of clay cuneiform tablets in the library of Nuzu that reveal dozens of details of daily life, including the custom illustrated above. The excavations at Nuzu are like a vertical mine shaft through four thousand years of history, a shaft that intersects with a strand of the biblical narrative in the ancient recesses of Genesis. For our purposes, Nuzu is of interest as lying along the route between Ur of the Chaldees, far to the east in the lower Mesopotamian Basin, and Palestine to the southwest, a route that Abraham followed in a move that was to change the history of religion and the world. Mesopotamia and the Fertile Crescent had been the center of civilization for centuries, its peoples had participated in some of the first agriculture on the planet, and its kingdoms had raised up vast temples of which the narrative of the Tower of Babel is a reminder. On all this Abraham turned His back and transferred the focus of God's religion to a new land, a remote and barbarian corner of the Middle East called Canaan, which we know as Palestine. Canaan was a conglomerate of tiny fiefdoms organized around towns of mud huts, each one no more than a few acres in extension and surrounded by barriers of boulders rolled together for protection from marauders who roamed the countryside. In exchange for the civilizations of Mesopotamia and a rich, well-watered valley of agricultural abundance, this was the inheritance of Abraham and His family, the forerunners of the Hebrews. Thus, in one fell swoop, Abraham founded a people, a lineage of Prophets, a homeland, and the Judeo-Christian tradition that would form the backbone of European civilization after the advent of Christ. And for some undetermined period in that exile from Ur, the story of Abraham and the culture of the Tigris valley around Nuzu intersected.

Now, the story above from the Nuzu library may sound familiar and suspiciously similar to the biblical account of Abraham and Sarah, His wife. Sarah had not conceived in many years and offered her servant Hagar to serve as child-bearer in her place, and thus Ishmael was born. When, by divine intervention, Sarah finally conceived and bore Isaac, it was he who enjoyed the rights of primogeniture and who carried forward the line of descent that gave rise to the Israelites. But Abraham and Nuzu only came to intersect again in the twentieth century when the library of Nuzu was excavated, leading archaeologists to conclude that Abraham's story in Genesis reflected customs of the region and so had a historical basis, long forgotten even by the recorders of the Old Testament stories in later years. If Abraham passed through Nuzu en route to the Promised Land, He did not tarry long here. He had more important things to do to the south, in Canaan, where God had prepared a momentous task for Him.

In a religious context that was polytheistic, Abraham is credited with introducing the concept of monotheism into religion, and this is His greatest, most original, and long-lasting doctrinal contribution to posterity. Most of us take monotheism for granted, not having lived in any other context, but it should be recognized as a vital step in the spiritual development of humankind, and a critical contribution to its subsequent social progress. To appreciate the impact of monotheism, let us use our imagination to visualize the limitations of a polytheistic culture, considering first an example that might occur closer to home.

Most of us have worked in some sort of institution with a hierarchical administration, and we have witnessed the strengths and faults of the administrators in the upper echelons. If those at the top are people of integrity, dedicated to their mission and disposed to self-sacrifice, we recognize them as true leaders and are inspired by their example. We respond to their calls for hard work because we believe that we are sharing the load with someone who has taken responsibility seriously. Even when we disagree with them on specific issues, we have learned to respect their opinions and we support them.

On the other hand, we have also seen what happens when the higher echelons of the hierarchy do not take things seriously. Perhaps we see that the bosses lack commitment to the mission of the institution and are more concerned with building a personal empire. They bicker among themselves over turf; they slough off and do not earn their salt. They come to the office at 10:00 A.M. and leave by 3:00 P.M. to play golf. Then they start to chase the secretaries around and have affairs that generate jealousies among themselves, making the head office a real hell. And what is the effect down the line? When the workers see this behavior at the top, their own morale slumps. They are not going to knock themselves out for the glory of some ignoramus who does not give a damn! They sit around the break room drinking coffee, and their commitment to the business evaporates. Why make an effort if it is all going to come to naught in the hands of these numbskulls?

This scenario above is what I imagine life was often like in an ancient society dominated by mid-eastern mythology. Zeus sees a good-looking chick and beds her, but she turns out to be the girlfriend of Dionysus who when he finds out is green with jealousy. Athena wants a piece of the action and schemes for power with Apollo, etc, etc. Soap operas may flourish with this kind of script, but this is no way to run a universe. Such a world has little direction, morality, reason for existence, or few rules beyond satisfying the whims of overgrown, self-centered god-hedonists. In brief, when the world is in the hands of gods who behave like children, how can adults take things seriously? If anyone actually believes that such gods exist and determine the course of events, the best that one can hope for in life is to resign oneself with nobility, or to appease the gods and get by with minimum damage. Thus, most ancient religions sought primarily to keep the gods placated through frequent sacrifices. This is a frankly pessimistic view of mid-eastern mythology and religion, which certainly represents a rich literary heritage, but my concern is with the impact of this sort of cultural baggage on the way people look at life. When man's vision of ultimate reality merely reflects human frailties, this puts a limit on our ability to conceive of anything higher and nobler. Furthermore, when the very gods in heaven are divided against themselves, this is not an environment that is conducive to social cohesion and real social progress on earth. Why make an effort if it is all going to come to naught in the hands of these numbskulls?

Abraham was the first to break through the limitations of a polytheistic mindset and establish the principle of monotheism, thereby making progress possible. Without monotheism it is difficult to visualize a moral code with the strength to hold an extensive society together. The unity of God opens the doors on abstraction and conveys a sense of the absolute—the existence of an ultimate good, an ultimate right, an ultimate justice, all of which have their source in God. Granted that we are limited in our capacity to comprehend the ultimate, and we must all practice mutual tolerance with those whose understanding differs from our own. Likewise it is obvious that monotheism alone has not done away with the social ills of mankind. But what do we prefer—a world in which we differ about what is right and wrong in God's eyes; or a world in which we can scarcely formulate the concept of right and wrong at all? Monotheism is the initiation and the cornerstone of a moral code. Without monotheism it would be impossible to introduce the concept of humanity as being children of one and the same God, a single family in which an ethical code should serve the good of all its members. Humanity is still struggling with this corollary of monotheism. When all the implications of monotheism are universally applied and we are willing to admit that followers of all religions worship one single God, this will be a powerful force in overcoming religious animosity.

Now, if the existence of one God implies an absolute value and the potential of a moral code, then it was the role of Moses to structure a moral code of ethics around Divine Law, as the expression of the will of the God of Abraham. It was Moses who brought the implications of monotheism home to daily life and to the community by revealing the Law.

God seems to be systematic in giving the least auspicious beginnings to His Cause in each age, as if to assure that no one mistakes the source of its success as originating in brute force or riches. Consider this paraphrased mandate of God to Moses, compiled from the narrative in Exodus, Chapter 4: "Moses, I want you to return to Egypt and free the Hebrews. Do not expect much help from the Hebrews themselves because they probably remember you as belonging to the oppressive ruling class, and in any case, everyone remembers you as a criminal and murderer. You will face up to the principal superpower of the age, and the combined opposition of state and religion. The state is defended with vast and well-equipped armies and you will have no more than a wooden staff in your hand. You will be accompanied by your wife and newborn son, and if you think that that stuttering tongue of yours is not likely to convince anybody much, then take your brother Aaron along to translate." But the source of Moses' power is other and deserves no paraphrase: "I will be with thy mouth."[1]

While the dating of the advent of Moses is not certain, archaeology indicates that many Canaanite villages in Palestine were destroyed in the thirteenth and twelfth centuries BCE, while new villages were founded in the same period. This appears plainly to mark the arrival of the Israelites, and Moses is assumed to have lived shortly before this period, followed by Joshua and the judges.

As Moses led the Hebrews out of Egypt and toward their Promised Land, we can highlight three points of medium- to long-term significance. First, Moses consolidated the tribal structure of the Hebrews, assigning to the different tribes their respective roles. The tribes are described as drawing their structure from the twelve sons of Jacob, and as Moses led these twelve extended families to the Promised Land, their significance as a social unit was enhanced, eventually resulting in the assignment of a geographic area within Israel. We know little about the internal structure of the tribes, but in the long run, tribal loyalty was an important part of Israelite consciousness. Even in the first century CE, long after the tribes had lost their social significance, the apostle Paul would identify himself with the tribe of Benjamin, illustrating the strength of tribal identification.

The second point to highlight is the institutionalization of worship in a priesthood centered on Aaron and his descendents, and around the tabernacle, which was a mobile temple. Just as the Hebrews were a nomadic people for at least one generation in the company of Moses, their God had to live as a nomad also. The tabernacle was a tent of poles, cloth, and hides built to precise specifications, wherein the Spirit of God would dwell when the Hebrews were at rest. The tabernacle had three sections according to function: the outer courtyard where the Hebrew men would gather; the inner courtyard where animal sacrifices were offered upon the altar of fire; and the inner sanctuary or Holy of Holies where the Tablets of the Law were guarded in the Ark of the Covenant and where the Spirit of God hovered eternally. The tabernacle would serve as a model for the permanent Temple, first built in the time of Solomon and reconstructed in the centuries before Jesus.

Third, it goes without saying that the Law was the most important contribution of this period to the future development of Judaism, including the period to which we will eventually refer, that of Jesus. In theory, the Law was eternal and not subject to modification. In fact, the Law led to amplifications, and amplifications led to commentaries, and commentaries led to expositions. These were eventually codified as the Mishnah and the Gemarah, which constitute the Talmud. However, despite its mutability, no one questions that the Law was the heart and soul of Jewishness.

When we think of the Mosaic Law, our thoughts tend to gravitate toward two areas. On the one hand, we think of the dietary laws—probably because we have all been to the delicatessen and have heard of kosher food. More significantly, it is the Ten Commandments that have found their way into the Christian consciousness and have been conserved in the Christian tradition as viable principles of ethics and social life. Other aspects of the Mosaic Law, such as the dietary regulations, were either discarded by the apostles or fell by the wayside as the church consolidated. But the Ten Commandments have stood the test of time because they are timeless principles that are recognized as necessary in any civilized society. Granted, we still struggle to build a society in which "Thou shalt not kill" is universally respected; "Thou shalt not steal" may be violated on every level of society, and so forth down the line. Despite humanity's apparent inability to fulfill principles that are three thousand years old, this detracts nothing from the principles per se, much less from their Author. Rather it is a testimony to the vision of Moses that He could formulate so succinctly the principles of social behavior for all time.

However, we would do an injustice to Moses if we did not recognize that the Law that He implemented went far beyond the Ten Commandments. And if laws dealing with crop rotation and fallow, or the suitability of meat for consumption, or treatment of beasts of burden are no longer highly relevant for a western urban society, they certainly had their place among the Israelites. Likewise, some social norms are no longer relevant, such as those regulating the treatment of slaves (who were more like indentured servants than slaves in our western tradition). Nonetheless, the unifying thread in these social norms was the application of justice and order to the daily life of the Hebrews. Nor was this the mere formula of "An eye for an eye and a tooth for a tooth" to be applied in dealing with offenses. Rather, the Mosaic Law sought to establish an organic justice that formed a part of the warp and woof of society—what in our western vocabulary we call social justice. And Moses did an admirable job, given the historical setting and the primitive social milieu in which He executed His Mission. The Bahá'í Writings pay glowing tribute to the sterling character and to the level of erudition of the Israelites educated in the teachings of Moses.

Accustomed as we are to assuming that an inherent relationship exists between religion and ethics, it readily escapes us that it was Moses who established an ethical tradition within a religious context. Outside of the Jewish tradition, and even up to the time of Christ, mid-eastern religion typically did not deal with human behavior. Religion focused on rituals to appease the "gods" and win their favor. A person practiced a religion to assure a successful cropping season, or fertility in his wife, or victory on the battlefield. Personal behavior and ethics, on the other hand, pertained not to the realm of religion, but to that of philosophy (and indeed, ethics is still a branch of philosophy today). Moses took a revolutionary step in the history of western civilization, not only in creating a code of law based on social justice, but doing so in the context of religion. This step put ethics into a cosmic context, and sought to bring man's behavior into line with the dictates of the one God of Abraham.

Following Moses, the Old Testament Prophets played a role, not so much in establishing new laws or principles or introducing new doctrine, but in making the Jewish view a worldview, to the extent possible at that time when the "world" only extended from the Mediterranean to Persia. For the religion that Moses left was decidedly tribal, revealed to a people that were not prepared to embrace other races and nations that readily could have absorbed them. Once the Jews were established firmly as a nation with a stable monarchy to lend it social cohesion, and an ethnic identity, they could afford to take a more benevolent view toward the rest of the world, a universal view in which God also loved and blessed those other nations. And this was the vision, much of it futuristic, that the Prophets provided to the Jews. "And many people shall go and say, Come ye, and let us go up to the mountain of the LORD, to the house of the God of Jacob; and he will teach us of his ways, and we will walk in his paths: for out of Zion shall go forth the law, and the word of the LORD from Jerusalem. And he shall judge among the nations, and shall rebuke many people: and they shall beat their swords into plowshares, and their spears into pruning hooks: nation shall not lift up sword against nation, neither shall they learn war any more."[2]

In that day, the blessings that God had reserved for the Jews would embrace the entire earth. Granted that the Jews would still play a favored role in the vision of the Prophets, but in the future day of the LORD, they would coexist with their neighbors in peace and mutual respect. It was this more tolerant and world-embracing view that pervaded the synagogue in the time of Christ, and that permitted sympathizers among the Greeks, Romans, and others to develop a deep respect for Judaism and, in some cases, to draw near as incipient practitioners of the Jewish faith, and some of these to eventually become Christians.

If the Prophets opened new perspectives to the Jews and offered them new attitudes toward their neighbors, the advent of Jesus broached new questions of doctrine. For just as Moses had built a small but just society on the foundation of monotheistic doctrine that Abraham had laid, so did Jesus take that society (now far from just, but firmly committed to the Mosaic Law) and lift it to new horizons previously unknown to it. For the primary role of Jesus was that of spiritualizing the Jewish ethical tradition, and extending this new tradition throughout the world. Now, this is a grandiose statement that is likely to go in one ear and out the other if we are not careful. What exactly does it mean that Jesus "spiritualized" the Jewish tradition? The terms "spiritual" and "spirituality" have been used and misused so often (for example, to describe the psychological state of human beings even within a totally materialist society) that it is preferable to take a moment and reflect on what "spiritual" really means. Forgive me if I belabor this point, and I hope not to make the topic too dry and overly objective, but we need to conceptualize "spirituality" clearly and (for lack of a better term) concretely to appreciate more fully the Mission and contribution of Christ.

The spiritual can be understood on several levels, all of which are necessary. First, in the simplest of terms, "spiritual" refers to that reality that is not material (and we include "energy" within the material, in the modern understanding that energy and matter are interchangeable). When we look at ourselves, we recognize that certain dimensions of the human being such as insight, thought, intuition, imagination, and creativity have such a non-material basis. We instinctively feel, at one time or another and in certain lucid moments, that we have a non-material dimension. In a way that we do not and cannot understand, the material and the spiritual mysteriously coexist and even interact; yet there is a qualitative difference between the spiritual and the material. "That which is born of the flesh is flesh; and that which is born of the Spirit is spirit."[3] So distinct are matter and spirit that, ironically, we often better understand the spiritual precisely by contrasting it with the material.

Second, and using the above definition of spiritual as a point of departure, certain derivatives or corollaries result from the acceptance of a non-material reality. The foremost of these is that a non-material reality is not subject to composition and decomposition, because these are traits of matter. For example, in the material world a seed germinates; as a young plant it accumulates minerals and organic compounds; it grows and produces leaves, stems, and flowers. But just as it is composed by the joining of minerals, molecules, and tissues, so does it die when its component parts dissociate once again. In contrast, the spiritual is not composed through the joining of component parts, thus the spiritual does not *de*-compose. Therefore, that which is spiritual is eternal: "and I give unto them eternal life; and they shall never perish."[4]

Since the spiritual is eternal, it is also the very essence of the human being. We change jobs, cars, and houses; we traverse childhood, adolescence, and maturity; and it all changes and passes away. But we are always who and what we are—our essence which is eternal and spiritual. Since spiritual reality is our essence, it is the dimension of our being that has true value and is deserving of our greatest attention. "For what is a man profited, if he shall gain the whole world, and lose his own soul?"[5]

Furthermore, spirit implies unity and harmony, because the struggle for existence and all that it implies of envy, competition, and wars is born of animal nature and of the material world. The physical world offers little basis for unity, and even if we could trace our family tree to a common primitive Eve and prove that we are all brothers and sisters in a physical sense, we know that siblings fight tooth and nail as well. Unity is born of the recognition of a common spiritual origin, a common heavenly Father: "that they all may be one; as thou, Father, art in me, and I in thee, that they also may be one in us."[6]

Finally, the spiritual is intrinsically good. Sin and evil result from the material world and from animal instincts. The traits of selfishness, greed, aggressiveness, lust, etc. are derived from the physical, animal nature of man and from the struggle for survival, while the spiritual is free from the defects of the material. "Watch and pray, that ye enter not into temptation: the spirit indeed is willing, but the flesh is weak."[7]

This is a dry, rational approach to spirituality, but the point is that belief in a non-material reality as the essence of a human being opens up many avenues of self-understanding (and theological doctrine!) that are not nearly so fruitful without a concept of spirit and a human soul. Once we appreciate this we can permit ourselves to think in more poetic, mystical, or subjective terms about human beings and their relationship with the absolute, and all the multiple expressions of the spirit in music, art, human relations, and service to humanity. These are experiences of the human spirit and manifestations of spirituality that need no rational argument to justify their existence. Yet we would do well to keep in the back of our mind that these are expressions of that non-material reality that is born of God. Otherwise we run the risk of equating spirituality with every expression of the human being, whether noble or selfish, and dubbing this as "spiritual." We fall into a trap of relativization that argues that every behavior and every artistic expression—be it harmonious or discordant, unifying or aggressive, uplifting or debasing—is equally legitimate and inherently beautiful because it is expressive of the human "spirit." The fundamental nature of the spirit—its non-material reality and origin in a Supreme Being—is the necessary point of departure for the development of the human being, as engendered by the Message of Christ.

The belief in the soul and its eternal existence, like the belief in monotheism, is easily taken for granted by most of us. Yet compared to a world in which this belief is lacking, it revolutionizes human thought and transforms the worldview of those that hold this concept. It offers an answer to some of the most acute existential questions about life: Why do we exist in the first place if only to be snuffed out? Is there no possibility of recompense to set right what in this world seems like an unending history of injustice? And at the root of it all, the essential question: Who am I? Belief in the soul offers to each individual a spiritual identity, a self-image to seek and discover and perfect, as opposed to a purely physical identity. Without confidence in this spiritual identity, man's struggle for self-perfection would be seriously inhibited and subject to pitfalls of self-doubt and doubts about the value of life itself. The soul puts an individual's life in a context of progress, with the potential to grow and mature eternally and infinitely. The value of this teaching cannot be underestimated in the effects that it wrought on those who accepted Jesus as their Messiah and Savior. And if its implications took years or centuries to articulate amply, every single Christian since the time of Jesus could have made the following statement, as the simplest expression of human experience: "I am a being created by God to live forever in the shelter of His love. I should strive through my actions to be worthy of these blessings, and my eternal existence is somehow influenced by my behavior." This represented no small milestone in human self-understanding.

Many of the statements above about spirit may sound like routine truisms of the church, but to appreciate the Mission and role of Jesus, we have to understand that, in general, they were precisely *not* truisms of traditional Judaism. The Jews did *not* have an explicit tradition of belief in the otherworldly. Granted that the "Jews" were a highly heterogeneous group and there were exceptions to virtually any statement that one could make about them, but mainstream first century Judaism (to the extent that we can tease out what this meant in the first century) did not understand the concept of spirit and soul as we do today. Obviously a belief in God is the first and most important element of such a belief, and the Jews were the depositories of the monotheistic tradition. However, beyond belief in the existence of God, the Jewish concepts of the spiritual were not well defined. Some (not all) Jews believed in angels as a sort of right hand of the Divine Will, and the cherubim were thought to hover over the Ark of the Covenant where the Tablets of the Law were guarded. Even the position of angels was far from clear. Furthermore, the Jews were quick to associate anything spiritual with the occult. In the Mosaic Law, witchcraft was a serious offense punishable by death, and other occult practices were severely condemned as abominations of heathen foreigners. "There shall not be found among you any one that maketh his son or his daughter to pass through the fire, or that useth divination, or an observer of times, or an enchanter, or a witch, or a charmer, or a consulter with familiar spirits, or a wizard, or a necromancer. For all that do these things are an abomination unto the LORD: and because of these abominations the LORD thy God doth drive them out from before thee."[8] Perhaps as a result of such warnings and a deep-rooted suspicion of the otherworldly, Jesus Himself was often denounced as a sorcerer or magician by His Jewish opponents, as attested by both the New Testament and later Talmudic sources.

More specifically, the Jews had a rather different concept of the human soul and its state after death, and this one aspect seriously limited Jewish concepts of the spiritual. True, the Old Testament has ample reference to the soul, and a respect for the Old Testament and its divine inspiration leads us to assume that the "soul" in the Old Testament is the same eternal "soul" that we read of in the New Testament. However, the Old Testament does not amplify on the nature of the soul, and the Old Testament contains virtually no reference to the continuing existence of the soul in a future life.

The Jews in the first century did not attribute all the characteristics of individuality to the soul, as we understand soul today. Among the different strands of Judaism, rabbinic Judaism deserves special attention, since it is that which has come down to us through the Talmud and is in turn derived from Pharisaic Judaism. Among the various Jewish sects, the Pharisees were probably the most innovative in relation to the Old Testament, and the most open to ideas of an eternal soul. Nonetheless, the morning prayer that was recorded in the Talmud a few centuries after Christ probably best reflects the viewpoint of early rabbinic Judaism toward the soul: "My God, the soul which Thou hast placed in me is pure. Thou hast fashioned it in me, Thou didst breathe it into me, and Thou preservest it within me and Thou wilt one day take it from me and restore it to me in the time to come."[9] The soul here is still more of a life force that comes and goes and will return, but it is not inherently part of one's own individualized being and identity, which is rather associated with the body. Soul was viewed as something like the electric energy that illumines a lightbulb; but if you throw the switch, the lightbulb turns cold and dark. The electricity is indispensable to the functioning of the bulb, but it is ethereal and diffuse, without individual identity. It is the bulb, not the electricity, which has individuality and real tangible being.

This perspective of the soul or spirit that goes out from God to give life to the world can be witnessed in Genesis at the very dawn of creation: "In the beginning God created the heaven and the earth. And the earth was without form, and void; and darkness was upon the face of the deep. And the Spirit of God moved upon the face of the waters. And God said, Let there be light."[10] And a few verses later, in the story of Eden, this Spirit is blown into the form of man: "And the LORD God formed man of the dust of the ground, and breathed into his nostrils the breath of life; and man became a living soul."[11] In Hebrew, "spirit" and "breath" are the same word.

Thus, against the backdrop of the Old Testament tradition, a firm and unequivocal belief in an eternal soul as held by the rank and file believer was the most revolutionary and far-reaching innovation of the teachings of Jesus, from which other innovations were derived. When Jesus introduced explicit concepts of the eternal soul and all the associated teachings referred to above, He truly created a revolution in the Jewish tradition. Whereas for the Jews the spirit was the breath of God blown over His creation, bestowing life until such time that it "blew on its way," what Jesus did for the concept of soul was to make it an individual entity, the very identity of the human self, an integral spiritual body. Jesus *individualized* spirit more firmly than before. And with this, Jesus was creating a new vision of the human being with such vast implications as to create a new world vision. Within this new vision, man is eternal and his sojourn in this world is but a brief step in his eternal journey unto God. This world is merely a staging ground for the spiritual world to come; yet our actions in this world and our ethical behavior are a determining factor in our eternal destiny. While firm ethical elements are clearly found in the very warp and woof of Judaism, viewing man as a unique and eternal spiritual being changed the whole context of ethics and the very purpose of life.

Many of the Jews, however, considered this new worldview as foreign to their own understanding of reality. Time after time, on issue after issue, these two worldviews clashed and sparks flew as the Jews expressed their disapproval, their disbelief, or their incapacity to understand what Jesus was saying. The introduction of a spiritual outlook into these issues is an aspect of the unique Mission of Christ, an aspect that we will explore in subsequent chapters.

Taking a step back for a moment, if we view our western religious tradition as growing from monotheism to ethics to individual spirituality, one might ask why is it that God chose to develop religion in this fashion? Why did the Jews have such a limited concept of the spiritual? Why was the introduction of belief in the eternal soul—with all its corollaries—delayed until the advent of Jesus? We cannot second-guess God's motives, but we can observe what happens when spiritual phenomena are explored independently of an ethical tradition: they often degrade into spook chasing or the occult. In other words, "spirituality" without ethics often becomes exactly what the Jews disliked and distrusted most about the spiritual, as outlined in the verse from the Pentateuch quoted above. Man seems to have a certain penchant for the mysterious and magical, and for making these central to religious practice, as Freud was wont to point out. Perhaps in the ancient pre-Christian world in which the occult, the magical, and even the demonic were the norm, it was wiser to first establish firmly the ethical principles of Moses, and then introduce the spiritual dimension in the time of Jesus. Perhaps it was necessary for man to mature in the ethics of the Jewish Law before being exposed to the specter of an infinite and admittedly mysterious world of the spirit and the afterlife.

Be that as it may, when the time was ripe, Jesus appeared with the "innovation" of the eternal human soul and all of its implications. And the circle of believers touched by this Message grew from twelve to hundreds to thousands to hundreds of thousands. Year by year the community of Christians multiplied, first within the synagogues, then in gatherings in private homes that served as primitive churches, where the first Christians shared fellowship and broke the bread of the Eucharist. With the passage of time these communities became semi-independent of the world around them to the extent that Gibbons described them as a republic within a republic. The community looked after itself, it had its own leaders or bishops who served as custodians of the nascent faith, and eventually it would sponsor institutions of public good such as orphanages and hospitals. Long before Constantine raised the profile of Christianity in the Roman Empire, the Christians were well on their way to creating a new civilization—not yet of vast constructions and monuments, nor of works of art and music, nor of trade and economic power. Rather it was a civilization of brotherly love and mutual support, when in the world outside of this community, Roman power was still the criterion by which civilization was judged. In the midst of a world that outwardly was ordered, but in which brute force was thinly disguised, Christians constituted a true civilization because Christians were truly civilized. They had a civilized attitude, civilized morals, and a civilized outlook on social relations. And eventually, this would flower—however imperfectly—into a visible civilization and empire.

When we survey the broad sweep of the history of Judeo-Christian religion over these two thousand or more years from Abraham to Jesus, an evolution of concepts and a maturation of faith emerge. The monotheism of Abraham led to the ethics of Moses, which in turn created an environment in which humankind could address spirituality as taught by Jesus with greater maturity. Monotheism, ethics, and spirituality—for those of us who grew up in a Judeo-Christian tradition, these are three indispensable and seemingly inseparable foundations of our western religious tradition. Monotheism we take for granted. Ethics is assumed to be the logical outcome of religious practice. And we never conceive of God without also assuming the existence of the soul. It would seldom occur to us that there was a time when any one of the three was not part of religion. In fact, this triad is the result of more than two millennia of religious evolution, a step-wise process whereby each new phase has built upon the gradual transformation in the collective soul of mankind to which the previous revelation contributed.

Monotheism, ethics, and spirituality are milestones of history and of civilization, the glorious peaks that mark the progress of humanity. Of course, even over-simplification cannot obscure the obvious—that deep valleys, centuries of tears, exile, enslavement, and suffering separate these peaks. The road from one peak to the next higher peak leads through hell, until humankind learns the hard way. This is one of the surest lessons of history—that the very lessons of history are learned with great difficulty and on a timescale of many generations.

I have focused on a period of some two thousand years and have used the example of religion from Abraham to Jesus, but I could have broadened my time scale and extended the scope of religious evolution all the way back to Noah, and before Him to Adam (in the Jewish tradition when the text states that "God was with" so-and-so, as in the case of Adam, this signifies a Prophet). The succession of Messengers and Prophets from Adam to Noah, to Abraham, Moses, and Jesus is the overriding scheme of God's faith, as if each Prophet is an Educator in a vast school for the spiritual training of humanity over the ages. In this scheme, each Prophet builds upon the progress of the previous Messengers and raises humanity to a higher level of consciousness and a greater degree of perfection.

Furthermore, the spiritual progress attained in this evolutionary process has a social dimension that evolves in parallel fashion. I referred briefly to the impact of Moses and Jesus in spawning a spiritual community, each in their respective period and within the social unit that was current at that time—Moses within the tribe, Jesus within the city state. The community that grew up around the spiritual

Message in each respective age was a new creation, with social commitments that contributed to new models of civilization. Social progress is driven by social conscience, the measure of which is the scope of the social circle. As we survey the progress of mankind from Abraham to Moses to Jesus, we see a broadening circle wherein the loyalties of humankind were at one time limited to the immediate family, later expanding to the tribe in the time of Moses, and then to the city-state in the age of Jesus. These ever wider social units and their corresponding loyalties and ethical codes reflect man's capacity to overcome egocentrism and view himself as part of a whole. These ever wider social units are themselves milestones of human progress. This evolution of concepts and this process of maturation of faith are called "progressive revelation" in the Bahá'í Writings—a term that we will refer to again in later chapters.

However, the claim that God's plan has an overriding scheme should not be construed to imply that the fate of God's Cause, much less that of the world, is determined mechanistically. What is predetermined is that God will fulfill His will to manifest His mercy and love through His Chosen Ones. But what happens after that is a mysterious interaction of divine and human wills that, from our standpoint, will always suffer from ambiguity. We will never know exactly where God's will in history stops and where the will of man takes over. The fact that God manifested Christ as an expression of His will does not alter the fact that Christianity developed within a specific historical context and milieu that influenced the way Christians presented, expressed, understood, and applied the Message of Jesus, and the way in which His Cause evolved. Christians adapted their presentation to their audience as was needed and it is clear that, at the outset, that context was largely Jewish. Thus the origins of Christianity are a mixture of God's intervention through the Message of Christ, and the efforts of early believers to implement His new faith within a given historical and social setting—an interaction of Divine will and the will of human beings who strove to fulfill as best possible their understanding of that Divine will, facing up to the challenges that their social setting put before them.

Returning to my theme of the origins of Christianity and its relationship to Judaism, progressive revelation is the overarching context in which to study the relationship between Jesus and Judaism. If revelation and religion are to be progressive, then Jesus was destined to bring innovations to the religion of Moses, and these were likely to irritate the Jews. They were thoroughly convinced of the unique nature of the Revelation of Moses and the one-time-for-all-time reality of their faith. What is more, in the centuries preceding the advent of Jesus, the Jews had sacrificed thousands of lives to defend their religion, which was the same as their national identity. They had resisted the worship of pagan gods such as Moloch and Baal, and had struggled long years to overthrow Greek domination in the time of the Seleucids and to purify the Temple. After such sacrifice, they would be slow to countenance what they viewed as unorthodox modifications in their faith. Granted that the Jews were divided into a diversity of sects with contrasting views among themselves on questions of doctrine, and they might well have viewed each other as unorthodox as well. That does not change the fact that they would receive the Message of Jesus with reservations rooted in their own particular sectarian orthodoxy. Just as surely as Jesus was destined to be manifest as the Messiah, so was He destined to confront serious opposition in the course of fulfilling His Mission as He brought new concepts to the Jewish tradition. In brief, it was orthodoxy versus God's evolving faith. The spiritual issues outlined above, among others, would form the basis for many a heated discussion in the Christian-Jewish dialogue.

In the remaining chapters we will examine the record of the Gospels in light of the Message of Christ and its innovative nature in relation to Judaism. This is not an attempt to review the entire range of issues that might have created tension between Jesus and the Jews, but rather those that grew out of the teachings of Jesus on spirituality. I do not pretend to say with this that the spirituality of Jesus was the central issue that caused the Jews to reject Him, but neither was it inconsequential—not necessarily because the Jews had anything against spirituality, although in some of its forms it might have been rather foreign to them. Rather, they had other priorities at that moment in history, and they just did not have patience with One that insisted on talking about eternal life of the soul when their here-and-now life situation demanded hard-nosed practical solutions.

On the other hand, it does not really matter how big an issue the spirituality of Jesus was at that time, nor whether it impinged seriously on the stance that the Jews took toward Jesus. That is not the primary issue that interests us here, although it will emerge frequently. The questions that concern us are the following. What impact did this conflict of worldviews have on the writing of the Gospels? And what implications does it have for the way that *we* understand the Message of Jesus, in our own time? If we find the doctrine of Jesus posed within the context of a conflict or a contrast of worldviews, it is not the conflict per se that should attract our attention, but the message that is implicit in the contrast. For it was through the use of these contrasts that the Gospel writers attempted to convey the message that they viewed as innovative and unique.

First we will return to the days before Jesus, to set the stage for the day of His advent.

CHAPTER 3

JEWISH ROOTS AND CAMELOT LOST

If Abraham, Moses, and Jesus represent a logical progression in the spiritual development of humanity, each nonetheless lived out His life and delivered His Message in a specific historical context. In the case of Abraham, certain customs that were current in the Middle East and that are documented in the cuneiform tablets from Nuzu and elsewhere can be observed in His story. Moses in turn established norms and practices that responded to the needs of a primitive pastoral-agricultural society. The historical context conditioned His Message, in the manner in which He presented His Revelation, and in the way it was understood. Moses adapted His teaching to the specific audience and its needs, according to the age and the social and religious milieu in which He lived. Far from detracting from the divine inspiration that moved each Manifestation of God (as the Prophets of God are known in the Bahá'í Writings), an understanding of the historical context permits insights into the spiritual message by viewing it in terms of the situation in which it was revealed. This permits separating the outer trappings of the specific situation from the inner essential meaning—the particular case from the eternal spiritual truth. The same occurs in the case of Jesus, and is the motive for studying the historical setting within which Jesus lived and taught. However, it is ironic that some of the most important factors of that social and religious milieu into which He was born, and that set the tone of the times, were defined some ten centuries earlier, in the early history of the Jewish monarchy.

The monarchy, as we understand it from the Hebrew Bible, was preceded by an obscure phase of tribal rule that followed the period of settlement of the Hebrews in Canaan. When each tribe was assigned a tract of land to occupy, the judges supposedly administered the Mosaic Law. When one thinks of the judges, one envisions a theocracy in which society was ruled by a unique class of wise men who applied the divine precepts. To what extent is this accurate? Hebrew scholars now question that the term *shofat*, translated as judge, implies a specific judicial function, rather a more accurate translation might be "ruler," in which case the tribal rulers would have been charged with implementing the Mosaic Law.

A parallel dimension of the social organization that is ill defined, but is implicit in the biblical literature, is that of the "men of Israel." This phrase appears with some frequency and probably reflects an assembly of the Israelites, a town meeting or council as it were. For example, when David aspired to assume the kingship he sought the approval of the tribal elders, demonstrating the existence of a traditional social structure. If such a formally constituted assembly existed, we know nothing about how it was constituted or how it functioned, or what the relationship among the several tribes would have been. This is a tantalizing topic, as we would all like to visualize more clearly the model that was employed to implement the Mosaic Law in a just society, but this period of history is mostly lost to us in the distant past.

However, the time came when the most significant feature regarding the period of the judges was the inability of the tribal structure (or any other that existed at the time) to cope with the threat of invasion that pressed upon the Hebrews, in particular from the Philistines who originated in the Mediterranean area and penetrated from the western coast well into the heart of the Israelite homeland. The Hebrews had battled their way into Canaan against local opposition that was armed much as they were, with bows and swords, but they could not deal as readily with the Philistines who were supported by horse-drawn chariots—a new dimension in military technology that struck terror in their adversaries, and that made the Philistine warriors fearfully effective. The Philistines even captured the Ark of the Covenant as a war prize, and so precarious was the situation that the very existence of Israel was at stake. As in modern times, the external threat resulted in a call for a strong central authority to rally the troops, to create unity, and to confront the threat effectively. Thus the monarchy was born.

The Old Testament portrays a certain ambivalence about monarchy at first, apparently viewing it as a necessary evil. Yet what was the option—annihilation by the Philistines? Under these circumstances, Saul of the tribe of Benjamin was "crowned" king. And in his election is a lesson in Jewish political science of the time. Saul was called to be king by a ceremony of anointing by the Prophet Samuel, who poured oil upon his head in an act reminiscent of Leviticus. Anointing was a prescribed ceremony for the priests of Aaron as a calling to their high office, and thus did God call Saul to his own office, giving to the monarchy a divine aura. Furthermore, the term *anointed* would later be applied to the Promised One in the Hebrew term that we transliterate as *Messiah*, or *Christ* in the Greek of the New Testament. To the Jews, the station of Christ—the anointed, the

Messiah—would be a combination of savior and political calling, a combination that would acquire ever more significance in the days of Jesus.

Under Saul, Israel adopted a monarchical system of rule, opening a new phase in its history that brought Israel's Golden Age and, in a few brief years, its division and downfall. Saul, David, and Solomon maintained a united kingdom that spanned nearly a century, but without a doubt David is the towering figure of this period, and of much of the Old Testament. He is a remarkable person, and as much as his historical role, it is his character that makes him memorable. He loves music and dancing and he is not averse to tossing down a few drinks. He can be lusty, and he has a ribald sense of humor, such as when King Saul conditions the hand of his daughter on David's bringing back a hundred enemy foreskins, and David shows up with two hundred! And in spite of his earthy character, his capacity for passionate devotion expressed in the Psalms knows no bounds. Some consider that David is a legendary figure and too good to be true, but to me he is too good to be a legend. Who could invent such a character?

For our immediate purposes, and for the state of Judaism years later in the time of Christ, David's historical role is one that would influence Jewish attitudes and thought profoundly. If David had limited himself to establishing a dynasty, he would have gone down in history as any other royal hero; but beyond creating his lineage, David gave the Israelites something they had never had before—a capital city. David conquered the city of Jebus, long a Canaanite enclave in the midst of an otherwise Hebrew homeland, and made it the seat of his government. The fact that Jebus had not belonged to any Israelite tribe prior to this time may have made it "neutral territory" and therefore more acceptable to the tribes as their common seat of government (just as Washington D.C. was created to be independent of any individual state by the founders of the American nation). Jebus was renamed Jerusalem, the first city in Jewish history to attain a prominent status as the capital and center of a Hebrew tribal confederation. Equally significant is the fact that David brought the Ark of the Covenant with the Tablets of the Law to Jerusalem, and set in motion the building of the Temple. This was constructed in the days of Solomon along the lines prescribed by Moses for the tabernacle, making it the focus of the institutionalized worship prescribed in the Law with its animal sacrifices and acts of atonement. Thus, David also made Jerusalem the spiritual center of Judaism and, by constructing the Temple, this spiritual status was given a permanency that had not existed previously.

By conferring on Jerusalem this dual political and religious status and uniting the administrative and spiritual centers of the Hebrews, David created a potent symbol expressing the concept that temporal government is an extension of God's rule. In brief, Jerusalem embodied the union of the temporal and the divine, a concept that is especially foreign and difficult to grasp for Americans who have been raised in the principle of separation of church and state. We Americans

27

tend to assume that ours is the only logical way for a modern civilized nation to operate, and forget that modern states such as the United Kingdom, the Scandinavian countries, and much of Latin America continue to recognize a state religion while protecting the rights of other minority faiths. However, the Jewish concept was different even from the reality of a modern state religion, whereby state and religion are two entities that are united by historical association, mutual consent, and/or convenience. The Jewish concept was that the state should be an expression of God's will, just as much as religion, that state and religion were organically interwoven, and that the king was responsible for assuring that God's will was carried out. For the Jews, Jerusalem was the visible embodiment of this concept and its focal point. Within a single generation, David raised the profile of Jerusalem from a renegade Canaanite city that resisted Jewish conquest for centuries, to the eternal symbol of Jewish nationality. David must have had a great sense of history to make history so effectively.

As years passed, David came to be regarded as the archetypical king, and his kingdom as the perfect example of God's intervention in history. Although it was Solomon that carried the kingdom to its fruition in a Golden Age, David and his kingdom would be the incarnation of the highest of Jewish hopes, and in a subsequent age, its restoration would be the culmination of end-time (eschatological) expectations. In a word, the kingdom of David and Solomon was a Jewish Camelot—a near mythical kingdom under the leadership of a wise king, a utopia with a superior moral quality that makes it the object of longing. The image would persevere with the Jews in later years as they sought to bear up under the yoke of successive oppressors, especially the Greeks and Romans.

However, the kingdom of David and Solomon was soon to be followed by division resulting in the dual monarchy of Ephraim or Israel (the Northern Kingdom) versus Judah (the Southern Kingdom, centered in Jerusalem). The disastrous split was precipitated by stubbornness, arrogance, and ambition between rivals, but when division came, the fault line occurred along tribal boundaries. Tribal loyalties were still strong and superseded the unity that might have been derived from a common law and faith under the united monarchy. Even in previous years when David suffered rebellion among the ranks, there were implications of tribal rivalries, and now when the confederation finally split in two, it was ten tribes to the north and two tribes (Judah and Benjamin) to the south. Technically, it is from this point onward in history that the term "Jew" is more properly applied, derived from the name "Judah" and referring to a resident of the kingdom of Judah.

The Northern Kingdom had disastrous years ahead of it as faction after faction and military leader after usurper all sought to gain the throne, until power finally stabilized. Judah at least continued to enjoy the stability of an established Davidic dynasty and avoided the bloodshed that racked the north. The Northern Kingdom would endure for about two hundred years until the Assyrians overran it in the late eighth century BCE, deporting most of its inhabitants to distant lands. Remnants of the ten northern tribes would survive in the Samaritans, who escaped exile, but who intermarried with invaders or neighboring stocks, although most northerners would be absorbed into other races and lost forever—a situation that would lend itself to creating myths about the destiny of the lost tribes of Israel. The kingdom of Judah for its part would survive for another one hundred and fifty years, but the movements of regional superpowers would eventually overtake Judah as well.

The final phase of Jewish history leading up to the time of Christ is a turbulent and unsettled period. It initiates with the exile of the Jewish elite to Babylonia under the Babylonian emperor, Nebuchadnezzar, giving birth to what we call the Diaspora, followed by the destruction of the Temple in 586 BCE. While a return to Palestine would initiate within the same century and continue through the next century, things would never be the same again. These six centuries would have ups and downs, although mostly downs from the Jewish point of view. The Jews in this six hundred year period appear like an aging boxer who dreams of a comeback yet suffers the indignity of defeat after defeat at the hands of younger adversaries of inherently lesser talent, but with the advantage of brute strength—the Babylonians, the Persians, the Greeks, and the Romans. Each successive defeat only generates more anger and frustration. This situation was especially intolerable in light of the position of the Jews as God's Chosen People. How, the Jews must have asked themselves, could these foreigners rule over God's own elect, much less oppress them?

Neither was there an internal unity that might have been generated from sharing in a common tragedy. It is ironic that when Cyrus the Persian conquered Babylonia and authorized the Jews to return and rebuild the Temple in Jerusalem, many and perhaps a majority chose to stay in Mesopotamia. (In the future, the Babylonian community would develop centers of Jewish learning that would rival those in Palestine in their brilliance, especially in the period after the destruction of the Temple.) Perhaps the Jews had become accustomed to the agricultural abundance of the region, or perhaps they felt more like Mesopotamians after one generation. And if it were not enough that many Jews were lukewarm about returning to Palestine, the few Jews who did return were met not by welcoming throngs of their brethren, but with opposition. The Old Testament indicates that conflict ensued between the returning Jews and the long-term residents of Palestine, and a Samaritan tradition confirms this. The Samaritans, being descendents of the northern tribes, denied worship at Jerusalem and held Mount Gerizim to be holy and the center of God's religion. Thus they had no interest in renewing worship in a restored Jerusalem. Hence the return of the Jews was an uphill battle to restore the integrity of the Jewish community based on the rule of divine law.

The entire Middle East, the Jews included, was reduced to the role of spectator as new superpowers vied for dominion over vassal states. The Greeks soon overcame the Persians, and when Alexander the Great died after a short but eventful life of conquest and high living, his far-flung empire was divided into three. The Jews eventually came under the domination of the Seleucids, a dynasty of Greeks that ruled from Syria. The Seleucid king, Antiochus, took it upon himself to humiliate the Jews to the utmost, sacrificing a pig upon the altar of the Jerusalem Temple. Such were the indignities that he piled upon the Jews that he drove them to desperation and to revolt. And when it came, it did not come from Jerusalem, neither did it flair up from either the priestly class in the Temple or the nobility. Rather, it came from the grass roots, from the sons of an aging and pious priest called Mattathias. Their story would be recorded in the Book of Maccabees, and they would come to be known as the Hasmoneans.

Legend narrates that a Seleucid agent demanded that Mattathias sacrifice to a pagan god and that Mattathias killed the Seleucid rather than commit this sacrilege. His sons picked up the cause and followed suit, becoming the spark that set off the tinderbox. A long and bloody war ensued in which many thousands died, but the unthinkable transpired. The Jews defeated the tyrant in an upset that rivaled the victory of David over Goliath. The Jews seemed to have bought their liberty with sacrifice, and at last were ruled not by outsiders and unbelievers, but by a Jewish king under Jewish Law, with Jewish worship in a rededicated and purified Jewish Temple. But what enemies do not destroy, you can trust in friends to squander, and herein lies the irony. The Hasmoneans spent their energies not in rebuilding Solomon's empire, but in fighting among themselves. Their dynasty was a trail of blood, assassinations, and unrest as brother rose against brother, son against mother.

And what of religion that should have been a unifying force, lending cohesion to a newly founded kingdom? Did it serve to subjugate to higher ends the political differences that emerged? Did it instill a sense of humility before a God who had permitted the Jews to overcome their enemies? Did the memory of thousands of martyrs, who gave their lives to defend the Temple and the faith that it represented, bring sobriety to those who built a new kingdom over the foundation of their sacrifice? Guess again. Jewish sect aligned with political faction, and the position of high priest became a political plum with which to reward one's co-conspirators in sedition. Rather than a renaissance of ancient glory, the experience of the Hasmoneans demonstrated—like the split in David's kingdom after Solomon's death—the sad internal divisions that had crippled the capacity of Judaism to regenerate itself, and this is one of the most important and telling lessons of this period.

If the Jews could have imagined what was on the horizon for them, they might have looked back with fondness to the tyranny of the Seleucids, for in the storehouse of historical despots fate had a real stinker lined up for them. The kingdom of the Hasmoneans and its infighting ended when an opportunist, Herod, convinced the Romans—now the ascendant power in the region—to support him as their puppet and to put an end to the bickering of this troublesome and unruly ethnic group at the margin of the expanding empire. Herod was not even a Jew by descent. He was an Idumean, from the region to the south of Judah, and he and his family were recent converts to Judaism. He was an ambitious, ruthless, and paranoiac ruler who murdered his wife in a fit of insane jealousy. If he was skillful in maintaining some degree of integrity of the Jewish kingdom in the face of the Roman steamroller, it was only for the sake of self-aggrandizement and not out of any love for the Jews. He had a penchant for construction, and modern visitors to the archaeological site of Masada can still see the remnants of one of his many grandiose palaces perched on a bluff overlooking the Dead Sea. It was Herod who, in an attempt to ingratiate himself with the Jews, expanded and embellished the Temple in Jerusalem, the beauty of which Josephus would expound, and that would witness the presence of Jesus less than a century later.

Meanwhile, the Jews fumed under the yoke of Herod, whom they viewed as a usurper and a traitor, and they longed for the restoration of the true Davidic kingdom. The hallmark of this period was frustration, which led to doctrines and a mode of thinking that scholars refer to as "apocalypticism." This is a set of ideas presented as a revelation from God and usually marked by expectations of His imminent intervention to set things right, accompanied by revenge on His enemies, restoration of His chosen people, and compensation for His faithful. It should come as no surprise that, as applied and interpreted by numberless sects in successive ages, apocalypticism became the expectation of God's vengeance on one's own enemies, the restoration of one's own people, and compensation for oneself.

The term "apocalypticism" is derived from the Greek for "revelation," which is also the title of the last book of the New Testament, and which also manifests these same elements. Apocalypticism is not precisely the same as the modern connotations associated with the term "apocalypse" and that imply an all-engulfing, worldwide destruction, without purpose or hope (on the contrary, apocalypticism implied hope and salvation for God's faithful in the midst of divine vengeance). These doctrines become a form of psychological support system to assure the downtrodden of their ultimate victory and to explain why God could have abandoned His loved ones to the intolerable and illogical situation of humiliation and conquest at the hands of the infidel. It is often assumed that the appearance of such literature reflects an oppressive environment to which the apocalyptic writing is a human response, and this assumption preempts the religious doctrine that such writings in fact represent content of divine revelation.

The Essenes and their literature that was uncovered at the Qumran colony best illustrate the apocalyptic point of view. Josephus named the Essenes as one of the three principal Jewish sects of the age (the others being the Pharisees and the Sadducees), but gave few details of them. It is accepted broadly that Essenes occupied the Qumran colony. This conclusion is supported, if for no other reason, by process of elimination, since it must have required a sizable sect to maintain such a large colony for nearly three centuries, yet it was certainly not the Pharisees or Sadducees that lived here. The Essenes might have been among the more extreme of sects in their apocalyptic viewpoint. However, we learn a great deal by looking at the extremes of a society, because these express explicitly and openly many of the same tendencies of more moderate elements—tendencies that in a given situation can bubble up and boil over. Given the discovery of the so-called Dead Sea Scrolls in nearby caves, the doctrine of the Qumran sect has been documented far better than any other in that period shortly before and during the time of Christ and thus permits us to speak with greater certainty and less speculation. The attitudes of the Qumran community, while revealing intense piety and humility, also have a violent side that contributes to the apocalyptic bent. Their writings reveal an unforgiving and unbending stance toward their perceived enemies, praying for God's vengeance and His unheeding disregard for their pleas for mercy—a far cry from the pronouncement of Christ on the cross: "Father, forgive them; for they know not what they do."[1]

It would be inaccurate to suggest that all Jews shared the apocalyptic view of the Essenes and indeed, in the broader context of Jewish society, a sizable sector of the upper classes were Hellenized and had adopted Greek customs, dress, sport, and language. It is even a fact that a majority of Jews lived outside Palestine in large Hellenistic urban centers like Alexandria in Egypt. However, in the context of Jewish religion, and perhaps more so in Palestine, the apocalyptic viewpoint played a critical role in the years surrounding and following the advent of Jesus. The Jews were discontented and were desperately awaiting the Messiah, in a mindset that demanded restoration and compensation.

The New Testament gives us a vision of the Jews as being meticulous in the fulfillment of the letter of the Law of Moses. The Jewish concern with strict conformity to the Law is illustrated in the code developed in the Qumran community. For example, in the Mosaic Law, water for purification rites was to be held in a receptacle made of carved stone. Elements made of fired clay were not acceptable for purification rites and would ritually contaminate the holy water. Now, in the understanding of the Essenes, if water were poured from the stone receptacle to some clay or other ritually unacceptable receptacle, the impurity that infected the water in the clay vessel would "swim upstream" as it were to the water in the stone vessel, making it ritually unfit. We can visualize ritual impurity as some super-virulent bacterium that spreads spontaneously to all that come in physical contact with it. Such an obsession with ritual purity, not unlike a modern, guilt-ridden psychological obsession, clouds one's spiritual sensibilities with infinite attention to detail, until one cannot see the forest for the trees—that God's forgiveness is unconditioned and proffered with both hands open. Although not all Jews were as radical in their application of the Mosaic Law, a similar concern with ritual purity comes through the New Testament as Jesus confronted the Pharisees.

While the Essenes were one of three important sects in the time of Jesus, in fact they are not mentioned at all in the New Testament, and it is the other two sects who would play a more active role in the New Testament story. These were the Pharisees and the Sadducees, and of the two, the Pharisees are the most prominent in the Gospel. Paul himself stated that he was raised in the Pharisaic tradition and, curiously, Paul is the only first century Pharisee contemporary with Jesus whose writings have survived to our time. We do not know as much as we would like about these two sects, especially the Sadducees who apparently were more attached to the temple rites and worship. The Pharisees placed relatively more importance on the study of the Law, and were disposed to a liberal interpretation that adapted the Law to distinct circumstances and permitted extrapolating to situations that were not explicitly foreseen in the Torah. At least one explicit doctrinal difference between these two sects has come down to us through the New Testament. The Sadducees did not believe in the physical resurrection of the dead since it was not an explicit part of the Mosaic Law, whereas the Pharisees accepted the doctrine of physical resurrection on the last day when the dead would rise and be judged. Furthermore, the Pharisees—or at least some of them, and in some degree—had adopted the concept of the continuing existence of the soul after death, a concept that we will return to later.

Besides these three sects, Josephus names a fourth group that he calls the Fourth Philosophy. This is apparently the group that came down to us in history as the Zealots, but their particular religious orientation is not clear, except that Josephus states that they were in agreement with the Pharisees. They may well have been motivated more by social revolution than by religious principle, since in their attacks they seem to have targeted upper class Jews as much as they did the Romans. They do not seem to have left any significant contribution to religious doctrine.

After the destruction of the Temple in 70 CE, the Sadducees lost the focus of their faith and their reason for existence, and dropped out of sight forever. The Essenes for their part had a passive view on life in the sense that they were waiting for God to intervene in history and were not prepared to take an active role in reviving a disastrously dispersed community of the Jews. Many Essenes must have died in the Roman onslaught when the Qumran colony was overrun. Of the three sects, only the Pharisees would survive in the form of rabbinic Judaism, and it is this form of Judaism that has come down to us today in its multiple manifestations. The Pharisees were more focused on the text as their source of inspiration, and thus were capable of regrouping and perpetuating a Jewish tradition through the formation of schools for the study of the Torah and its reinterpretation in the Talmud. In the midst of the vacuum created by the destruction of the Temple, the rabbis would craft the greatest revolution in Judaism since the appearance of Moses Himself. The rabbis claimed for themselves the authority to establish the normative interpretation of the Judaic Scriptures. Yet, being one of many sects, it took the rabbis several years to establish their credibility across the Jewish community in general, and this process may have extended into the second century.

Modern scholarship focuses on these three principle sects as representative of first century Judaism. In fact, what little we know of their doctrines may still not say much about what the masses of the Jews believed, or the way they understood their religion. If we take Josephus as a reliable source, he cites only four thousand Jews among the Essenes, and in another passage he refers to six thousand Pharisees. If it is accurate to associate the Sadducees with the priestly class, they might have been much more numerous—it has been estimated that there might have been tens of thousands of priests in Israel! Yet, summing all these sects, we would not account for even 1 percent of the seven million Jews in that period. Josephus credits the Pharisees with having great influence over the masses, but archaeological evidence suggests that this was certainly not universal. Synagogues of the period display elaborate frescoes and mosaics with images of Moses and other heroes of the Old Testament—a violation of Jewish Law that prohibited the use of human images and that the Pharisees would have opposed if they had had the power to do so. Rather, in the early first century, Pharisaic Judaism was still a minority movement, as was Christianity, each struggling to promote its doctrine and its influence. The Pharisees were obviously far better established than the Christians and were numerically superior, at least at the beginning. As both groups sought to spread their doctrine, they would come into conflict time and again.

So again, what did the masses of the Jews and the man-on-the-street believe? There is really no way to know, but I suspect, despite what Josephus says about the influence of the Pharisees, that the unlettered masses were heavily influenced by the priestly class and by Temple ritual. Jewish practice centered on the Temple was the status quo, and a religion of ritual as mediated by a priestly class was readily accessible to most Jews. While the Jewish masses were subject to multiple and conflicting influences, it is probable that the Judaism of the masses would have been traditional and attached to the Temple and its animal sacrifices and its observance of Jewish holy days. This question is important in the sense of understanding the audience to whom both Christians and Pharisees directed their messages, but in another sense, it does not really matter what branch of Judaism was most numerous or most popular at a given moment. What is important to remember is that these various currents existed, and that early Christianity probably came into contact with all of them at some point in its development. With this perspective, different verses of the New Testament might reflect encounters or clashes of ideas with different sects. One verse might reflect a Christian response to traditional Old Testament Judaism, another verse might be a reaction to Pharisaic doctrine. These are the influences on the Gospel text that we will attempt to tease out of the Gospel story.

What can be stated with certainty is that the Judaism into which Jesus was born was severely divided against itself. It is misleading to refer to the "Jews" in the time of Jesus as if they were a monolithic movement with a united leadership and common doctrine. This present tract might be guilty of this fault as well on occasion, and the reader should bear in mind that Judaism was in fact diverse. Despite this diversity, one recurring theme that was shared by nearly all Jews was a longing for the advent of the Messiah, in the tradition of the Davidic throne. This longing is expressed in the Gospels by the disciples and by the multitudes of Jews who greeted Jesus with "Hosanna to the son of David"[2] when He entered Jerusalem. In the world outside of the Gospels this messianic longing boiled over into revolt against Rome on multiple occasions, and the messianic dimension was made explicit in 135 CE when Rabbi Akiva, foremost of the Jewish sages of his day, proclaimed the leader of the revolt, Bar Kochba, as the Messiah.

When we survey the milieu into which Jesus was born, it was David who contributed one of the most salient features of that society. Other aspects of first century Judaic society traced directly to Moses, of course—the Law and the mode of temple worship. These were still present under Roman rule in the first century and continued without interruption, more freely than they had under Greek Seleucid rule. David's contribution to first century Jewish society was so important precisely because it was *absent*. The Davidic throne, the monarchy that was the symbol and expression of Jewish autonomy, the political entity that accompanied the worship of Yahweh and was its complement in this world—this was what was missing in Jewish life and it was this for which the Jews hungered. As so often happens in the lives of individuals, the Jews were shaped and driven not by what they had, but by what they did not have. In the final analysis, it did not matter whether or not David's Camelot actually existed in history. What was important was that the Jews *believed* that it did, and that they no longer enjoyed its benefits and glory and the self-esteem that it afforded. David supplied the image and the dream and the vision and the hope that contrasted with the subjugation to which the Jews were submitted. Driven by their frustrations, their patience wearing thin, the Jews awaited the Messiah to fulfill their highest hopes. Yet the Jews were driving by looking in the rear view mirror. Their vision of the future was by and large their vision of the past.

So when Jesus was born in a stable in the humblest of beginnings, He had a tall order waiting for Him. In the eyes of the Jews He would have to restore

Jewish autonomy, defend the Jewish Law, and reinstate the Davidic dynasty, in the face of outward oppression and inward division. He would have to follow in the footsteps of David who established Jerusalem as the seat of a Jewish kingdom, and had united the spiritual and political centers in a single central site. In his person, David combined inspired guidance and temporal authority, and any deviation from this model was inconceivable. The pressure was intense, the demands were high, and the Jews were expecting the best from their Messiah. And the last thing that the Jews were expecting or willing to accept from the Son of a Nazarene carpenter was innovation in doctrine, law, and ritual. This was the setting into which Jesus was born. This was the situation that awaited the King of the Jews.

CHAPTER 4

THE SYNAGOGUE:
SOMETHING NEW UNDER THE SUN

In the last two chapters, I referred to the evolution of worship from the tabernacle in the time of Moses, to the Temple of Solomon, and finally to the second Temple, which Herod subsequently remodeled shortly before the time of Christ. There is little question that, as long as the Temple existed, normative Judaism (which is to say, mainstream Judaism) was centered on God's House of Worship. Solomon made the Temple the center of Jewish religion and culture, fulfilling the vision of David and uniting the administrative and spiritual centers of Judaism in one and the same city. After Nebuchadnezzar destroyed Jerusalem, Ezra and Nehemiah returned from exile in Babylonia in the fifth century BCE and reestablished the Temple and its precincts as a requisite for the continuation of Jewish culture. Later, a major event in the age of the Hasmoneans was the purification of the Temple after the Seleucid Antiochus had desecrated it, an event that the festival of Hanukkah commemorates. The New Testament rounds out the picture with its images of loud pageantry surrounding the Temple, recently refurbished by Herod.

Although various currents of Judaism existed in the time of Christ and put varying degrees of emphasis on Temple worship, virtually none would have considered the Temple as unimportant. The Sadducees put the greatest emphasis on Temple worship, but this does not mean by any stretch of the imagination that Pharisees had turned their backs on the Temple. The Sanhedrin, or Jewish high court, where the most distinguished doctors of the Law met, including the foremost of the Pharisees, gathered in the very precincts of the Temple and certainly drew prestige from this proximity. Even the Qumran sect, which withdrew from

Jerusalem and considered the Temple to be desecrated by the clique of priests that presided there, revealed in their protest against the perceived impurity of the Temple, their concern with the Temple per se. The only current of Judaism that did not consider Temple worship important was that of the Samaritans (which if we are strict about the derivation of the term "Judaism," did not have anything to do with Judah and so was not strictly "Judaism"). The Samaritans occupied a part of the ancient kingdom of the north and worshiped at Mount Gerizim, in accord with instructions in Deuteronomy. For the Samaritans, the Temple was not relevant in the least and, to the contrary, represented competition to Gerizim.

The priority of Temple ritual resides in the central role of the animal sacrifices as stipulated by the Mosaic Law to be carried out at appointed times of the year. In the ancient world, both in Judaism and in pagan cultures, such sacrifices were at the core of man's relation to God and served to set one right with God in the purification from sin (atonement), to give thanks at harvest, etc. Without sacrifices, God's religion was incomplete, and the Temple (as the inheritor of the heritage of the tabernacle) was the only place where these could be properly offered. Reference to these sacrifices can be seen in the New Testament when Jesus visits the Temple and casts out the moneychangers and the vendors of doves. More than to satisfy ancient bird lovers, these doves were for use as sacrificial animals before the temple altar.

At some point in the period of the exile and thereafter, something of great historical and spiritual significance occurred. Like many events of long-term impact, this phenomenon developed quietly and almost imperceptibly at first, and in terms of recorded history, very much in the shadow of the Temple. As such, its origins are obscure, and only when it was well established do we have any evidence that it existed at all. This was the development of the synagogue.

It is suggested that the synagogue came into being during the exile of the Jews in Babylonia, and this hypothesis holds a certain logical appeal. We know from the biblical text, as well as from scant archaeological records, that the first exiles removed to Babylonia were not run-of-the-mill Israelites, but were of the nobility and the educated priestly classes. These were certainly Jews familiar with the Holy Text and its study, and derived a firm national consciousness from that Holy Text. Once separated from their traditional site of worship in Jerusalem, one would expect the Jews to have sought some alternative to fill the void left by the loss of the temple ritual. And where would they have turned but to the Holy Text itself, studying this in an organized fashion? Hence, the synagogue would have developed during this period out of a need to share the Holy Text systematically with the community of exiles, as a survival strategy to draw strength in time of trials and to fortify their identity during their absence from Palestine. When the exiles returned to Palestine two or three generations later, they would have brought this renewed scriptural interest with them, together with a nascent institution that was centered on study of the Holy Word. And since there was a delay of many years in the completion of the Temple, the vacuum of temple worship still would have been felt and the synagogue would have continued to fill this vacuum, even in Palestine.

It is important to stress that at this point in history and in the early first century, the synagogue was *not* a temple as we think of it today, any more than a Christian Science reading room is Saint Peter's Cathedral. The Temple was located in Jerusalem on Mount Zion and it was essentially unique. In our own day and age we equate a synagogue with a church or a mosque as a primary site of worship, but this was far from the case as long as the Temple existed. The Jerusalem Temple held pride of place with regards to worship, but the synagogue was a center of the local community, especially outside Jerusalem where Jews had no other option for community life. According to one Talmudic source, eighty synagogues were in Jerusalem itself when Titus destroyed the Temple in 70 CE, and several synagogues have been excavated in Jerusalem from this period. Synagogue and Temple co-existed side by side with no apparent contradiction or conflict.

The synagogue has three names that describe its functions and that say much about its importance in the community. The synagogue is a House of Assembly, a House of Study, and a House of Prayer, although again, while the Temple existed, it probably overshadowed the function of the synagogue as a House of Prayer. The term "synagogue" is derived from the Greek for "assembly," and in its function as a House of Assembly, it is tempting to view the synagogue as a grass-roots organization where the community discussed its common issues, an ancient forum of primitive democracy, but we cannot know to what degree this was the case. Nonetheless, the Old Testament refers to the assembly of the men of Israel in the time of Moses, and later David, and implies a consultative function of this assembly, so that such a function of the synagogue at a much later date is not unthinkable.

Most importantly, the synagogue was the House of Study, the place where the revealed Word was read and the Torah was expounded to the entire community. The reality of the synagogue was inextricably bound up with the Hebrew Bible, which in itself was a unique set of writings. The scriptural tradition of the Jews was unequalled in the Middle East and in much of the world, in the sense that the Jews had a written text attributed to God, unlike the mythology of other peoples. Jewish tradition held that the Hebrew Bible (or at least its most important sections) could be traced directly to Moses and the Prophets, who in turn were inspired directly by God. The Jews enjoyed a sense that the link to God through Jewish Scripture was direct, and that the Word of God was exactly that—words of God enunciated through a chosen instrument. While other groups had mythologies of gods, most of these were essentially legends of how things came to be (etiology) and did not have the sense of superior beings communicating with mankind. And although the Greeks had the tradition that the gods spoke to man through the oracles at Delphi, revelation in this case was such an ad hoc daily occurrence that it detracted from any individual "revealed" message, which in any case often dealt with the most mundane issues of no spiritually transcendent value. In this vein, it must be emphasized that Jewish Scripture conveyed a firm sense of righteousness, morality, ethics, and justice. It was not merely an etiology designed to explain the origins of the Jews, but a purposeful expression of what God desires for and of His creatures.

Furthermore, Jews considered their own history to be the history of God's periodic intervention in human affairs, both in terms of His direction of those affairs and His guidance to His chosen people. Mythological traditions had a static quality about them that did little to convey a sense of progress that was accompanied by the Supreme Being. The Jewish tradition traced the intervention of God over time as He accompanied His chosen children in the discovery of their destiny and spiritual path. The Hebrew Bible was not static, but progressive, and was unique in this sense, too. The Jews possessed a unique scriptural tradition in the Middle East, and this tradition took on new importance and a fresh dimension with the development of the synagogue as a center of study. In a typical service in the synagogue, a teacher would read from the scrolls of the Law in the presence of the congregation and give some exposition on the text that he had read. At least in later times, when the Talmud was being codified, it was custom to read the entire Torah in the synagogue on a cycle of once every three years in Palestine, or once a year in Babylonia.

This structured form of study in the synagogue implies a clear focus on the Torah, a focus that was even incorporated into the architecture of the synagogue. The scrolls of the Law, massive and imposing objects compared to a modern Bible, were held in a wall niche at the front of the assembly in sight of all. We catch a glimpse of the scrolls and the Holy Word as the centerpiece of the synagogue in the Gospel of Luke when Jesus entered the synagogue at Nazareth and, standing before the assembled worshipers, opened the scrolls to a verse of Isaiah—no small task considering their size: " . . . he went into the synagogue on the sabbath day, and stood up for to read. And there was delivered unto him the book of the Prophet Isaiah. And when he had opened the book, he found the place where it was written, The Spirit of the Lord is upon me, because he hath anointed me to preach the Gospel to the poor; he hath sent me to heal the broken-hearted, to preach deliverance to the captives, and recovering of sight to the blind, to set at liberty them that are bruised, to preach the acceptable year of the Lord. And he closed the book, and he gave it again to the minister, and sat down."[1]

The role of the synagogue in the study of the Torah is a subtle point, the importance of which cannot be overestimated, although it is easy to overlook its significance. The study of the Holy Text in the synagogue may not sound novel or revolutionary, precisely because in our own times the study of the Sacred Writ is a standard activity among the faithful in synagogues, churches, cathedrals, temples, mosques, centers, or whatever name is given to a house of worship. But prior to the existence of the synagogue, the Sacred Writ was the domain of a narrow priestly class, the function of which was to interpret and transmit that Holy Word to the masses. In primitive Judaism, or in other religions for that matter, the masses were exposed primarily to the judgments of priests or governors, and the revealed Word was transmitted through the lens of the priestly class. Although in ancient times the Law was read to the entire community of Israelites, this occurred on infrequent occasions and without a study of the same. And while it may appear that this pattern of priestly interpretation continued in the synagogue with the teachers, in fact this was not exactly the case. Just as the synagogue was not a temple, neither was the teacher a priest. Rather he was a student of the Law who had attained enough knowledge thereof to be recognized as a learned person whose own authority and position depended upon the study of the Law. And as we have seen in the account in Luke, the focus of the synagogue service was the Hebrew Bible per se, holding priority over any sermon or interpretation.

In this context, the special significance of the synagogue is this. Direct contact with the Hebrew Bible was not an option for the masses in ancient times, until the synagogue or its ancient equivalent came to be. The synagogue was probably the first opportunity in the history of the world whereby the masses of humanity were exposed extensively, directly, and systematically to the revealed Word. Implications of this phenomenon are primarily spiritual, but also social. Long centuries of experience with the revealed Word demonstrate that it has the potential to inspire the soul and to transform human character. This capacity to transform reflects the combination of the power inherent in Scripture, and the faith that humankind places in it as God's Word. Hence the importance that is universally placed on its study in the diverse religions and at all levels of the community—young and old, rich and poor. As an extension of its spiritual impact, the study of the Word in the context of the synagogue made that spiritual transformation a shared experience and created a community centered on a deeper consciousness of God, and dedicated to fulfilling His principles precisely through an enhanced awareness of the revealed Word.

Unfortunately, history is seldom written from the standpoint of the masses, and the impact of the synagogue on the community of believers before the Common Era must be deduced indirectly from other sorts of observations such as the social coherence of Jewish communities in the Diaspora. For example, a huge Jewish community existed in Alexandria two to three centuries before Christ, where synagogues were well established. Much later, the New Testament refers frequently to the synagogue in the time of Christ. The synagogue and its scriptural orientation come to the forefront in the post-temple period, when the synagogue becomes the sole focus of Judaism. The custom of studying the Holy Word there fit the inclination of the rabbis well with their own scriptural orientation, and eventually the rabbis were able to implement their own brand of Judaism through the institution of the synagogue. Thus, the synagogue would become the vehicle for the survival of Judaism, of which rabbinic Judaism would be the only form to come down to us today.

So significant was the development of the synagogue to the course of Judaism, that several authors have stated that "two Judaisms" existed in the time of Christ—that of the Temple and that of the synagogue. Such a statement results from the contrast in the focus, and especially the attitudes, of religious practice in each respective setting. The Temple was the site of formal, ritualistic worship, characterized by the blood of animal sacrifice, whereas the synagogue offered reverent reflection on the Holy Word. A professional, hereditary priestly class directed Temple worship and might well have guarded their position jealously, and frequently abused their power. The synagogue represented a lay religion, in which any devoted student of the Law might rise to a position of honor through his acquired wisdom. The Temple attracted throngs of unfamiliar crowds on feast days, when Jerusalem swelled to overflowing, whereas the synagogue was warmed by the fellowship of a local community. Temple sacrifices manifested a tribal religion and hearkened back to a day when the Hebrews struggled to distinguish and separate themselves from other surrounding Semitic tribes. In contrast, the synagogue threw its doors open to sympathizers of Greek, Roman, or other origins. The Temple was a stage whereon to parade the opulence of the privileged classes; but in the synagogue, all gathered as equals before God.

The contrast that we can visualize between Temple and synagogue seems to justify the idea of "two Judaisms." Yet it must be stressed that this reference to two Judaisms is a modern view of Jewish religion two thousand years after the fact. It would have made no sense to Jews of the first century, who would have seen both institutions as part of their faith with no contradictions or conflicts, and who would have continued to turn to the Temple as their spiritual center, even as they attended services in the synagogue.

Both types of Judaism—Temple and synagogue—appear in the New Testament and play a role in the story of the Gospels. Jesus frequented synagogues on many occasions and initiated His public Mission in the synagogue in Capernaum according to Mark. However, the most dramatic events of His Ministry (casting out the moneychangers, His own crucifixion) occur in the vicinity of the Temple, while events in the synagogue are on a second plane, reflecting the reality of Judaism per se and the preeminence of the Temple in normative Judaism. It is no coincidence that Jesus is portrayed as being well received and admired in the synagogue of Nazareth, while it was in the Temple precincts that members of the priestly class judged and subsequently crucified Him. The synagogue lent itself to an atmosphere of openness and receptivity among the "common people," whereas in Jerusalem, Jesus came into direct conflict with the hierarchy of the Jewish establishment.

For our purpose of elucidating the origins of Christianity, the immediate significance of the synagogue is that it was the venue where Christians and Jews met and interacted most intensively. We have no documentation of this interaction in the first century outside of the New Testament itself, and even here details are scant. But in the New Testament we find a few references to reveal the nature of this relationship, both in its positive aspects and in its negative and conflictive elements. In the Gospels, this interaction in the synagogue occurs within the context of Palestine; while in Acts, we see this interaction occurring in cities outside Palestine, in Diaspora communities in Asia Minor and Greece. These references, combined with some reading between the lines, and all put into the general historical context, permit us to visualize what was happening in and around the synagogue as the first century advanced.

An appreciation of this interchange among Christians and Jews is indispensable to understanding the origins of Christianity, because it colored the way that Christians presented their faith to their audience, which was often either Jewish or Christians of Jewish origins. In time, this presentation came to be set down in Christian Scripture, and eventually, the origins of Christian Scriptures would influence how later Christians would understand their own faith. To visualize better how this interaction might have unfolded and how it might have impacted on Christianity, let us use our imagination and draw upon the Book of Acts to reconstruct the atmosphere within the synagogue and that surrounded the first Christians.

The traveler and his companion raise their eyes toward the horizon. Dusk is settling and it is not wise to be on the road late after sunset. They can scarcely distinguish the roofs of Antioch and a few dim lights. They had best hurry, not to be caught too late outside the protection of its walls. They walk faster, making the dust swirl around their feet.

"Dust!" muses the traveler. "Well did the Lord say, 'Shake their dust from off thy feet.' Dust is what a missionary journey is made of!"

Tomorrow evening the Sabbath will initiate. They will rest tomorrow and attend the service in the synagogue the following day to see what the Lord has in store for them.

On the Sabbath day they enter the synagogue and take seats close to the front in full sight of all, yet make no other effort to attract attention. If the Lord so desires, they will have their opportunity. A few of those present do not appear to be Jews; perhaps they are Greeks or possibly Romans who sympathize with the religion of the Jews. Here no sincere seeker of the truth is denied entrance. The building is simply organized and sparsely decorated, yet is permeated with an air of reverence as those present speak in hushed tones. As is the custom, the scrolls of the Law are guarded in a niche in the front wall, the focal point of the congregation.

After a few minutes, the leader of the synagogue enters, walking with dignified, measured steps to the front of the House of Assembly. His long white beard testifies to his age, his countenance reflects the wisdom garnered from years of study of the Law and the Prophets. He acknowledges the presence of his visitors with a circumspect nod of the head, but gives no other indication of recognition. Does he suspect their identity? Does he imagine their mission and purpose in attending? He gives no indication, continuing with the service, opening the scrolls to the Book of Exodus and reading from the story of Moses and the salvation of the Hebrews in Egypt. When he finishes, he adds comments of instruction for the congregation and then returns the scrolls to their place. A hymn is sung and the formal service ends. Then he turns to the visitors. Would they care to address the congregation, he asks. Do they have counsels that they would like to share with their brethren?

The traveler does not lose any opportunity to deliver the Message, and when the Lord opens the door, he is quick to take advantage. He leaves his seat and moves to the front of the synagogue. He turns to his audience and, although he looks into their eyes, his gaze seems to be set on some horizon beyond his hearers. The topic of salvation that the leader of the synagogue has expounded serves his purpose well, and he picks up the theme. Although he has delivered this topic a thousand times before, each time that he speaks it is as fresh as if it were the first time. The words well out of his heart as if emanating from an invisible plane, and they surge upon his audience as the waves of a mighty ocean. The speaker is transformed, a tool in the hands of a greater power, a reed through which the Divine pipes His song. For this is Paul! Paul the veteran, Paul the itinerant teacher, Paul the unlikely convert. His delivery is impassioned and reflects the depth of his training in the Law. Quotations from the Prophets spring effortlessly from his lips, yet it is not so much his choice of words that moves the heart, as it is the spirit that his audience senses. Even the illiterate detect the fire of his conviction and feel the heat of his faith.

All are witness to the power that emanates from the speaker, but do they understand his intent? Some nod their heads in assent, yet their faces register no change, suggesting that they have not grasped the weight of his message. Others comprehend his intention, but their eyes betray suspicion and doubt. They would express their resistance, only no such reaction is forthcoming from the leader of the synagogue who listens patiently, and none dares raise his voice in protest without leave from the leader. A number of those present show both assent and the great joy of Good News. They have captured the essence of Paul's message and have understood its implications: the Messiah has appeared! Their prayers have been answered and their souls soar above their immediate surroundings in the joy of their newfound knowledge. They eagerly flock around Paul and express their awe and gratitude. Would he return to teach them in the synagogue on the next Sabbath, they ask.

Paul will linger a few weeks with the new believers in Antioch before he moves on to carry the Gospel to others. Once he has gone, the newfound converts will continue to attend the Torah readings in the synagogue—and why not? Did not the Lord Himself visit the synagogue frequently? Did not their teacher Paul introduce them to the Gospel in this very House of Study? Is the Torah not the Word of God? And is not the synagogue the place where our families and neighbors continue to assemble? Jewish-Christians will continue to worship side by side with Jews for some years yet, while they differ from their brethren in their understanding of the advent of the Messiah.

Soon, Jewish teachers from Jerusalem will come to "set the record straight," seeking to undo what Paul has done. No matter, the seed is sown. It has fallen upon fertile ground and, God willing, will continue to grow and flourish until a rich harvest is forthcoming.

While the dramatization above of Paul's story from Acts 13 is necessarily fictional in many respects, what I consider to be a critical detail—that Paul was *invited* to speak in the synagogue by its leader—is in fact lifted directly from the New Testament.[2] This illustrates an aspect that must be appreciated, that the synagogue presented a potentially open and receptive atmosphere in which the Christian Message could be propagated. I do not mean with this to over-exaggerate the receptiveness of the synagogue as a generality. Indeed, the New Testament reports other instances in which Paul was rejected and even stoned in synagogues, but neither was the response in Antioch unique. "Now when they had passed through Amphipolis and Apollonia, they came to Thessalonica, where was a synagogue of the Jews: and Paul, as his manner was, went in unto them, and three sabbath days reasoned with them out of the scriptures, opening and alleging, that Christ must needs have suffered, and risen again from the dead; and that this Jesus, whom I preach unto you, is Christ." "And the brethren immediately sent away Paul and Silas by night unto Berea: who coming thither went into the synagogue of the Jews. These were more noble than those in Thessalonica, in that they received the word with all readiness of mind, and searched the scriptures daily, whether those things were so."[3]

Compared to Temple worship, the synagogue was a decentralized institution, and each synagogue probably enjoyed autonomy, each was free to develop its own character and inclination, and so it was possible for Paul and others to find those receptive audiences among the Jews by visiting synagogues at every opportunity. And since the Jews in the Diaspora were already spread throughout the Mediterranean world in most important urban centers, and had established their synagogues wherever they had formed a community, these provided an existing stage set in the midst of the Greco-Roman culture from which Paul could launch his forays into the gentile world. And we note that Acts states that it was *"the manner"* of Paul to do so, implying that this was his preferred method of spreading the gospel.

Neither did the role of the synagogue end when a Jew accepted Christ as the Messiah. It is generally accepted that, in the first years, Jewish-Christians attended the synagogue alongside Jews. For example, James, brother of Jesus and bishop of Jerusalem, refers to proper Christian behavior when in the synagogue (which is translated from the Greek as "assembly").[4] James could have used the term *ekklesia*, which also means "assembly" and is more common in the New Testament, so why does he say "synagogue?" Was James referring to attendance in a Jewish synagogue or was he using a Jewish term to describe a Christian gathering? Even in the latter case, the use of the term "synagogue" implies a conceptual dependence of Christian meetings on the Jewish House of Assembly, and this conceptual dependence is even more telling as would be the physical presence in the Jewish synagogue.

In light of the relatively liberal atmosphere in the synagogue (that is, in comparison with the environment in Jerusalem around the Temple), the dialogue of Christian and Jew had the opportunity to grow and develop here. One can visualize the Jews of Antioch or other cities crowding around Paul, Barnabas, or Peter, eagerly posing their questions; the doubters pouring through the Scriptures looking for the arguments to debunk the Christian claims that Jesus was the promised Messiah; the Christians in turn responding with counter-arguments gleaned from the very same Scriptures to substantiate the circumstances of the life and death of Jesus.

Such a scenario might have continued for at least thirty-five years—a generation more or less—starting some time after the crucifixion in the year 30 CE or so, up to the year 70 CE when the Temple was destroyed by the Roman, Titus. Christians saw this calamitous event as a fulfillment of the prophecies of Jesus ("There shall not be left here one stone upon another, that shall not be thrown down."[5]) and therefore as an act of divine retribution upon the Jews for their rejection of the Messiah. The Jews for their part were devastated and were in no mood for what they viewed to be an offshoot, junior branch of their own to be telling them, "I told you so!" when they were already smarting from the loss of the Temple. The Jews regrouped around schools of rabbis now hurriedly established outside of Jerusalem where a new mode of life was formulated. In the following centuries, Jews would have to get used to being a minority living amongst the Gentiles with no homeland or Temple of their own, and this required a reexamination of the Scriptures and a reinterpretation of their own reality to adjust to the new circumstances. And in the course of their reorganization sometime toward the end of the first century, the Jews threw the Christians out of the synagogue once and for all, implementing a ritual curse upon heretics (Christians), the Birkat-ha-Minim, to be read in the synagogue service.

This is a simplistic version of how the split between Judaism and Christianity came about. It no doubt has a degree of validity, and it is tempting to opt for the simplistic explanation when history offers us watershed events that appear to explain the ultimate result. In fact, the separation of Judaism and Christianity was probably a more gradual process that occurred over several decades. Processes by their nature involve complex interactions of multiple factors and are notoriously difficult to understand in detail, and how much more so two thousand years after the fact. Furthermore, it would probably be an error to assume that relations evolved (or deteriorated) uniformly throughout the ancient world of the Christian and Jew. Different environments, situations, and intensity of external forces would have existed in different communities, and between communities in Palestine and in the Greco-Roman world. Although the destruction of the Temple was a "milestone" in the separation process, it is also possible that the Christian-Jewish dialogue that existed in the synagogue continued for a few years more. For example, Justin Martyr, a Christian apologist of the second century living in Rome, wrote a text entitled *Dialogue with Trypho*, in which Trypho is a Jew to whom Justin addresses his arguments drawn from the Old Testament. While Justin's knowledge of Jewish history is faulty, he displays sufficient knowledge about then-current Jewish arguments in a Christian-Jewish debate to suggest that he did in fact obtain information from Jewish sources, directly or indirectly. The very fact that Justin structured his major work around the format of a Christian-Jewish dialogue suggests that this was still a reality in the second century. Be that as it may, the first century saw an ever-widening gap develop between Christianity and Judaism, and this separation received a significant stimulus in 70 CE when the Temple was destroyed.

To visualize this change in relations between Christians and Jews in the course of the first century, let us pick up where we left off after a lapse of some thirty odd years. Let us return to the synagogue with Barnabas, Paul's companion in the days of his evangelizing in Antioch, but now a generation or more later and after the destruction of the Temple. What has happened in the course of these three decades? Again, we will exercise our imagination and put the evolution of events into the context of the synagogue at a time near the end of the first century.

Barnabas draws himself up from his seat slowly. The years have taken their toll; his hair is now thinning and his eyes growing dim. Many things have changed in the thirty years since his missionary travels with Paul. That first generation of apostles have nigh well disappeared—Peter, Paul, James, and the rest. They were the original heroes that first gave their lives for the cause of the Lord. Now their mantle had fallen to a "younger" generation. Barnabas could muse about that term.

"Younger, indeed. How long has it been since I have felt younger?" he chuckles.

Faithful to those who bequeathed on him and his companions their sacred trust, he would not complain, only give thanks for that eternal honor.

Yes, much has changed since his travels with Paul, and more significant than thinning hair. Those had been magical days, when they would visit synagogues and carry the good news for the first time to the remotest corners of Palestine and beyond.

Barnabas had witnessed many miracles of the spirit with Paul—pure hearts that were enlightened at their first knowledge of Christ, souls that remained faithful unto death. There was opposition to be sure, but there were also times when tens or hundreds came to the cause spontaneously. He remembers the response in the synagogues of Antioch and Berea, how the new believers eagerly received the Gospel, how they crowded about and sought the truth with pure hearts.

Such magical times still occur, but less frequently now, at least in the synagogues. Barnabas still visits the friends in the synagogue, but division often interrupts such visits. The Jewish teachers have established their seat in Jabneh, to the west of Jerusalem, and they send their emissaries throughout the region to garner allegiance to the rabbis and obedience to their decisions. Paul in his day would reason with the Jews, but it is ever more difficult now. In the past there was occasional opposition, now it is more organized. The rabbis bring their arguments and even convince a few of the brethren to recant. The Scriptures speak of the Lord, but these use those same Scriptures to discredit Him! The believers must be protected, nonetheless, and even if the Jews will no longer listen, Barnabas returns to the synagogue to strengthen the faith of the Jewish-Christian brethren. Tomorrow is the Sabbath, and we will see what the Lord has prepared for us.

Barnabas enters the synagogue and sees familiar and friendly faces. The loving eyes of old friends greet him, but other faces betray distrust. After the reading of the Torah, one of the Christian friends rises to recite the Lord's Prayer. He starts to pray when he is interrupted.

"This is no scripture fit to recite in the House of Assembly," says one. "These are words of the great deceiver, Jesus of Nazareth who used sorcery to cast spells upon the innocent, working in consort with the Evil One."

Barnabas is not disposed to debate, but he rises to defend the name of the Lord.

"Oh friends," he says, "have you not heard how the Scriptures referred to Him? Were not His words fulfilled when the Roman legions threw down the stones of the temple, leaving not one upon the other?"

His opponent grows angry.

"Deceit!" he cries. "Our Scriptures promise the kingdom of David, not a kingdom of a sorcerer, least of all of one who destroys our temple. Our Messiah must free us from oppression and restore our nation to its rightful place among the races of the world. He who is not with us is against us."

He argues forcefully, and the Jews murmur assent among themselves. The call to political independence strikes a receptive note with them. Even a few of the Jewish-Christian brethren appear to join them in their murmuring. Barnabas has heard these accusations many times before, for the rabbis have consolidated their arguments and diffuse them widely. Barnabas responds as his experience has taught him.

"Did the Scriptures not foretell clearly that the Savior would be born in Bethlehem? Did your fathers not witness His entry into Jerusalem seated on a humble ass, as the Prophet had foreseen?"

He cites several other prophecies gleaned from the Old Testament, and the believers are assured. Are any of the Jews convinced? Time will tell. Barnabas has no taste for debate and dispute, but he bears with them. The believers must be protected, and perhaps even among the Jews a few will hear and respond to the call.

These confrontations are tiresome and, more, they sadden the heart. Did not Paul harbor in his innermost being the hope that his own race would draw near and recognize the Messiah? Rather, time has estranged them more than ever from their true Savior, and dialogue with them is almost impossible now. No, these are not the same times that our brother Paul witnessed.

With these vignettes we attempt to visualize relations between Christian and Jew in the first century within the venue of the synagogue as those relations evolved toward their ultimate state of alienation. In following chapters I will refer to this period and its antagonisms as the critical environment for the development of the Gospels. However, we should not leave the topic of the synagogue without recognizing two huge debts that Christianity has with Judaism in general, and that probably filtered through the synagogue in particular—on the one hand, the very concept of Scripture, and on the other, the orientation toward scriptural study to which I have referred.

When I refer to Christians as having inherited a concept of Scripture, I do not refer to simply the inheritance of the Hebrew Bible from Judaism, as rich and profound as this may be. Rather, just as the Hebrew Scriptures were unique in the ancient world, so was the attitude of the Jews toward that Scripture, and the view that the Jews held that God had set down His will in a written text, which was part of God's presence in this world. Reverence toward Scripture was a traditional Jewish value, which was given expression in the synagogue where the Torah was shared with the community. It was in the synagogue that the Jews carried the study of the Scripture to the masses of the believers and created communities focused on the Revealed Word.

As nascent Christian communities grew out of the synagogue and developed a life of their own, they nonetheless maintained much of the same structure of worship. Evidence indicates that the first Christians, even in their Christian meetings that were apart from the synagogue, would employ an agenda that included scriptural readings, and indeed, at first the only writings that were considered "Scripture" were drawn from the Hebrew Bible. In other words, the Christians adopted not only the Old Testament, but also a model of worship and the reverence for Scripture that was implicit in that model. The custom of reading the Old Testament in a community gathering was grafted directly from the synagogue to the nascent church.

Subsequently, when Christian Scripture came into being, that same vision of a Holy Text was transferred from the Old Testament to the Gospels and the letters of the apostles. Indeed, one can speculate whether that very scriptural tradition of the Jews did not serve as a stimulus and a motive for Christians to set down their own sacred story. The Hebrew Bible was the model that served Christians as they sought to consolidate the foundations of a new faith as a separate religion.

Now, it may appear that Christianity was bound to adopt this scriptural orientation in any case, that Scripture would eventually take its rightful role and place in the community and would become the center of community worship. Perhaps, but not necessarily. In a Mideastern world in which religion outside of Judaism was focused on magical elements, Christians could well have become carried away with the mystical (or pseudo-mystical) elements of Christianity. For example, Paul's letter to the church in Corinth indicates that some believers there were putting heavy emphasis on charismatic practices such as speaking in tongues or prophesying. Such ecstatic states of religious fervor were commonly a part of pagan religions, and Christians in the Greco-Roman world readily would have felt that these practices were a natural part of religious experience. Such practices could have absorbed Christianity in the gentile world. Or Christians could have become obsessed with rites of purification, as seems to have been the case with the Ebionite sect of Christians who were firmly attached to Jewish traditions. Christian commentators in the second and third centuries refer to sects of Jewish-Christians that by that time were considered non-orthodox, and whose focus was on Jewish practice of frequent bathing to maintain a state of ritual purity.

The point is that other options were open to those first Christians besides making the study of Scripture central to their faith. I suspect that the environment in the synagogue that was conducive to a sober and reflective approach to the Scriptures was extended to Christianity in its formative years. And just as this scriptural orientation represented a moral force within the synagogue that was unique and not to be underestimated, the inheritance that was passed on to the church was likewise as significant, in assuring a sober and reverent approach to spirituality, and its application to human moral character. This is a heritage whose profound influence cannot be underestimated.

In sum, the early church emerged from a Jewish matrix, and in some cases it probably emerged slowly and painfully. It drew on its Jewish heritage and on some of its healthy aspects, especially those associated with experience in the synagogue. As long as the church had one foot in Judaism and one foot in a new revelation, it suffered an identity crisis, and what is more, it had to confront its old identity, its Jewish face, both in dealing with Jewish-Christians and with Jewish opposition. These were the central, burning issues of the church in the first century, and were some of the important factors that shaped Christian Scripture for all time. I will deal with this evolving relationship more fully in the next two chapters.

CHAPTER 5

THE EARLY CHURCH:
TWO POLES OF A NEW FAITH

Just as we can talk about "two Judaisms" in the first century, one focused on the Temple and the other on the synagogue, we can also talk in broad terms about "two Christianities." I alluded to Jewish-Christianity when I referred to the synagogue, and indeed this early version of Christianity was firmly rooted in Judaism. I attempted to visualize the environment in the synagogue and how Christians might have viewed their own participation there. Few people doubt that at least some Jewish-Christians continued to attend the synagogue, and the Book of John makes explicit reference to this in the time of Christ. When Jesus bids farewell to His disciples in John, He warns them: "They shall put you out of the synagogues."[1] Other evidence of the presence of Jewish-Christians in the synagogue is indirect, such as the curse against heretics to be recited in the synagogue that the rabbinical authority promulgated toward the end of the first century, a curse that would have inhibited the presence of Christians.

The initial followers of the Jewish-Christian church, including the disciples, had been born as Jews and raised in the Jewish tradition, under the Jewish Law. Even after becoming Christians (and we should be careful about projecting our own concept of what that conversion might have meant to them), most would have been essentially indistinguishable from Jews, with the caveat that they had accepted Jesus as Messiah. Yet they did not see in this fact any reason to abandon Jewish practice. On the contrary, for them Jesus was the Messiah to the Jews, fulfilling Jewish expectation and having appeared to purify and restore Judaism to its pristine state, thereby confirming Judaism and its tradition. Abandoning Jewish practice would have been an act of infidelity with that same tradition and therefore a contradiction of the very act of having accepted the Messiah.

The case of Peter is an example of this attachment to Jewish practice among early Jewish-Christians. In the Book of Acts, Peter is recorded as visiting the Temple for worship even after the crucifixion. And remember that Peter was a native of Galilee and not Jerusalem, so before coming to Jerusalem with Jesus, he would not have been in the habit of going to the Temple, except possibly on special feast days when he might have traveled from Galilee for the occasion.

The champion of the Jewish-Christian church was James, brother of Jesus and first bishop of the church of Jerusalem. He is a little known figure about whom there is scarcely mention in the New Testament, outside of his encounter with Paul, his position as a pillar of the church, and one epistle attributed to him. He resurfaced rather unexpectedly in the twenty-first century when an ossuary (a stone coffin for bones) was uncovered, inscribed with his name and identifying him as son of Joseph and brother of Jesus. Josephus, the Jewish-turned-Roman historian, records that a brother of Jesus was the leader of the church in Jerusalem and was unjustly martyred—one of only two or three facts about Christianity that he bothers to record. It is a rather interesting detail for a non-Christian to be aware of and to be passing on to posterity, but perhaps indicative of the prominent role that James must have played in the early years.

Apart from the Jewish-Christian church, the "other" Christianity was gentile Christianity, and Paul was its creator and its champion. Although, according to the New Testament, Paul was not responsible for the conversion of the first non-Jews to Christianity, it was he who made conversion of non-Jews a widespread phenomenon and therefore an issue for the church. Paul made three extensive missionary journeys throughout the Mediterranean world, penetrating deep into Asia Minor and visiting several cities in the Grecian peninsula. The Book of Acts says that he made his way to Rome, but his own letters do not confirm this, and in his letter to the Romans he expressed the intention to go as far as Spain in his efforts to evangelize. Once having established those Christian communities of Asia Minor and Greece and having moved on, Paul would write to his spiritual children offering them his insight and guidance as the need arose. It is evident from these letters that he is writing to communities that are more than a few isolated individuals. These are communities that have grown to the point of having problems of dissent and factions.

After Paul, it was Luke who contributed to consolidating the foundations of gentile Christianity, at least from our perspective some two thousand years later, by recording extensively in Acts the efforts of Paul. The Book of Acts serves to confirm Paul's role as the channel of God's will to the non-Jews, and is our primary historical source of Paul's activities, giving an overview of his missionary work within which we position Paul's own letters as snapshots of specific churches at given moments.

Even in the Greco-Roman world, Paul taught first in the synagogues of cities such as Thessalonica where the Jews represented a minority living within their own quarter in the city. The first Christians even in these cities were probably either Jews or gentile sympathizers of Judaism who were accustomed to Jewish monotheism, Jewish worship and, even more importantly, Jewish Scripture. Thus, early on, Christian worship in these communities might have borne considerable resemblance to synagogue worship even in the house church, a nascent institution that was developing outside of the synagogue. We have the most evidence of house churches among the gentiles in Greece, Asia Minor, and Rome, largely from references to these in Paul's Epistles, but we cannot rule out the possibility that house churches coexisted with synagogue worship in the Jewish-Christian world as well.

In simplest terms, the house church was a meeting place in the home of a believer who facilitated his or her house for community gatherings. Different modes of the house church might have evolved, as likely happened in a decentralized system. Worship might have varied from church to church, but evidence suggests that sermons, hymns, exhortations, and prayer all formed part of the early church meetings. Within the church, certain individuals had specific functions and leadership roles (deacons, bishops, etc), but these were still different from our modern version of a church hierarchy, and letters written by bishops even in the second century indicate a consultative leadership style rather than the authoritative role that the position would eventually assume as the church administration consolidated itself. Some of the characteristics of the house church were probably dictated by the economic status of the house owner. Aquila and Priscilla were faithful Christians from Rome who moved to Ephesus and then back to Rome. They were close associates of Paul and even shared his trade as tent makers. One can imagine that they were not wealthy and did not have a dwelling that could accommodate many, yet Paul sent greetings to the church in their house. On the other hand, if a well-to-do Greek or Roman became a Christian, as appears to be the case of Philemon, and made his house available as a church on occasion, his status as house owner, and as lord and master of family, servants, and slaves would have carried over to his position as host of a house church. In the Greco-Roman world, the household was the microcosm of society, and the head of the household held a position of unquestioned honor and respect within his domain.

If the same spirit of brotherhood animated Jewish-Christian and gentile Christian alike, the challenges that faced these two poles of Christianity were very different! In gentile Christianity, the challenges of the gentile church were those of a nascent community fending off the vices of a freewheeling polytheistic world. The pagan environment out of which Christians came to the church was extremely liberal in a moral sense. Pederasty was widely practiced, at least among the Greek upper classes, and prostitution, both male and female, was not uncommon. Alcohol and excess were part of the "good life."

This external environment spilled over into the life of the Christians, and Paul resorted to frequent exhortations to morality in his letters to these churches. Corinth was the extreme example of the challenges of this "liberality" and Paul upbraided the church roundly for its multiple indiscretions. For example, some of the Corinthians had become carried away with the Eucharist ceremony and had taken to drinking to excess in the service. Somebody was actually getting tipsy during worship! Someone else was guilty of incestuous relations, sleeping with his mother-in-law. The problems of vice are the most obvious negative influences of the pagan world on the early church. However, other more subtle problems also arose, such as social relations that filtered into the church and that were not entirely consistent with Christian love, such as those between master and slave or between rich and poor social classes. We can well admire the faith of those first pioneers of western Christian civilization, but we should not get overly romantic about the reality that the young church lived at that time.

Why did Paul need to make these fervent calls to his converts? Had they not understood the simple and basic tenets of a Christian community and a moral life? Were these young Christians not sincere in their faith? This conclusion would be too harsh a judgment on these young churches—essentially, this was not a problem of sincerity, but of the reality of a young religion. The trials of the young gentile church were the natural outcome of the conversion of individuals who came from an undisciplined lifestyle, and should not surprise us. For the most part, new converts to a religion are slow to assimilate fully the changes implicit in a new belief system. There are exceptions to be sure, such as Paul himself, whose life was revolutionized in a brief moment, but the kinds of changes in culture and moral standards that the Christian Message demanded of its converts usually are assimilated only over one or more generations.

Note, too, that conversion in the ancient Greco-Roman world was not comparable to what we might call conversion to an existing church in our own times, in which an established congregation sets the tone, moral standard, and atmosphere, and offers the peer support of an existing community. The first Greco-Roman Christians were breaking new ground within their cultural setting. They had little model to follow, except for that of the Jews and the synagogue in cases where Paul had initiated his teaching there, and that connection must have become increasingly tenuous as the church grew and attracted mostly gentile believers. Paul attempted to train leaders in those early churches and leave the congregation in able hands, but it was no easy task that those first church leaders faced, to nurture an environment reflecting the moral standard that they were called upon to manifest.

Thus the early gentile church in the Greco-Roman world mirrored the weaknesses and vices of the surrounding environment in that first generation of believers, but the Jewish-Christian community, set in the midst of a largely Jewish culture, faced a very different situation. The society in which the Jewish-Christians lived and moved, and in which Jesus Himself was born and taught, already exercised a high moral standard. If there were problems associated with moral questions, these were concerned not so much with overcoming vice as with overly zealous application of laws dealing with personal conduct and morality. This is conveyed pointedly in the story of Jesus and the adulteress, where the judgment of Jesus is formulated as, "Let him who is without sin cast the first stone."[2] In this environment, Jesus sought to moderate a rigorous and judgmental application of the Law with patience, understanding, and forgiveness.

Ingrained traditions and religious orthodoxy, rather than vice and immorality, were the challenges that the Jewish-Christian church faced. In the external environment, orthodoxy manifested itself as opposition from the Jewish establishment, which argued against the Christian claims that Jesus was the long-awaited Messiah. The New Testament contains explicit references to opposition in those early years after the crucifixion, most graphically in the martyrdom of Stephen, a young Christian who had invoked the ire of Hellenistic Jews (i.e., Jews who had adopted elements of Greek culture) and who as a result was stoned to death. Luke states that shortly after the martyrdom of Stephen, the disciples were forced to flee from Jerusalem. Other acts of aggression were directed against Peter, and eventually Paul, who in his own letters states that he was flogged no less than four times. If we had only the New Testament accounts to inform us, we might ask ourselves if these were isolated incidents, but a review of the times only serves to confirm that Christians must have found themselves in a precarious position.

In retrospect, we might tend to focus on the early church as central to the events of the first century. However, the tone of Jewish history at that time was dominated not by the relationship with Christians, which for Jews must have been a minor sideline of the day, but by Roman oppression and the longing of the Jews for their independence. Romans had held sway in Palestine for over a century and had ground their boot heels into the Jewish nation since the days of Herod who lent himself to Roman designs in return for their support. When Herod died in the year 4 BCE and left a brief power vacuum, the Romans brutally repressed Jewish revolt and crucified thousands. Life was in turmoil and the birth of a carpenter's son did not rank among the signal events of the day, at least not to any contemporary observer. By the mid to late first century of the Common Era, Jewish nationalism was coming to a boil. The Jews were looking for relief wherever they could find it.

The New Testament portrays the expectations that the Jews held in the time of Jesus for a nationalistic Messiah and a restoration of the Davidic throne that would liberate the Jews from foreign domination. These nationalistic aspirations broke out in open revolt against the Romans in 66 CE, and what next occurred defies reason. The greatest power on earth, with a seasoned army that had conquered Egypt and had brought vast hoards to their knees, delayed four years in putting down the revolt of an insignificant minority in an impoverished corner of the realm. First the rebels overran the local garrison in Palestine. Then a Roman legion was dispatched from Syria to establish order, but was driven out in humiliation. Vespasian, the Roman commander and conqueror of Britain, at last was sent to put down the rebellion. After wasting Galilee, he corralled the Jewish forces in Jerusalem. Surrounded with no escape, starvation started to take its toll among the hapless Jews. Josephus tells bloodcurdling tales of the suffering that the Jews experienced within the walls of David's city, and this agony would have dragged on but for the fact that Vespasian, having returned to Rome to seize the emperor's throne, needed some political capital to strengthen his popularity. Thus, his son Titus, in search of a quick victory, drove his legions to suicidal attacks that saw Roman and Jewish blood mix in the gullies that descended to the Valley of Kidron. Titus moved in for the kill and desecrated the holy city in August of the year 70 CE. Stragglers escaped to Masada where the Zealots held out for another three years, until their legendary mass suicide. Titus returned to Rome triumphant, and a victory arch erected in his honor still bears images of Jerusalem's inhabitants in chains, and of the city's treasures being carted away, including a huge menorah pilfered from the Temple.

Our attention is naturally riveted on the one hand to the tragedy of the destruction of the holy city and its sanctuary, and on the other to the intense suffering that accompanied it, both during the siege and afterwards when Jews were slaughtered or enslaved. Underlying these calamities, there is a lesson here that is just as relevant for us, and it is this. The very fact that the Jews could resist Rome for four years, and time after time preferred death to defeat, is more than a history of heroism or a reliving of David and Goliath. It is an indicator of the intensity of the Jewish effort and their zeal, and is very telling about the atmosphere that prevailed in the first century. Fanatical Zealots were in the driver's seat and set the tone of Judaism and the whole of Jewish history in that moment. This fanaticism was not limited to a hatred of the Romans, but was extended to Jews who did not share their commitment. Josephus was an eyewitness to the fall of Jerusalem and records that more moderate Jews, who desired to come to terms with the Romans in the midst of the siege, were slaughtered as readily by their Jewish brethren as by the Romans themselves.

Nor did this nationalistic fervor end in 70 CE when the Temple was destroyed. Revolt was rekindled in 115-117 CE, and decisively in 132-135 CE in the rebellion led by Bar Kochba with very broad popular support. The name of Bar Kochba (Son of Star) is rooted in an Old Testament messianic promise of Isaiah and implies messianic expectations associated with national liberation. Rabbi Akiva, the foremost of Jewish sages, himself proclaimed Bar Kochba to be the Messiah, confirming those associations in the minds of the Jews. And once again, the Jews were remarkably successful in that last revolt in holding off the Roman legions for more than two years, but the handwriting was on the wall and independence was not to be their lot.

The point of this historical survey is that for almost three full generations the Jews were seething with fervor to obtain their freedom from foreign domination. Their enthusiasm must have had its ups and downs in the face of disastrous defeats, but the fact that it could resurge so vigorously only confirms its depth. Within Jewish society, this was the force that dominated the first century, and even though there were more moderate elements among the Jews, their voices were drowned out. The feverish atmosphere was all embracing and inescapable.

What of the Christians in this environment? We can only imagine and must read between the lines to visualize what the Christians might have been experiencing, but one overriding fact of the early Jewish-Christian church is undeniable. This fact is not recorded explicitly in any tract or history of that age, nor is it emphasized in the writings of the apostles. And still it is a reality that set the tone of the church in that first century, and it is this—that compared to the Jewish population, Christians were a tiny minority in the land of the Jews and even outside of Palestine. One estimate puts the number of Jews in first century Palestine at around two million, and outside of Palestine in the Diaspora at about five million. The very highest estimate of the total number of Christians at the end of the first century is around five hundred thousand while other estimates are as few as seven thousand including gentile Christians in other regions. Jews outnumbered Christians by a factor of *at least* 10 to 1, and probably much, much more. In particular, within Palestine there is no question that relatively few Jews had accepted Jesus as Messiah, and here the Christians were an even smaller minority. Religious minorities often suffer marginalization and prejudice even at the best of times. And this minority status in the midst of an increasingly unsettled political and social climate put the Jewish-Christians in an even more delicate position.

What would have been the position of the Christian leadership as the political atmosphere was heating up? We assume that they sought to avoid participating in agitation against Rome, if for no other reason than because they no longer shared the Jewish view that overthrowing the Roman yoke would be part and parcel of the advent of the Messiah. If the Jews felt that their revolutionary efforts would be confirmed when the Messiah appeared, the Christians obviously held no such expectations because they had already accepted Jesus as Messiah. Thus the continuing expectations of the Jews held no validity for the Christians. Much less had Jesus advocated any such action against Rome.

Apart from theological reasons for not participating in the revolts against Rome, the church had other reasons. Christians had already felt the sting of Roman repression when Nero made them a scapegoat for the burning of Rome in 64 CE. Having set a sector of the city aflame to open an area for the building of his palace, Nero needed to placate the populace and give it a defenseless victim on whom to vent its wrath, and to divert suspicions from his own act of arson. His glance fell upon the Christians who were hounded down, assassinated, tortured, or driven from the city. After this firsthand experience with Roman brutality with no justifiable cause, the Christians were careful not to give the Romans any additional pretexts for further repression.

The reticence of Christians to support the Jewish revolts was probably a source of irritation to the Jews, perhaps more important than we imagine after two thousand years. We have seen that the Zealots had little patience for those who did not share their revolutionary fervor. Just as the fanatical factions murdered moderate Jews, radical Jews must have viewed Christians as shirkers who were avoiding their responsibility before God. This issue might have been a flashpoint between Christians and Jews in this period, more even than theological issues. The Christian-Jewish tension in this regard is presented rather subtly in the Gospel when the Pharisees ask Jesus if it was lawful to pay taxes to Caesar, and Jesus replies: "Render therefore unto Caesar the things which be Caesar's, and unto God the things which be God's."[3] In other words, the Jews were expressing their anti-Roman sentiment in their resistance to taxation, while Jesus is represented as being rather ambivalent toward Rome.

This is not to say that the question of Christian "neutrality" before Rome was the only issue that divided Christians and Jews. The latter would hardly have been indifferent to the Christian claim that Jesus was the Messiah, and they certainly must have opposed this claim vigorously for several reasons. However, the all-consuming issue of the day for the Jews was the Roman occupation, and the reticence of Christians to participate in the revolt as a corollary of having accepted Jesus would have made the Messiahship of Jesus all the less palatable to the Jews. Faced with demands to defend the motherland, the Jewish-Christians were on the defensive. In their minority status, the Jewish-Christians were caught between the Roman repression that fell upon all, and the restive Jewish Zealots who viewed them as potential traitors. There is some evidence that in the time of Bar Kochba Christians were persecuted, perhaps for their reticence to support rebellion. This overt pressure is likely symptomatic of social pressure that was brought to bear on Christians for many years, as long as Jewish revolutionary fever boiled.

This social pressure on Christians, especially in Palestine, would have been a potent force to deal with, and the church fathers must have dedicated considerable effort to sustaining the faith of their young flock and consolidating their Christian identity. The members of the congregation, having accepted the

Messiahship of Jesus as central to their faith, found themselves in varying degrees of comprehension on secondary points of doctrine. In other words, early Christians as individuals were in varying degrees Christian and Jewish, on a continuum as it were. One might even speculate that the prospect of throwing off the Roman yoke once and for all indeed attracted some Jewish-Christians, and that they were receptive to the arguments of Jewish nationalism. The ties of tradition would have been strong, especially among the Jews who for centuries had thought of themselves—had felt like—a chosen people. The cause of Jewish freedom must have been a powerful siren call for anyone born into that millennial tradition! The church fathers would have struggled to keep the Jewish-Christians from getting embroiled in revolt: "Put up again thy sword into his place: for all they that take the sword shall perish with the sword."[4]

Consequently, the congregation of Jewish-Christians, the man in the street, the rank and file, existed in a tug-of-war between the church fathers, who sought to maintain the integrity of the church, and the Jewish society that sought to absorb them once more into the mainstream of Jewish tradition, doctrine, and national aspirations. It was a struggle for the souls of the faithful, who were pulled in two directions. On the one hand, they were attracted to a Jesus who had touched their hearts, and whose doctrine had illumined a dark and hopeless age. On the other hand, the inertia of tradition pulled them toward the observances and laws that their fathers had followed for centuries, toward the aspirations of freedom that their Jewish brethren manifested, and toward family ties and old friendships. It was in light of such pressures that the Gospel writer felt compelled to record statements such as: "If any man come to me, and hate not his father, and mother, and wife, and children, and brethren, and sisters, yea, and his own life also, he cannot be my disciple."[5] As the intensity of the struggle grew, the task of holding the church together became more difficult.

So central is this situation to an appreciation of the early church in Palestine, that it is worthwhile taking a moment to let our imagination fly once again, and to visualize what the man in the street Jewish-Christian must have been experiencing during those years.

Zachariah settles into his seat in the synagogue, at the side of his aging father and mother. His parents have never espoused the faith of Jesus, although they have always shown great respect for the apostles when they have had the good fortune to receive one of those chosen few in their humble place of worship. Zachariah, in his turn, has great respect for his parents, and bears in his breast the hope that they, too, may one day accept Jesus as the Promised Messiah.

These are troubled times, and no peace is to be found in Palestine. Fifteen years have passed since the Romans razed the Temple in Jerusalem. Zachariah has heard from his Christian teachers that Jesus referred precisely to this tragedy, and that it is

God's judgment upon those who stubbornly refuse to recognize God's chosen Messiah. On the other hand, he is also pained at the grief and anger of his parents at this sacrilege committed against their ancient traditions.

Today, a rabbi from the Jewish school at Jabneh has arrived to speak in the synagogue. He is received as is befitting one learned in the Law, and is accorded a seat of honor in the front of the synagogue. His theme is one that stirs the audience and raises emotions, for he speaks passionately of the deliverance of the Hebrews from the Pharaoh. The rabbi's message is indirect, but his intention is clear to his Jewish audience. Just as God rescued the Hebrews in days of old, so too will He liberate His chosen people in the days of the Messiah! He ends with a veiled warning against a false messiah by citing the command in Deuteronomy to hang an executed criminal from a tree: "He that is hanged is accursed of God."[6] This is a frequent jab that the rabbis use to reject the claims that Jesus is the Messiah. How can a man executed on a wooden cross be the Messiah and a deliverer, if the very Word of God testifies that such a one is cursed?

Zachariah's father is absorbed in the sermon that he is hearing. Like most of his neighbors, the old man also lost family members in the war with the Romans nearly two decades ago, and his years have not erased that memory. His head moves in approval and his eyes glisten with tears as he listens to the age-old story of liberation. The repetition of tradition affords both comfort in trials and hopeful expectations for the future. Yes, the time will come again! Yes, it is time for the Messiah, and of course, the Messiah could never be an executed criminal!

Zachariah looks at his father. He is moved by his father's longings, and his own eyes fill with tears. How he desires to satisfy his father's hopes! Can his father's instincts be wrong? Will God not redeem His chosen people? Are those ancient traditions that are their millennial heritage to be abandoned? Is the blood of his father's family to go unavenged? These are the thoughts that course through his mind and perturb his heart as he listens to the sermon and watches the emotions reflected in his father's face.

In this environment, apostasy was a serious concern and a problem in the early church. The First Epistle of John is primarily concerned with apostasy, to the extent that those who have turned their backs on Christ and abandoned the church are denounced as antichrists: " . . . as ye have heard that antichrist shall come, even now are there many antichrists . . . They went out from us, but they were not of us; for if they had been of us, they would no doubt have continued with us."[7] Although much legend has arisen around the term "antichrist," its meaning in this context is concrete. The term "antichrist" is applied to those apostates who have betrayed Jesus and the church, and is extended to all those who deny the Messiahship of Jesus: "Who is a liar but he that denieth that Jesus is the Christ? He is antichrist, that denieth the Father and the Son."[8] "Every spirit that confesseth that Jesus Christ is come in the flesh is of God: and every spirit that confesseth not that Jesus Christ is come in the flesh is not of God: and this is that spirit of antichrist, whereof ye have heard that it should come; and even now already is it in the world."[9] There may be a hint here of resistance to a group called the Docetists who argued that Jesus was pure spirit with nothing of the flesh, but the Docetists became a problem later in the second century. A more straightforward explanation is that it is the Jews who denied that the Messiah had been made manifest in the person of Jesus, and that this latter verse is directed against them, and is meant as a warning to those who would submit to their arguments.

Apostasy is also an important theme of the Book of Hebrews, which appears to have been directed specifically to Jewish-Christians in the mid-first century. A central motivation of this letter is to warn the Jewish-Christians against the dangers of falling away: "Take heed, brethren, lest there be in any of you an evil heart of unbelief, in departing from the living God." "For it is impossible for those who were once enlightened, and have tasted of the heavenly gift, and were made partakers of the Holy Ghost, and have tasted the good word of God, and the powers of the world to come, if they shall fall away, to renew them again unto repentance; seeing they crucify to themselves the Son of God afresh . . ."[10] The degree to which the problem of apostasy plagued the church is impossible to ascertain, but where there is smoke, there is fire. And remember that this was only twenty or thirty years after the crucifixion, when the early church was still in its formative years and most of its membership in Palestine had been born into the Jewish tradition.

Such were the external and internal environments and the challenges of Jewish orthodoxy. Since Jewish-Christians still shared many concepts and customs with Jews, when the church fathers dealt with their Jewish-Christian congregation, their situation reflected many or most of the same issues as did teaching the Jews in the synagogue. Many of the cases of Jesus confronting the Jews that I will refer to in subsequent chapters we will view through the lens of being meant for consumption by a Jewish-Christian audience instead of the Jews per se.

Even within the church, it was not merely the rank and file that displayed a reticence to detach from Jewish custom. The church leadership was also slow to abandon Jewish orthodoxy at the same time that they were called upon to diffuse the innovative spiritual teachings of Jesus. No less a figure than Peter continued to worship in the Temple, and many in the church insisted on circumcision as a requisite to entering the covenant of God. The Book of Acts records a vision of Peter in which he was commanded to abandon the dietary restrictions of the Law, but we can only imagine that behind this account was an agonizing struggle that challenged many Jewish-Christians. The Jewish-Christian church continued with one foot in Judaism and one foot in the new Revelation. While the Jewish-Christians were undoubtedly sincere in their convictions, this ambiguity probably made the task of the church fathers in defending the church against

Jewish orthodoxy all the more difficult as they sought to walk a tightrope between being Jewish enough, but not too Jewish. This kept the church in a fuzzy middle ground wherein it neither separated from Judaism nor acquired its own distinctive identity as an independent religion, while the gentile church, unshackled by such conceptions, was free to evolve its own Christian identity.

Thus, the two poles of the church—Jewish and gentile—suffered from different pressures. The religious orthodoxy of the young Jewish-Christian church contrasted with the relative laxity of the gentile church and its problems of morality, alcohol, etc. As the Jewish-Christians looked at the gentile converts, they were quick to prescribe the application of the Law, and especially circumcision, as a cure-all for their spiritual ills; while gentile Christians, championed by Paul, were reticent to adopt the Law as part of their daily life. This created the tensions between gentile and Jewish-Christians that are recorded in the Book of Acts and some of Paul's letters. Paul explicitly complained of the narrowness of those Jewish-Christians who insisted on Jewish norms for gentile converts, and together with the apostles and James, sought a compromise whereby Jewish-Christians could continue to follow their conscience and abide by Mosaic Law, while Christians of gentile origin need not do so. This solution was a stopgap measure with its own internal contradictions that could only perpetuate the tensions described in the New Testament. Yet the very tensions suggest an important and fundamental situation to be dealt with in the primitive church: how to reconcile a new religion and a new revelation with the Jewish-Christians that were just that—half Jewish and half Christian.

Modern scholarship has emphasized the tensions that existed between these two poles of the church, and the differences in outlook regarding the role of Judaic Law for Christians. Yet despite real tensions, I suspect that the Jewish-Christian church continued to hold pride of place and the love and respect of the gentile church, for most of that first century of the Christian era. At this point, permit me to speculate. As I attempt to visualize the situation of the early church and put myself in the position of the first Christians, I must imagine that the churches in Palestine, and particularly in Jerusalem, enjoyed a certain special prestige in that early Christian world. Certainly all Christians of any origin, both Jew and gentile, held Jerusalem in reverence as the site of the passion of Jesus. Peter, and perhaps other apostles, continued to reside in Jerusalem for some time, lending additional prestige to that community. The church of Jerusalem must have been widely respected as the guardian of those original traditions so closely associated with their Savior, and as the mother church to which others looked as an example. All these factors would have made the Jerusalem church the spiritual center of a faith that was spreading around the world of the Mediterranean. Indeed, if after twenty centuries Christians still look to Palestine with reverence, how much more would they do so in an age when there were no other centers, neither administrative nor spiritual, to compete for the attention of the faithful.

This is precisely the way in which Luke portrays Paul's attitude in Acts, where we see Paul, the Apostle to the gentiles, returning to the Jerusalem church for validation of his strategy for the entry of gentiles to the faith. Paul had been spreading the Gospel among gentile communities for several years already, and he was apparently taking some heat for his methods and for his claim that gentiles need not be circumcised nor be subject to traditional Jewish Law. Paul sought the approval of the apostles for his views, which, if conferred, would have implications for the church far beyond what even Paul could have visualized. A council of the apostles was held for this purpose in about 48 CE in Jerusalem, this being the only sort of centralized governing body that the Christian faith had at that moment. (One wonders if the council was not viewed as the equivalent of the Sanhedrin, which was the supreme Jewish body at that time, and which also met in Jerusalem.) Quite happily for western Christianity and the future of the gentile world, the apostles gave their assent to Paul's point of view.

Thus, even Paul (and Luke in his role as Paul's historian) looked to Jerusalem for decisions about such matters of policy. This is particularly significant considering that Luke was a gentile Christian writing in the latter half of the first century. Despite his origins and the fact that he was writing some four or five decades after the time of Jesus, he still looked to Jerusalem as his spiritual homeland. In relation to the timing of the writing of the Gospels, the Acts were written after all the Gospels except that of John, and this attitude would have been current while the Gospels were being set down.

This may sound perfectly logical, and it probably is if the apostles were concentrated in Jerusalem. However, it is indicative that Christianity, even as it attracted more and more gentiles, continued to view Jerusalem as its mother church, and to a certain extent as its standard and judge of what normative Christianity ought to be, to the end that the approval of Jerusalem was sought on policy matters. It probably is not surprising, then, that the Jewish-Christian church (or at least someone in this church) also viewed itself in the role as guardian of normative Christianity, since Jewish-Christian emissaries went out to circumcise the new gentile believers, much to Paul's chagrin. For our purposes, the self-image of these Jewish-Christians is the other side of the coin, but it confirms Luke's view of Jerusalem being the authoritative center of the faith. Furthermore, in the Epistle to the Galatians, Paul is upset with a gentile church in Asia Minor that has adopted the practice of circumcision under the urging of Jewish-Christians. While attention is usually focused on Paul's view in this letter, the attitude of the Galatians is just as significant, since this represents a gentile church that was receptive to the arguments of the Jewish-Christian emissaries who sought to implement the Law. This most certainly reflects their respect for the church that those "Judaizers" claimed to represent, just as Paul and Luke held that church in veneration.

Neither should the prestige of the Jerusalem church be viewed simply in the sense of an incipient church hierarchy with the authority to decide on matters of doctrine. We must suppose that gentile Christians felt a spiritual link to that community of Palestine and that all Christians held a special love for the brethren in Jerusalem. This is evidenced by the fact that throughout Paul's ministry, and even up to the end of his life in the mid-first century, he was making a collection of funds among the gentile Christians to buy food for the Jerusalem church, which was exceedingly poor. According to Luke, this was a mission that would take Paul back to Jerusalem and ultimately to arrest and one final imprisonment. However, Paul himself referred frequently to this fund-raising in his letters to the churches over several years and evidently gave it high priority, perhaps as a mechanism whereby the gentile churches could express in tangible terms their appreciation and respect for the mother church in Jerusalem.

Thus, despite tensions, strong bonds united the Jewish and gentile churches. And, in light of all the above, the situation of the Jewish-Christian church in Palestine would have been of general concern to all Christians as Palestine became progressively more violent. (Remember that travel and communication over Roman roads was actually efficient, and news would have spread throughout the empire within weeks.) Even if most Christians in Palestine would not have participated in the revolt, this did not make their situation in the midst of a war zone any less worrisome. The attention of Christians everywhere must have been riveted on the events unfolding in the cradle of their faith as Palestinian Jews stubbornly refused to buckle under to the Roman legions, as the Temple was destroyed, and as the Jews regrouped for another turn. And as Jewish pressure came to bear more insistently on the Jewish-Christian church, its potential negative effects also would have concerned Christians everywhere. On the one hand, gentile Christians would naturally have sympathized with the Jewish-Christians who were subjected to intense social pressure, both before and after 70 CE. On the other hand, the central role of Jerusalem in Christianity made even modest levels of apostasy among Jewish-Christians a high profile problem, a painful loss, and an embarrassment to all the church. It served no one in the church, neither gentile Christian nor Jewish-Christian, if the Cause of Christ was weak and vacillating at its very storm center. Persecution of the Jewish-Christian church was a serious concern and a problem for *all* the church.

The situation in Palestine would have occupied all Christians, no matter what their origin or where they lived. It was this environment of social pressure, persecution, and apostasy that colored the Christian literature that came out of the second half of the first century. Its authors would be primarily Jewish-Christians, in spite of the accelerated expansion of the gentile church, for although the gentile church grew much more rapidly, it continued in the shadow of the Jewish-Christian branch for some time yet. Just as new converts mature slowly as individuals, so must communities mature to produce the intellectual environment with the potential to generate new minds and new genius. In the mid-first century, and up to the end of the same, the Jewish-Christian church still held the moral authority and intellectual leadership, producing literature to strengthen the faith of the believers and to defend the young church.

It would not take long for the gentile church to overtake the Jewish-Christian church as intellectual leader. By the second century, many or most of the Christian writers, apologists, and theologians whose writings have come down to us were gentiles. They bore very un-Jewish names such as Justin, Ignatius, Ireneus, Polycarp, and later, Eusebius. Curiously, it would be the continent of Africa that, in the fourth century, would contribute the greatest theologian of all Christendom, Saint Augustine. Just as the Jewish-Christian church was overwhelmed numerically in the late first century by gentile Christians, so were the Jewish-Christian thinkers overwhelmed by their gentile counterparts in the second century. The Jewish-Christians would produce no more theological geniuses. The intellectual dominance of the Jewish-Christian church would scarcely outlive the generation of the disciples themselves.

The Jewish-Christian church would soon be a thing of the past. Its demands for circumcision would fall on deaf ears; its insistence on Jewish Law would become an anachronism. It was the gentile church that would eventually occupy the field, and Rome would displace Jerusalem, both as administrative center and spiritual guide. The tensions between the two poles of the church were never really resolved; they simply disappeared with time as the Jewish-Christian church faded away. How could this happen, and why did the Jewish-Christian church die out? Perhaps the barriers of orthodoxy that confronted the Jewish-Christian church were more formidable than those of vice and free living among the gentiles. Perhaps that was why Jesus preferred the company of wine bibbers, prostitutes, and tax collectors to that of the scribes and Pharisees. Be that as it may, the Jewish-Christian church of the first century might have been forgotten altogether except for one timeless contribution with which its intellectual leaders endowed humanity as its testimony to posterity—Christian Scripture, and in particular, the Gospels of the New Testament.

CHAPTER 6

LOOSE CANON ON DECK:
CHRISTIAN SCRIPTURE IN THE EARLY YEARS

The adoption of Christianity by non-Jews or gentiles is sometimes said to have been the most important event of Christianity in the first century. Unquestionably, this development freed the church from Jewish orthodoxy and eventually determined the face of the church. The long-term effects of this are still felt today in the twenty-first century, for without the entry of large numbers of gentiles into the faith of Jesus, Christianity would have been constricted to the bounds of Judaism, and would never have developed into the world-embracing moral and spiritual force that it has become. The vast majority of Christians alive today would not be Christians if this had not occurred. However, the other development of the first century that continues to shape Christianity involved significant participation of the Jewish-Christian church, and this was the setting down of Christian Scripture.

What we know today as a single volume of the New Testament evolved over a number of years and in response to forces inside and outside of the church. The books did not appear at once, nor in an organized, systematic way, but randomly (short of God's guiding hand in the matter!). A far greater number of tracts circulated among Christians, and were read and used in worship services, than eventually found their way into the New Testament. One of the most difficult and potentially contentious questions for early Christians was that of determining which writings among those available in the first two or three centuries were to be considered as canonical, which is to say, recognized as authoritative Scripture. How some were accepted and others were marginalized and designated as apocryphal was undoubtedly a complex story that cannot be reconstructed with any certainty. In any case, complete consensus on the question of canon did not exist within the church for three centuries or more.

The question of canon was not unique to Christianity. In the first century there was not even consensus among Jews as to which books of the Old Testament were authoritative. While there was no question about the Pentateuch and the books of the Prophets, lesser books such as Maccabees were disputable (and as a result, even today Protestants and Catholics use slightly different versions of the Old Testament, having used different compilations of Jewish Scripture as their point of departure). How much more confusing would it have been in the first century to determine what Christian Scripture was legitimate and worthy to be called holy, at a time when that Scripture was still being written! If we know little about this situation, it is almost certain that it was a hot topic.

Fortunately for us we do not have to face this problem. We have been raised in a culture in which the New Testament is published as a single, uniform volume, at least with regard to the books that are represented there. It never enters our minds to ask if this or that book was truly inspired or should be distrusted as the product of someone's imagination. It is difficult to even envisage what it was like without canonical Scripture—but let us turn the clock back and put ourselves in the shoes of a nascent Christian community in the second half of the first century, and try to visualize what sorts of discussions could have occurred.

The friends walk silently through the streets, drawing no attention. It is dusk and the other members of the community have started to gather in the home of Theophilus. They arrive one at a time so as not to arouse suspicions. They have had no problems of direct persecution here in Thessalonica, but the neighbors are not sympathetic and caution is warranted. Once inside they drop the coverings from their heads and greet each other with broad smiles and loving eyes. Associates and family members may have turned them away, but here is their true home, their true family.

After a few moments, they gather in a circle for worship. They pray as He taught them: "Our Father, who art in heaven . . ." Then they listen as a letter from their brother Paul is read. They have heard it many times, but it continues to evoke his memory and revive the spirit that he sought to infuse in them. It comforts them in their trials and gives them strength. Finally they break bread in memory of their Savior and, once the Eucharist is completed, they sing one last hymn.

They also have in their possession the apostle's letters to Corinth and to the friends in Galatia. They have heard that a letter to the friends in Rome is being copied and they look forward to obtaining it. On other days they read from the Books of the Prophets in the Septuagint, the Greek translation of the Hebrew Scriptures, and the erudite among them expound upon the promises of Scripture and their fulfillment in Christ Jesus. Often this offers the context in which they recite the stories that have been passed on to them about the Savior Himself. They used to rely on oral traditions, but a few years ago their brother, Mark, collated many of these stories and they were fortunate enough to obtain a copy, while other narratives they continue to pass on by word of mouth. Today, news of a new compilation has come.

"Matthew has taken the work of Mark and added more material that he has obtained. Have you seen his work? The friends in other churches have used his collection for some time now."

"What are his sources?" someone asks. "Are they reliable? We trust in Mark's history of the Savior, but what does Matthew have to add? And by what authority does he alter Mark's version?"

It is not unusual that some meet a new compilation with skepticism. Many versions of the story of Jesus exist, and differences between them are evident. Even heresies circulate in some circles—some say that the Lord was never crucified in the flesh! Thus, caution must be exercised in accepting new versions. They say that the apostle John has had visions—is this true? He speaks of a reign of a thousand years—is it possible?

Many questions of the friends have no answers. Meanwhile they cling to the handful of writings that they have at hand—the letters of Paul, the compilation of Mark, the Books of the Prophets. And of one thing they are sure, beyond all doubt—that they are bound together by the memory of the Savior whose story gives them strength and faith.

For the very first Christians, Scripture meant the Greek translation of the Hebrew Bible, given their Jewish roots and their synagogue tradition of scriptural study. Even many of the first gentile Christians came to know the new faith in the context of the synagogue and were thus familiarized with the Hebrew Bible. Among Christians, Old Testament readings were supplemented by oral traditions of Jesus, which eventually were set down as the Gospels. Apparently, several different sets of traditions coexisted, both of sayings of Jesus that communicated His teachings and doctrine, and of the events associated with His life. The Gospel writers drew on these several oral traditions, and successively constructed their different but parallel accounts that have come down to us. The letters of Paul, including some that Paul himself refers to, but that we no longer have in existence, were directed to specific communities. Other books that were widely used in the first century, such as the Epistle of Barnabas and the Gospel of Thomas, eventually were rejected from canon and fell by the wayside. We can only imagine the polemics that accompanied the use, critique, acceptance, or rejection of what many considered to be Holy Scripture at one time or another. Eventually, sometime between the third and fourth centuries, consensus was reached and a final list of New Testament books was established.

Now, if we know little of the process of the writing of the Gospels and their selection as canon, an overriding fact about them that is critical for their understanding is this. Much of what we consider Holy Scripture of the New

Testament, and that determines what we believe *today* in the twenty-first century, developed primarily within the Jewish-Christian "branch" of the early church. In the simplest terms, the authors of the New Testament books were Jewish-Christians, if not in conviction and practice, at least in an ethnic sense and in the setting in which they wrote.

Traditionally, Matthew and John have been identified with the disciples of Jesus of the same names (although there is no hard evidence of this). Mark is assumed to be the companion of Barnabus mentioned in Acts, and was supposedly a secretary to Peter. Mark and Matthew were both concerned with announcing Jesus as the Jewish Messiah, as the Promised One of the Jewish prophets. Matthew in particular is considered to have an especially Jewish viewpoint, taking pains to present Jesus in the same light as Moses. For example, Matthew relates the story of the flight of the holy family to Egypt and a subsequent return from that country, reminiscent of Moses coming out of Egypt. Even Paul, whose mission was focused on the gentile churches, received a thoroughly Jewish education and preparation prior to his own conversion experience. Paul used the same vocabulary derived from a Jewish tradition as the Gospel writers, and a large part of his mission was extending the Jewish messianic tradition to non-Jews. Paul interpreted the advent of Jesus in the light of Jewish tradition and Law, and also reinterpreted Jewish tradition and Law in light of the advent of Jesus. For Paul, the significance of Jesus still had to be understood within a Jewish context to make sense.

Every single one of the authors, if we accept the traditional attribution of authorship, was an ethnic Jew. Every single one was born into the faith of Moses, and was trained under Jewish norms up to some point in his life: Every single one, *except* . . . Luke.

According to tradition, Luke was a Greek physician who accompanied Paul on some of his travels. As a Greek and a gentile, Luke is the exception to the rule that the New Testament was written by Christians of Jewish background. Regarding the Jewish-Christian outlook and influence on the New Testament, Luke is the exception that *proves* the rule. As we saw in the previous chapter, Luke is faithful to the central role of the Jewish-Christian church, and in his writing of Acts, he respects the role of the Jerusalem church as the "mother church." Even for Luke the gentile, the point of reference was the Jerusalem church, which was Jewish-Christian par excellence. Writing in the second half of the first century at a time when the gentile churches were well established, Luke did not look to Thessalonica or Ephesus or even to Rome for norms about what Christianity ought to be, or what a good Christian ought to do. He looked back to Jerusalem, much as a modern Catholic looks to the Vatican.

Luke displays a keen Jewish insight in his Gospel. One parable in particular, that of the Good Samaritan, illustrates this, as it is just such a Jewish insight that is necessary to appreciate the message therein. In this well-known parable attributed to Jesus, a traveler is attacked and lies wounded by the roadside. Representatives of the Jewish upper class pass by and refuse to help him, but it is a Samaritan who succors the traveler and provides for his care. Who, Jesus asks, exemplifies the Old Testament commandment to love thy neighbor as thyself? Christians read the parable as a lesson that one should be kind and loving, but within a Jewish context the message is much more intense. From the Jewish point of view, the Samaritans were the lowest social class imaginable, the untouchables of ancient Palestine. They were descended from survivors of the northern kingdom that had separated from the Davidic throne upon the death of Solomon. They had intermarried with non-Hebraic stock and so had sullied their blood. Furthermore, they worshiped at Mount Gerizim and not in Jerusalem, and had their own version of the Old Testament. The Jews considered the Samaritans political traitors, racial half-breeds, and spiritual pariahs, and held them in the very lowest regard. It was precisely this fact that was central to the point of the parable. In other words, one must appreciate how despicable the Samaritans were to the Jews to appreciate the intention of Jesus, that even a Samaritan could be spiritually superior to a socially positioned and well-heeled Jew, if he loves his neighbor and does God's will.

From any but a Jewish point of view, the Good Samaritan could just as well have been a good Roman, or a good Athenian, or a good Joe Blow—in brief, any good person—which is exactly what the term Good Samaritan represents in our own non-Jewish society. The intensity of the message can only be appreciated by reading with Jewish eyes, and Luke apparently appreciates the full impact of the story that he is relating to have conserved it as such. Even as a gentile, Luke understands the Jewish context of Christianity very well, and writes within much the same mindset as the other Gospel writers. Even as Luke projects the Mission of Jesus into the gentile world, he maintains Mark's essential scheme of the Gospel and does not stray far from the Jewish-Christian context of the early church.

In their role as writers of the Gospels, it was the Jewish-Christians that held the intellectual leadership of early Christianity, and in the context of the subsequent decision about what constituted canonical Scripture, this is a fact that may almost have been by design. Church fathers of a later age who were faced with the question of deciding what writings to accept as authoritative showed a strong preference for Scripture that had supposedly developed under the influence of the apostles. This essentially limited Christian canon to the first century, and to the Jewish-Christian environment within which the disciples lived and moved, with the exception of Paul and perhaps Luke. Hence, with these exceptions, most Scripture was not only attributed to the disciples or their companions—all of them Jewish-Christians—but also reflects the environment of that church, described in the previous chapter.

Although our interest is primarily with the Jewish-Christian church, an important lesson is to be found in the circumstances surrounding the letters of

Paul. A significant portion of the New Testament is directed to the gentile church and is derived from Paul, either by his personal authorship or possibly through his students and associates who wrote in his name. In his extensive missionary travels, Paul established churches over a wide geographical area. It was impossible for him to visit each of these churches frequently, but safe travel under the Roman Empire permitted communication. It appears that Paul would frequently receive inquiries from his converts seeking counsel about problems or challenges that arose in the churches. As noted in the previous chapter, these epistles occasionally address the state of the gentile church and its disciplinary problems. Paul's purpose in writing the epistles is to correct problems of morality, to encourage unity among the believers, or to offer guidance on the application of doctrine.

The important point to recognize is that Paul's Epistles often responded to the specific needs of a young and struggling church. Paul did not write as if he were revealing divine guidance for all time, nor even for all congregations in his own time. While Paul might have been drawing on general principles with wide utility, he was also bringing those principles to bear on concrete situations that real live people were experiencing at a given moment. The letters of Paul, with the notable exception of Romans, were written in response to then-current needs of the church, and as such reflect the state of a given community at that time in its history. It is through these very letters that we learn a great deal about the struggles and trials of those nascent congregations that in many ways were very different from the church that we know today. Many of these differences arise from the fact that the Christians at that time were still a small minority in relation to the world around them, and they struggled valiantly with the influences of the pagan world and its excesses and mores.

As we look at the Gospels and their origins in the Jewish-Christian world, we see an analogous situation, in the sense that the writers of the Gospels also sought to address, some more than others, the problems that were facing the Jewish-Christian church. Again, the tests of the Jewish-Christian church were not those of immorality, but rather of orthodoxy both within and outside the church. In the previous chapter we looked at the environment of the Jewish-Christian church and its tug-of-war with Jewish orthodoxy. We saw that the Jewish-Christian church existed in an environment in which a significant challenge for the church fathers, more than moral questions, was time-honored, hide-bound traditions inherited from centuries of Jewish practice. Early Christians did not attempt to dissociate themselves from Jewish tradition, rather they viewed themselves as the true Israel. They did not reject Judaism per se as a misguided doctrine, but insisted that Jews had misinterpreted and misunderstood their own Scripture. Christians on the other hand were the true Israel, the real Jews, and the real children of Abraham. This stance kept them just at the threshold of Judaism, or even at its very center, as they saw themselves. The challenge that church leadership faced in the Jewish-Christian world was a community that was still immersed in Jewish tradition and thought, and so was susceptible to returning to the Jewish mainstream.

Within this context the church fathers struggled to maintain the loyalty of the church to Jesus, and to establish the tenets of the Christian Message that were novel to members of the congregation that were not yet deepened in Christian doctrine. I referred at the outset to the fact that the some of the spiritual teachings of Jesus, particularly those associated with the soul and its immortality, were novel and did not form part of the traditional Jewish worldview at the time that Jesus appeared. Some of the implications of these teachings were inherently foreign to a Jewish audience, and the church fathers sought to educate their Jewish-Christian believers in these teachings.

Another point that was perhaps even more problematic for many Jewish-Christians was Christology, or the spiritual station of Christ. Jews were firmly committed to monotheism, and viewed the Prophets, including Moses, as men inspired of God, but essentially equal to the rest of mankind. The doctrine that Christ occupied a station above men and at the right hand of God was difficult for Jewish-Christians to assimilate. They could accept Him as Messiah despite His having been crucified contrary to general expectation, but the idea that He was just one step away from God Himself was still blasphemous for some Jewish-Christians.

Thus, the day-to-day work of the church leadership in the Jewish-Christian milieu was to wean the community gradually off Jewish concepts and nurture those spiritual concepts and teachings of Jesus as expressed in their respective symbols. And this is a significant part of the Gospel message that has come down to us—teachings that are designed to raise the Christian consciousness of new believers gradually, from first- or second-generation Jewish converts to seasoned and deepened believers. In the situation in which a Jewish-Christian community was still not fully indoctrinated into the teachings of Jesus, many of those essential truths of the Christian Message were clothed in terms that were familiar to a Jewish-Christian audience. In subsequent chapters we will explore the use of terms drawn from the Jewish vocabulary, such as "kingdom," "life," and "resurrection."

This evangelizing task of the church fathers might have advanced at a steady, progressive pace, were it not for the crisis in the external environment precipitated by the evolution of events in Palestine. As we saw in Chapter 5, the first century in Palestine was dominated by the struggle of Jew against Roman, and the repression of Roman over Jew. As the first century advanced, the Jewish community was becoming more restive, more rebellious against its Roman masters. It was also becoming more impatient with the Christians. This increasing aggressiveness toward Rome might have demanded even stricter adherence to Jewish orthodoxy.

It most certainly demanded active support of revolutionary aims: "If you are not with us, you are against us." And as the political situation of the Jewish community came to a boil, it must have been the source of confusion to many Jewish-Christians as they felt attracted to the cause of their Jewish brethren. As pressure increased, many must have been tempted to return to Judaism. This represented even more acute tests for the Jewish-Christian community and more challenges for its leadership to maintain the integrity of the community against demands for apostasy, and to keep the Christians from embroiling themselves in the politics of the day.

Such was the evolving political environment that surrounded and accompanied the development of the Gospels and a few other books of the New Testament, and in these books we see reflected the tensions generated by this environment. Even in Paul's letters, which were written before the crisis came to a head, we see evidence of tension and opposition. But the Gospels per se are dated somewhat later than Paul's writings, during a period from shortly before 70 CE through a couple of decades after that watershed date. The critical period for the composition of the Gospels coordinates closely with the crisis that surrounded the rebellion of the Jews against Rome and the destruction of the Temple. And this event represented a turning point in Jewish history. In our own experience, the fall of Jerusalem is comparable only to 9/11 in the way that it disrupted orderly life and shattered all sense of stability. Palestine was turned upside down, Judaism lost its center of gravity in the Temple, and a vacuum of faith was suddenly created. The world was in flux, the crush of history was deciding the course of men's lives, and whoever did not have a clear concept of what he believed would run the risk of letting others dictate his belief for him. This was a period that called for intense reflection and redefinition, certainly within the Jewish community, and very likely among Jewish-Christians who were still attached to the Temple and Jewish custom. The Pharisaic rabbis, for their part, were reorganizing in Jabneh to the west of Jerusalem and were mounting an effort to extend their own understanding of Judaism to Jewish communities throughout Palestine and beyond. The church leaders were likewise called to respond to the situation, defining better who and what they were as Christians, and what they were not. It was in response to this situation and a generally repressive environment that the Gospels were written.

It is generally accepted that the Gospel of Mark is the oldest of the four, possibly written shortly before 70 CE. Mark's account is a straightforward, down-to-earth description of the actions of Jesus and the events surrounding His life. Matthew would have followed Mark a few years later, after the destruction of the Temple, taking most of Mark's Gospel and amplifying it with other materials from yet another oral tradition (or from written material that is now lost to us). Luke's Gospel and Acts (also attributed to Luke) followed, likewise drawing upon Mark's Gospel and editing it, and adding other "new" materials. The fourth Gospel, that of John, was the last to be composed and dates to sometime near the end of the first century. Compared to the other Gospels it is a unique creation and was designed to accentuate the theological elements of a truly new religion. In particular, John emphasized elements of Christianity that highlighted the spiritual stature of Christ. Thus we have today four Gospels that are not entirely consistent among themselves, and yet have much common material.

The works that became the New Testament, from Paul to John, were set down over a period of some fifty to sixty years, during which the relationship of Christian and Jew was deteriorating rapidly, from relatively tolerant discussion and disagreement that occasionally flared into anger, to strident rejection and mutual vilification. And as time advanced and the rift became a gulf, the Gospels are increasingly blunt about the Jewish rejection of Jesus. In Mark's Gospel, it is the scribes and Pharisees who are seen as the culprits, singling out a small segment of the Jewish population that actively opposes Jesus. By the time John sets down his Gospel years later, he uses the broad brush of "the Jews" to refer to the opposition. In John's time, rejection is no longer the responsibility of a few stubborn and misguided elements, but of an entire nation. In the time of John, the environment is more decidedly one of "us-and-them."

Since the Gospels were written over a period when Jewish-Christian relations were worsening, or had broken off substantially, the confrontations between Jesus and the Jews that are represented in the Gospels reflect not only the interaction of Jesus with Jews thirty to fifty years earlier, but the issues that continued to be current in the period in which the respective author was writing. This view on the origin of the Gospels, within a setting that influenced the composition of each writer, naturally gives rise to a significant question: does the content of the Gospel originate in the words of Jesus, or in the words of the Gospel writers? I will give the Gospel writers the benefit of the doubt and assume that they are doing their utmost to convey the Message of Jesus as best they understood it. In other words, the Message is from Jesus. The Gospel writers, however, finding themselves in difficult times, have drawn upon their collective memory to find the answers that Jesus might have used to deal with the situations that they themselves were confronting. They took the words and teachings of Jesus and formulated them in the context of situations that were like their own. The structure that the Gospel writers use to present the words of Jesus is their own, and often the structure is as informative as the Message itself, both with regard to the circumstances and to the very meaning of that Message.

One structure that is common to all the Gospels to some degree is the scheme of contrasting the ideas and doctrine of Jesus with those of Judaism. The Jewish context serves as a backdrop to highlight Christian doctrine, a backdrop against which the Gospels are to be understood. The writers have used the Jewishness of the New Testament environment to convey some of the most distinctive points of the Christian Message. One frequently gets the feeling that the Gospel writers are saying to their Jewish-Christian audience, "*That* belief is Jewish doctrine, but *we* believe in *this* doctrine . . . look over *here*." The purpose of this method, in the context of the early church and in the face of Jewish pressure to recant, was to educate those first- or second-generation Christians in the doctrine of Jesus, to gradually wean them away from millennial doctrines and the ideas of their forefathers.

Although all the Gospels use this model, special attention should be addressed to John, whose Gospel is the most distinctive. He includes unique material not found in any other source and excludes much material common to the other Gospels. John takes a very different point of presentation, yet in a sense John's Gospel is just as Jewish as Mark's and Matthew's, because his Gospel likewise depends so heavily on the Jewish context for *contrast*. John sets Jesus against a backdrop of Judaism like a crescent moon against the night sky—delicate, gentle, and beautifully ethereal, yet sharp and incisive. In a literary sense, John's Gospel is the most carefully crafted, and is the subtlest in its presentation of contrasts. Whereas Mark might say, "The Pharisees said this, and Jesus said that," John is a dramatist who uses a story and its elements to convey his message. John is wont to create carefully staged scenes in which the setting, the characters, and their actions are as much a part of the message as is the dialogue. John carries the reader to a climatic point in his short dramas, to a fork in the road, as if to say, Jewish doctrine follows that road, and the doctrine of Jesus is this way.

Tradition holds that John wrote his Gospel from Ephesus in Asia Minor and if this was the case, he might have dealt with a more gentile environment on a day-to-day basis. Yet John addresses the relationship between Judaism and Jesus and Christian doctrine head-on, as if he has taken this as his unique calling. Was he dealing with Hellenistic Judaism that was spread throughout the world of the Diaspora? Or is he concerned with making a contribution to meeting the tests that the Jewish-Christian church is facing in Palestine? One way or the other John has a special concern for Jewish thought, and one must ask if this does not reflect a special concern for the Jewish-Christian church in its dealings with the Jewish community.

We have in the New Testament the answers that the Christians offered to Jews and/or Jewish-Christians within this historical context, but what were the questions that the Jews were formulating? Jews were increasingly anxious to see the advent of the Messiah to fulfill their expectations of national liberation. In this environment Jews must have either demanded proofs of the Mission of Christ based on Scripture, or they attacked the Christian claims as incongruent with the Old Testament criteria for the Messiah. In either case, the Gospel writers were highly sensitive to these demands and sought to respond to them at every opportunity, and their resource for this purpose was Hebrew Scripture. They responded in terms of a reinterpretation of the Old Testament, seeking to convince their audience, or to assuage their lingering doubts, to show how the advent of Jesus was in agreement with the Hebrew Bible. As a result, the Gospels are peppered with statements like, "that the Scriptures may be fulfilled" or "as was written by the Prophets," referring back to the Old Testament and justifying the Mission of Jesus in this way.

Furthermore, the citation of Hebrew Scripture by Christian writers appears to evolve over time from Paul to John as Christian-Jewish relations deteriorated. When Paul cites Scripture to the Romans he does so in an essentially instructive vein to convey a concept: "Wot ye not what the scripture saith of Elijah? how he maketh intercession to God against Israel," "But what saith the answer of God unto him? I have reserved to myself seven thousand men, who have not bowed the knee to the image of Baal."[1] Paul cites God's election of a few faithful among the ancient Hebrews as an example of what was happening among the Hebrews of his own day, but certainly not in the context of a prophecy that was destined to be fulfilled. In this case, Paul's use of Scripture serves to draw a parallel for the purpose of making a point and so is more a rhetorical use than one that recurs to Scripture as a defense. Similarly, in Corinthians, Paul refers to the Old Testament in a theological sense referring to the sacrifice of Christ. "For I delivered unto you first of all that which I also received, how that Christ died for our sins according to the Scriptures."[2] The essence of this reference to Scripture, which in any case does not cite any specific Old Testament verse, was that Jesus was destined to serve as a sacrifice for the expiation of sin. Paul again uses Scripture instructively in a theological context.

The epistle that is ascribed to Peter is not much more specific in its use of Scripture. Peter refers to Jewish Scripture in a prophetic sense, but again in general terms without clear reference to any specific prophecy: "Of which salvation the prophets have inquired and searched diligently, who prophesied of the grace that should come unto you."[3] This is rather similar to the use that Paul gives to the Old Testament, citing Scripture in a theological context to emphasize the redeeming role of Jesus.

When we look at the four Gospels, a change occurs—a change that could well be associated with the evolving conditions of the times. In this age, the Gospel writers were more concerned with defending the truth of the historical Jesus, gleaning details from the Hebrew Bible, and applying these to the circumstances of the life of Jesus. References to the Old Testament in the four Gospels are cited almost exclusively in the context of prophecy, which is to say, ancient predictions of then-future events surrounding the historical Jesus. These are highly specific prophecies in contrast to the general statements mentioned above from Paul and Peter. The citation of prophecies in the Gospels often has no particular theological significance outside of being a statement that, "Jesus was foretold by the Prophets, and therefore must be the true Messiah." Even John, who is far more concerned with subtle theological points, refers extensively to Old Testament prophecy.

A prime and illustrative example of the use of prophecy is a passage from Matthew describing the entry of Jesus into Jerusalem on Palm Sunday, which is an adaptation of a narrative of Mark. Expanding on Mark's version, Matthew has added a mention of the Scriptures that is absent in Mark, in reference to the Book of Zechariah where we read of the promised advent of a king. "Rejoice greatly, O daughter of Zion; shout, O daughter of Jerusalem: behold, thy King cometh unto thee: he is just, and having salvation; lowly, and riding upon an ass, and upon a colt the foal of an ass."[4] This latter phrase is a particular literary form, repeating a thought and making the "ass" to be equivalent to the "foal of an ass." But Matthew understands the "ass" and the "foal of an ass" to refer to *two* animals, and so represents Jesus as entering Jerusalem riding simultaneously on two such beasts, in an attempt to comply with Jewish Scripture to the uttermost detail. Matthew quotes Jesus as saying: "Tell ye the daughter of Zion, Behold, thy King cometh unto thee, meek, and sitting upon an ass, and a colt the foal of an ass. And the disciples went, and did as Jesus commanded them, and brought the ass, and the colt, and put on them their clothes, and they set him thereon."[5]

Apparently Matthew has poured over the Old Testament to glean from it whatever details he can find to apply to the appearance of Christ, however theologically insignificant they might be. It appears that the Gospel writer has felt compelled to justify the truth of Jesus based on the Hebrew Bible. Furthermore the innocent error that he commits in misinterpreting the Hebrew text, and adapting to it the story of the entrance into Jerusalem, betrays a certain overeagerness to comply with Scripture. Why did Matthew and the other Gospel writers display this concern with Scripture? Apparently they are addressing an audience composed of Jews and Jewish-Christians who had a firm scriptural tradition, and who demanded and/or benefited from this sort of evidence.

This interaction of Gospel writer with his audience—most likely Jewish-Christians or possibly the critics of the young religion—colored the way the New Testament was composed and presented to the audience. This fact is of particular significance for us, as it is that same New Testament text that we seek to understand in the twenty-first century, and therefore, the events of the first century continue to impinge on our understanding of the New Testament. Herein lies the urgency of returning to that first century context to tease out the Message of Jesus from its Jewish-Christian milieu.

I suspect that in this context we find keys to at least a couple of riddles that scholars have posed for a good part of the twentieth century. The first of these regards Mark and his portrayal of the disciples of Jesus. In the Gospel of Mark, the disciples display a remarkable incapacity to grasp what Jesus is saying or who He is. On point after point, the disciples just do not understand, in such manner that Jesus upbraids them frequently with words such as, "Are ye so without understanding also?"[6] "perceive ye not yet, neither understand? have ye your heart yet hardened?"[7] They do not comprehend His words, nor even His power when they are witness to it, as when He rebukes the wind. This portrayal contrasts with the other Gospels, where the disciples evince at least some degree of capacity and insight. So why does Mark offer such an unflattering image of the followers of Jesus? Would not the Cause of Jesus be better served if His inner circle of confidants displayed at least the minimal spiritual capacity? What is going on here?

I think that what Mark has done is to make the disciples surrogates for his own Jewish-Christian audience. The words of Jesus that are directed against His disciples are meant in fact for a Jewish-Christian congregation, as a wake-up call for their own lack of insight, and as a warning to those who, like the disciples in Mark, still do not grasp the significance of the teachings of Jesus in contrast to Jewish orthodoxy, or who are incapable of appreciating the power that resides in Him. If we look carefully, we often see in the disciples' misunderstanding of Jesus some issues that have their roots in Jewish tradition, and would have been issues in dealing with a Jewish-Christian congregation.

For example, when the Pharisees accuse the disciples of not respecting the Jewish custom of washing before meals as a purification rite, Jesus first upbraids the Pharisees roundly for overemphasizing the material aspects of purity, and then addresses the populace saying: "there is nothing from without a man, that entering into him can defile him: but the things which come out of him, those are they that defile the man."[8] Still, the disciples do not understand and they come to Him for clarification, at which He in turn upbraids *them*, saying "Are ye so without understanding also? Do ye not perceive, that whatsoever thing from without entereth into the man, it cannot defile him; . . . That which cometh out of the man, that defileth the man."[9] Note a special irony here, that it is the behavior of the disciples in not washing that precipitates this entire discussion, yet they cannot even understand the significance of their *own* actions in disregarding Jewish standards. I suspect that Mark is driving his point home at the disciples' expense, for the benefit of his Jewish-Christian congregation, and that the real target of those words, "Are you so without understanding also?" is the Jewish-Christian audience of his own day, whose members continue to follow Jewish custom meticulously.

A second riddle concerns Paul and the historical Jesus, and is an apparent discrepancy between Paul and the Gospels. While the Gospels focus on events in the life of Jesus and on His words and sayings, Paul's writings take a totally different approach. In his several extant letters that we have in hand, Paul expounds on the role of Christ as universal savior, but makes minimal reference to events surrounding the life of Jesus. Nor does he often refer explicitly to the teachings of Jesus, as we know them in the Gospels, although we can read between the lines and find the essence of those teachings in many of his letters. With regard to the historical Jesus, why does Paul not refer more amply to the life of Christ? With all that he wrote, did it not occur to him to make more than scarcely a dozen passing references? This has led to speculation that Paul had minimal interest in Jesus outside of His cosmic role as world savior, or even that Paul was creating a religion that was virtually independent of the Christianity of Jesus and of the Jewish-Christian church.

In defense of Paul we should note that he was not alone in remaining silent about the historical Jesus—neither Peter, nor Jude, nor James (Jesus' own brother!) expounded on Jesus at length. Nor did Matthew, Mark, Luke, or John say anything about the life of Jesus for thirty or forty or fifty years!! Scholars can wonder why Paul did not write more about the historical Jesus, but Paul was certainly not alone in de-emphasizing the historical Jesus in those first years. In an age in which Scripture was limited to the Old Testament, at least Paul wrote *some* uniquely Christian literature in those first thirty years.

I think that a clue to Paul's silence on the historical Jesus lies in standing the question on its head, and asking, why did the Gospel writers address the question of the historical Jesus? Why, after a lapse of thirty odd years, did someone finally set about recording the stories that had been passed on as oral traditions? Again, I think that the answer lies at least partly in the general milieu of the early Jewish-Christian church, and the questions that the Jewish orthodoxy was bringing to bear on the Christians as the first century advanced. For the Jews, the essential question about Christianity was whether or not Jesus was the Messiah, and the Jews expected a Messiah who would intervene dramatically in history—a living, breathing, worldly governor-king. In turn, Jewish-Christians would be wondering, "Just who was this Jesus if He did not fulfill what a Messiah should be?" These demands put upon the church fathers required a response in terms of a historical figure. The Christians were pressured to come up with some description of the historical Jesus, as well as the arguments to defend their understanding of how this very same historical Jesus fulfilled the Old Testament promises. Their answer was formulated as the Gospels.

In summary, the Gospels reflect multiple tendencies, intentions, and influences. The Gospels contain spiritual truths derived from Jesus, and narratives of the interaction of Jesus with the Jews in His own time. They also reflect the state of the Jewish-Christian church some thirty to fifty years later, when the Gospels were set down, and the attempts of the church fathers to educate their Christian communities in the midst of a Jewish milieu, as the Jewish establishment was becoming more aggressive and was seeking to stamp out what they considered a heresy in their midst. While the content of the Gospel stories has its origin in

Jesus, the structure that the Gospel authors have given to the narrative is likely their own, in their attempts to apply the teachings of Jesus to their own period of history. The rest of our study will be dedicated to observing how the Gospel writers carried out this task, walking the tightrope between the Jewish majority and the Jewish-Christian minority, with one foot in each of two worlds.

CHAPTER 7

THE KINGDOM OF CHRIST: SURPRISE ANSWERS TO JEWISH QUESTIONS

When we look at the New Testament in the context of the first century, probably few points of discussion between Christians and Jews were as heated as that of the kingdom of Christ—a subject that is closely associated with the historical setting of His advent. I have mentioned that this period represented the low point in history for the Jews, or so they thought. They had passed through almost six centuries of subjugation, humiliation, and insult, and they were ready for a change, which according to their Scriptures, they had a right to expect when the Messiah appeared. The Jews fed their hopes on the traditions of their glory days, their days of empire under David and Solomon. Even after the empire had faded, the Davidic dynasty continued to give coherence and visible substance to the nationhood of the Jews for another three centuries. Since the conquest by Nebuchadnezzar, the Jews had been deprived of the Davidic line and most of their glory and, therefore, they wanted the restoration of David's kingdom, and they wanted it *now*. It is in the context of the kingdom that the Jews viewed the Messiah. Who is the Messiah? The King of the kingdom! The very name Messiah means "anointed" and refers back to David who was the anointed of God to establish his throne. These doctrines are summed up in what scholars refer to as Jewish apocalypticism, which saw the disastrous state of the Jews in the first century as a sign of God's imminent intervention.

And what is the kingdom, material or spiritual? For the vast majority of Jews, it was a material kingdom, not only with political implications, but complete with agricultural abundance, plenty of water, and even natural wonders. Jewish hopes were set on Old Testament texts such as: "The wolf also shall dwell with the lamb, and the leopard shall lie down with the kid; and the calf and the young lion and the fatling together; and a little child shall lead them. And the cow and the bear shall feed; their young ones shall lie down together: and the lion shall eat straw like the ox. And the sucking child shall play on the hole of the asp, and the weaned child shall put his hand on the cockatrice' den. They shall not hurt nor destroy in all my holy mountain: for the earth shall be full of the knowledge of the LORD, as the waters cover the sea."[1]

In brief, the Jewish view of the kingdom and of the role of Messiah was largely material and this worldly, in line with their overall worldview. And indeed, the Jews were willing to put their money where their mouths were. They banked on a worldly kingdom and a worldly Messiah in the person of Bar Kochba, who led them to near victory, but eventual disaster, in 135 CE.

What did Jesus offer to His disciples and to the Jews? He spoke at length about the kingdom, but at the same time He did not offer immediate relief from political oppression, prescribing on the contrary to pray for one's enemies and to "render therefore unto Caesar the things which be Caesar's."[2] His view of the kingdom was rather one of a spiritual kingdom, in the midst of the world, but not part of it. As one would expect, this was a vision of the kingdom that was not shared by the Jews, and they must have scratched their heads in disbelief more than once to hear the doctrine of Jesus. If that were not bad enough, Jesus promised the destruction of the Temple—the last remnant of Judah's glory days and a reminder of Solomon, son of David! This was a major step backwards in establishing the kingdom that the Jews awaited.

Thus, the kingdom and the role of the Messiah represent still another example of the clash of two worldviews between the Jews and Jesus. This clash is recorded in the Gospels and most likely continued throughout the first century and well into the second. It was undoubtedly one of the first questions that Jews put to Christians when the latter insisted on the Messiahship of Jesus. If the Messiah has come, the Jews would say, then where is the kingdom that He should inaugurate? It was also one of the questions to which Jewish-Christians would have been sensitive, and with which the church leadership would have had to deal to maintain the loyalty of those early believers.

Thus, two critical questions relative to the kingdom made it very difficult for Christians and Jews to understand each other in the first and second centuries, and the church fathers were pressured to answer them. These two questions can be summarized as:

1. *What is the kingdom?* Is it spiritual or material? Or both? And if spiritual, what does that mean? An invisible heavenly kingdom in a world that is beyond the senses?

2. *When is the kingdom to initiate?* At the advent of Christ as Messiah? With Easter and Pentecost? With the growth of the church? Or with the return of Christ?

These were burning questions for the early Christians, for several reasons. They had to respond to criticisms from Jews about the apparent non-fulfillment of the kingdom, and, from a Jewish standpoint, the questionable position of Jesus as the Messiah. Similarly, the church leadership was pressed to protect the Jewish-Christians from pressure to recant, based on those same objections from Jews. Finally, the Christians themselves were undoubtedly anxious to see relief in this world from the pains and trials of their day-to-day life, and wanted to know when God might inaugurate His worldly reign.

From Christian texts that have survived from the second century, it appears that not all Christians had the same answers. Many may well have expected the worldly kingdom to materialize in their own lifetime. We might be critical of them and even scoff at their naivety in expecting the kingdom to appear just around the corner, but the fact is, after two thousand years, Christians still do not have much better answers. And we can split hairs and argue about how early Christians answered these questions, but do we really expect a uniform opinion to emerge from the record of their writings—if after two thousand years there is still no consensus? Jesus said it best: "of that day and hour knoweth no man . . ."[3] Or was the kingdom all that remote and beyond the hopes of the first Christians to witness? Was it a futuristic state of the world and an expression of Utopian dreams? Jesus seems to have said something different.

We are told that as Jesus initiated His Mission, He declared that: "the kingdom of heaven is at hand."[4] This statement alone might have generated expectations of an imminent appearance of God's rule and the material abundance associated with it, but in fact, the Christian response was quite different. One of the answers that Christians offered regarding the kingdom is found in the Gospel of Luke, where the Pharisees confront Jesus. The Jewish and Christian concepts are contrasted in the following vignette: "And when he was demanded of the Pharisees, when the kingdom of God should come, he answered them and said, The kingdom of God cometh not with observation: neither shall they say, Lo here! or, lo there! for, behold, the kingdom of God is within you."[5] Modern translations replace "within you" by "in your midst," but both versions convey the idea that the kingdom already existed, and in a sense that was foreign to the traditional Jewish understanding, since this kingdom "cometh not with observation" as the Jews apparently would have thought, but is invisible and therefore spiritual. Numerous other verses likewise refer to the kingdom as already existing in the lifetime of Jesus: "And from the days of John the Baptist until now the kingdom of heaven suffereth violence, and the violent take it by force."[6] "But if I cast out devils by the Spirit of God, then the kingdom of God is come unto you."[7] "And into whatsoever city ye enter, and they receive you . . . say unto them, The kingdom of God is come nigh unto you."[8] "the kingdom of God is preached, and every man presseth into it."[9] Jesus even spoke of the kingdom as eternal and pre-existent: "Come, ye blessed of my Father, inherit the kingdom prepared for you from the foundation of the world."[10]

All the foregoing references implied that the kingdom was already a reality while Jesus lived and was not a distant hope or an event to be realized in some future age. This suggests a spiritual reality in a kingdom beyond the physical senses, and this was in fact one answer that Christians offered to explain the apparent non-fulfillment of the kingdom expectations. It is also significant that the references cited above come from two Gospel writers with rather different perspectives: Matthew, who is writing in a very Jewish environment, and Luke, who is concerned with a message for gentiles. It appears that Christians of different backgrounds and in different sorts of early congregations shared this understanding of the kingdom.

A fuller exposition of this perspective is found in the famous parable of the sower, in which the distinctive nature of the Christian kingdom is explicit. Jesus intimates to His disciples that He is going to share with them the "mystery of the kingdom" and proceeds to relate the parable. The Christian doctrine that is expressed here holds that the kingdom is spiritual, as is clear from the context in which it is posed by Mark—as a phenomenon of the heart and of its receptivity to the Word as offered by Jesus: "The sower soweth the word. And these are they by the wayside, where the word is sown; but when they have heard, Satan cometh immediately, and taketh away the word that was sown in their hearts."[11] Others hear the word and "immediately receive it with gladness," but abandon it due to "the deceitfulness of riches, and the lusts of other things," or under pressure from "affliction or persecution." This latter reference sounds very much like a warning to those Jewish-Christians who might be tempted to give up the treasures of the kingdom under duress from their compatriots. Only a few "hear the word, and receive it, and bring forth fruit, some thirtyfold, some sixty, and some a hundred." These are the truly faithful that make the Word a productive, vibrant, and positive force in their life. In sum, the kingdom is not the visible world of material abundance expected by the Jews, but an interior world whose inhabitants lived the life of the spirit as engendered by the Word.

This parable appears first in Mark's Gospel (remembering that it is the oldest of the four), but is repeated in the Gospels of Matthew and Luke. Here too, we see that different Gospel writers shared this perspective. Indeed, the fact that all three included the parable in their respective Gospels suggests that they considered this to be an important concept, a suggestion that is confirmed by the words that Mark attributes to Jesus: "Know ye not this parable? and how then will ye know all parables?"[12] Furthermore, Mark tells the parable not once but *four* times in different variations, one after the other[13], as if to say to his audience, "This is really important, so get it right!" Clearly, Mark and the other Gospel writers felt that this was a highly relevant teaching for them and for their times. Finally, the gravity of the theme is again emphasized at the end of the parable when Jesus says, "If any man have ears to hear, let him hear."

Apart from the content of these passages, note the following observation about their *structure*. In the first verse quoted above from Luke, we read that Jesus "was demanded of the Pharisees" and Jesus responded to them saying that the "kingdom of God is within you." This confrontation of Jesus with the Pharisees introduced a contrast in the Jewish and Christian concepts of the kingdom, and the clash of Jews and Jesus is really a clash of views. Although Mark's parable has no direct confrontation with the Jews, it is implicit in an "us-and-them" sense of the people on the outside who cannot understand, and the inner circle of believers who have been given insight to see. "Unto you it is given to know the mystery of the kingdom of God: but unto them that are without, all these things are done in parables."[14] We assume that those on the outside must include the Jews, and the sense of Jews-versus-Jesus is implicit. However, this is a contrast not merely of the faithful and the unfaithful, but more importantly of Christian doctrine and Jewish doctrine. In other words, the confrontational structure is as much or more a tool to contrast ideas and concepts, as opposed to being merely an anti-Jewish outburst.

Whereas the Old Testament conveyed a vision of a kingdom of material abundance, a vision on which the Jews set their hopes, Jesus taught His disciples that it was through detachment from the demands of material existence that they could attain the kingdom: "take no thought, saying, What shall we eat? or, What shall we drink? or, Wherewithal shall we be clothed? . . . But seek ye first the kingdom of God, and his righteousness; and all these things shall be added unto you."[15] Indeed, the kingdom of God is "not of this world,"[16] but rather pertains first to that inner spiritual world, for "except a man be born of water and of the Spirit, he cannot enter into the kingdom of God."[17] And in one of his earliest letters, which predates the Gospel of Mark by a decade or more, Paul likewise takes a spiritual view of the kingdom saying, "flesh and blood cannot inherit the kingdom of God."[18] And again, when addressing the Romans: "for the kingdom of God is not meat and drink; but righteousness, and peace, and joy in the Holy Ghost."[19]

The requirements of citizenship in that kingdom are purity of spirit and divine qualities: "Blessed are the poor in spirit: for theirs is the kingdom of heaven."[20] Humility is a foremost requisite of entrance into that realm: "Whosoever therefore shall humble himself as this little child, the same is greatest in the kingdom of heaven."[21] And do not imagine that this is any easy task. It requires all of the mettle that God has placed in the human spirit, and is no job for namby-pambies who give flight at the first test: "No man, having put his hand to the plow, and looking back, is fit for the kingdom of God."[22] "For I say unto you, That except your righteousness shall exceed the righteousness of the scribes and Pharisees, ye shall in no case enter into the kingdom of heaven."[23] The kingdom of God was a new relationship with God, more intimate than had existed in ancient times, a New Covenant that was proclaimed to the world, a New Covenant centered on the divine law of love. Bahá'u'lláh, Prophet-Founder of the Bahá'í Faith, echoes the concept of the spiritual kingdom that springs from the souls of men when He addresses the kings of the nineteenth century saying, "By the righteousness of God! It is not Our wish to lay hands on your kingdoms. Our mission is to seize and possess the hearts of men."[24] Still, we are talking about a kingdom the signs of which are manifested here in this visible world, not merely in the invisible world of spirit! Thus, the one who "shall enter into the kingdom of heaven" is the one "that doeth the will of my Father"[25] while here on earth.

While Jesus stressed the spiritual requirements of citizenship in the kingdom, He also referred to its manifestation in a visible community. In one of only two explicit references to the church in the four Gospels, He addresses Peter saying: "thou art Peter, and upon this rock I will build my church."[26] Remember that in the first century the term "church"held no connotation of denominational affiliation or ecclesiastical hierarchy, but rather referred to the corporate body of the believers—a given Christian community or congregation. This allusion refers to Peter's role in the nascent community of believers. Jesus follows this reference to the church and amplifies on Peter's role, adding, "I will give unto thee the keys of the kingdom of heaven."[27] While this second charge to Peter conjures up visions of the pearly gates, a more sober consideration of its significance invites the following reflection. Through reference in these verses to the role of Peter, Jesus has associated the church with the kingdom. Is not the church the visible manifestation of the inner kingdom, the joint expression of the spiritual qualities of the soul, manifested as unity among the believers? Is not the church the earthly kingdom, a nation apart from the Greeks, Romans, Syrians, and other nationalities that surrounded them? From this perspective, discussions of whether the kingdom is material or spiritual have less significance. The kingdom is essentially spiritual, no doubt, but must manifest itself in tangible acts, in tangible communities, in tangible institutions that are the expression of the inner spirit.

Nonetheless, despite all His references to the here-and-now kingdom of His own time, Jesus undeniably spoke of the kingdom as a future event as well that would be associated with His return. "Verily I say unto you, There be some standing here, which shall not taste of death, till they see the Son of man coming in his kingdom."[28] As to the nature of that future kingdom, in the only prayer that He left to His followers, Jesus taught them to pray for an earthly kingdom: "Thy kingdom come. Thy will be done in earth, as it is in heaven."[29] This prayer for a worldly kingdom echoed the numerous prophecies of the Old Testament, such as that of Isaiah cited above. And still speaking of the future, Jesus also implied a spiritual renovation in the day of His return. A new salvation would await on that day: "And when these things begin to come to pass . . . your redemption draweth nigh . . . know ye that the kingdom of God is nigh at hand."[30]

So for Jesus what was—or is—the kingdom? Did Jesus teach a spiritual kingdom, or a material, this-worldly kingdom? Did He teach that it already existed, or that it was imminent, or that it would appear in the distant future? In brief, we return to those two questions posed before: What is the kingdom? And when would it appear?

Part of the difficulty in understanding the kingdom (and perhaps this applies to Christians in many different ages) is to be found in the article, "the"—"the" kingdom, *one* kingdom. In fact, there is not a single kingdom. Just as in nature there is a mineral kingdom, a plant kingdom, and an animal kingdom, all of which coexist and form part of one natural reality, similarly God has many kingdoms: spiritual, material, this-worldly, other-worldly, a here-and-now kingdom, a future kingdom. But none of these different kingdoms are mutually exclusive. In Chapter 2, I dealt with the concept of progressive revelation, whereby the Mission of every Prophet or Manifestation of God is essentially spiritual and creates a spiritual kingdom of devoted hearts governed by the love of God. The spiritual rebirth in turn spawns a material civilization or kingdom in the form of a community that carries the spiritual precepts to practical application, in a process that repeats itself time and again throughout history. In a more abstract sense, the kingdom is universal, beyond time and space, and represents the spiritual life of mankind that evolves from age to age, both the interior and subjective kingdom, and the external and visible kingdom as expressed in communities and social institutions. One phase of the kingdom was manifest in the days of David and, before him, in the days of Moses. Another phase initiated in the time of Jesus, still another is to dawn upon the world in the day of His return.

The Gospels give us a vision of the kingdom that is both here-and-now, first-century, and in the future, and both spiritual and material. Reflecting on history, we can see how Christianity passed gradually from the stage of "the kingdom is within you" to World Empire. We are witnesses that Christ spiritually revitalized a community of His followers, inspiring high morals and a standard of brotherly love that defied the Roman standard of "might makes right." We testify to the steadfastness of their faith at the risk of martyrdom, and we know that, with time, the Christian standard eventually "conquered" Rome and established itself as the moral standard of western civilization. Thus, we see the spiritual kingdom initiated by Jesus become a firm community of hundreds, thousands, and hundreds of thousands of believers, until Constantine appeared and Christianity was itself transformed into an empire.

It is easy enough for us to see this—right? It is easy enough to talk about spiritual kingdom and its transformation into a visible civilization. It is easy enough for us to sort out the different strands of the Gospels and fit them into tidy pigeonholes, and classify verses as present and future, because we can see how history unfolded, what was imminent, and what was futuristic. As clear as this might be for us, early Christians may or may not have had ready access to all the Gospels to effect the sort of analysis presented above. More importantly, they certainly could not benefit from the perspective of hindsight that we enjoy. They were standing on the brink of epoch-making events that would shake the world, so they thought, and they were right. But the nature of those events was perhaps distinct from what they expected. It was likely difficult for them to appreciate the significance of their simple, homespun gatherings of twenty or thirty believers where bread was broken and the Eucharist shared. They were so close to the history that they themselves were making that they could scarcely recognize it as history. They did not imagine that within a few short generations the empire that persecuted them would espouse their religion. They could not visualize that same empire imploding on itself (except perhaps through that divine retribution that they awaited) and their own church hierarchy eventually filling a vacuum left by its ineffectiveness. It is no more than natural that they should look elsewhere for the events that would turn the world on its head, and they looked to the return of their Lord and all the events associated with it. As the second century advanced, the view of an imminent, material kingdom that would accompany the return of Christ came to dominate the vision of several of the most prominent of Christian writers, a material kingdom as visualized in the Old Testament and reiterated in the Book of the Apocalypse.

So let us return to the first century and to the Christian-Jewish dialogue, and put ourselves in the shoes of those second- or third-generation Christians. Regarding the Jews, we can say with a degree of certainty that their expectations for the kingdom were high but, compared to the situation of the Christians, they experienced relatively less ambiguity about the kingdom, since the only one that they expected was a worldly one. Furthermore, the Jews still looked to the future for the kingdom, while Christians had to explain why the material kingdom had not appeared with the advent of Jesus.

Christians had to face up to the dichotomies of present or future, material or spiritual, which for the Jews were non-issues. We can imagine that as Jews and Christians drew further apart toward the end of the first century and in the course of the second, the Jews must have harried the Christians on the point of the kingdom. The Jews were demanding to know where the kingdom was as promised by Isaiah and the Prophets—exactly as is represented in the Gospel of Luke: "he was demanded of the Pharisees, when the kingdom of God should come."[31] As we move into the second century, the response that most Christian apologists offered had less and less to do with a spiritual kingdom. Although the Gospels record far more words of Jesus stressing the spiritual dimensions of the kingdom, the second century Christian theologians, Justin Martyr and Irenaeus, apparently minimized this dimension. One no longer finds the central idea to be "the mystery of the kingdom of God"[32] as "the word that was sown in their hearts."[33] Rather, they seemed to adopt a more Jewish view of the kingdom than that presented in the Gospels, and for these Christians—like the Jews—the kingdom would be futuristic and material, and it would only take a few more years until Christ appeared again for it to be realized. This line of thought was later opposed by Origen in the third century and eventually reversed with the appearance of Augustine in the fourth century, but meanwhile, this tendency to emphasize the material kingdom made Christian aspirations almost identical with Jewish expectations.

It is likely that the shift toward a material emphasis in the kingdom during the second century reflects Jewish influence at least in part. Evidence shows that the church was still losing converts to Judaism, perhaps into the third or even the fourth centuries. Remember that, although Palestinian Judaism was devastated by wars, the greater number of Jews actually lived outside Palestine. Thus a competition between Christianity and Judaism continued beyond the first century in urban centers of the Greco-Roman world.

This is evidenced in the second century by one of Justin's foremost works, *Dialogue with Trypho*, to which we have referred and in which the Christian apologist argues for a material kingdom with its seat in Jerusalem that is to last for one thousand years. However, just why this Jewish outlook came to dominate the viewpoint of Christians (or at least of certain prominent Christians to whose writings we have access) is not clear. Was it a response to Jewish criticisms and demands for explanations about the kingdom, a concession to the Jewish viewpoint that appeared to have a firm scriptural basis and was difficult to refute? Or was it acquired independently of Jewish demands and directly from the Hebrew Scriptures per se, which presented visions of a peaceful world of plenty? Or was it still an attempt to calm the concerns of Jewish-Christians who were restless at the non-fulfillment of their own version of Jewish expectations? Of course, these options are not mutually exclusive, and all might have contributed. One way or another, the imagery of the earthly kingdom—so explicit and graphic in the Jewish tradition, so timely and urgent at that moment in history, so cherished and attractive in a world ravaged by injustice and oppression—was so powerful that it overshadowed the subtler meanings with which Jesus had invested it.

Another aspect of the representation of the kingdom in the Gospels that does not deal with substance, but with the form and structure of the Message of Jesus, merits reflection. Throughout the Gospel narrative, Jesus adopted a thoroughly Jewish vocabulary to communicate His Message. In the case at hand, Jesus gave ample and repeated usage to the term "kingdom" that formed a firm and very visible part of the Jewish apocalyptic vocabulary. For the Jews, there was little ambiguity about what the kingdom represented. The kingdom was the kingdom, the restoration of the Davidic throne—and if there was a diversity of views on how it might come about, there was certainly consensus that it would exalt the Jews to their former glory. Jesus, in addressing a Jewish audience that was steeped in Jewish Scripture and tradition, used a traditional Jewish vocabulary that had an especially urgent and timely significance at that point in history. Moreover, He made the "kingdom" the very central issue of His Mission.

However, Jesus injected into the vocabulary of the Jews new meanings, totally foreign to their common usage, appropriating the Jewish vocabulary and adapting it to His own Message. Moreover, the meanings that Jesus gave to the "kingdom" were intensely spiritual, and could only be understood from a spiritual point of view, which is to say, from the standpoint of His doctrine of the human soul. "The kingdom of God is within you" and is born of "the word that was sown in their hearts." This implied a whole interior world to be explored, an inner self that was couched in terms of the most cherished of Jewish aspirations. To someone who had little concept of an inner being independent of the physical self, who looked for the restoration of Jewish political independence, this probably sounded like gibberish. Yet Jesus drew freely upon that time-honored expression of Jewish political status, and converted it into a symbol of a new sort of citizenship that began at the most fundamental level of the self—the human soul. This was part of His Mission in introducing new concepts and new teachings under God's plan of progressive revelation.

This spiritual adaptation of established terms would add new and profound dimensions to the Jewish vocabulary, yet it would leave the door open to ambiguity in those terms, as in the case at hand of the kingdom. Jesus spoke of the kingdom in new contexts and with new implications about its spiritual content, its moral standard, and the spiritual bonds among those who enter that kingdom. But with the passage of time, it was relatively easy for His avowed believers to "backslide" and revert to a simplistic understanding of what the kingdom represented. And they reverted to the Jewish understanding of a worldly kingdom in which the faithful are rewarded with eternal peace and material abundance—a vision that still escapes us, and for which we long, but which stops short of the spiritual kingdom that Jesus was trying to communicate.

Here we see a pattern of the presentation and misunderstanding of New Testament doctrine: the appropriation and use of a Jewish vocabulary, the application of totally new and spiritual meanings to that vocabulary, and the subsequent misunderstanding by Christians themselves of the spiritual content of that message and reversion to a Jewish interpretation. We will see that this pattern will be repeated in other aspects of the Christian Message, in regard to issues that are central to Christianity.

Furthermore, we have seen in this first and very important example of the kingdom and its multiple meanings, a pattern used by the Gospel writers to convey the Message of Jesus by contrasting it with Jewish doctrine in short vignettes that are represented as face-offs between Jesus and different elements of the Jewish community. The Gospel writer has enshrined in the very structure of the text, those intentions and meanings that he seeks to convey. The first example was taken from the Gospel of Luke, in which the Pharisees demanded when the kingdom would appear and Jesus responded in terms that were evidently foreign to the Pharisees, but that represented His own doctrine. In the case of the parable of the sower, in the Gospel of Mark, the Jews are not represented as confronting Jesus, but the "us-versus-the-Jews" sense is clear. Such antagonistic face-offs are often thought to be evidence of anti-Semitism or anti-Judaism in the New Testament. I think that their intention is not so much to set Jesus against Jews, but rather to contrast Christian doctrine with Jewish doctrine, especially for the sake of those Jewish-Christians who were still struggling with the implications of having accepted Jesus as the Messiah. Rather than stories to ingrain hatred for Jews, they are didactic tools focused particularly on those early Christians of Jewish origin who were still attached to the doctrines and belief systems that were represented by the scribes, the Pharisees, and the Sadducees. This is a didactic tool that Mark and Matthew often use, and Luke much less frequently. John, in turn, also employs some point-blank confrontations of Jesus and the Jews to contrast doctrine, but what is more, he presents well-arranged dramas, as we will see shortly. In subsequent chapters, we will explore this structure of antagonistic vignettes as a vehicle for teaching Christian doctrine, and the intentions of the Gospel writers in specific cases.

CHAPTER 8

RESURRECTION AND SPIRIT:
OPTIONS FOR THE AFTERLIFE?

Even at its best, Old Testament Judaism was firmly this-worldly, putting priority on justice and ethics in the earthly plane. The limited Jewish perspective on spiritual reality circumscribed the outlook of the Jews on many fronts. This was especially pertinent to the subject of life after death. Since the ancient Jews did not have a well-defined concept of soul as a spiritual entity independent of physical existence, they had even less concept of the eternal existence of the soul in a spiritual world after death. Indeed, the Old Testament contains minimal references to life after death. Although concepts varied from sect to sect, for most Jews the soul referred to a sort of life force that animated the body, but that disappeared or dissipated with death.

Nonetheless, two independent concepts were derived from the Old Testament and can be associated with eternal life. The first dealt, not with the continuance of an individual's identity in some afterlife, but in the continuance of life itself in the posterity that one leaves in this world. Hence, Abraham might die, but His seed lives on and perpetuates His heritage. This may be the original and more ancient concept of life's eternal continuity among the Jews. This outlook perhaps predominates in the Qumran writings, where eternal existence is often mentioned in conjunction to a reference to one's descendents.

The second concept of eternal life, which was apparently associated most closely with the Pharisees, was that of resurrection, or the reappearance and revival of the dead at some future date when they return from Sheol. Heaven and hell, as we think of them, had no place in Jewish thought, but there did exist the idea of a place called Sheol where "souls" accumulated at death. The term "Sheol" at

---

times could be interpreted as "the grave," at other times it seems to be a nether world, but in general it does not have the connotations of punishment that "hell" does in the Christian tradition, and as it is often translated. However, not all Jews accepted the doctrine of resurrection, and the Sadducees rejected resurrection as being foreign to the teachings of Moses.

The Old Testament contains a small number of explicit references to resurrection, but these are few and far between, most notably in Ezekiel 37 in the vision of the dry bones that return to life, and in Daniel 12:1. This latter reference perhaps best typified the stance of the Pharisees about resurrection, in that it is set in the context of the advent of the Messiah, and the reward of the Jews in the last days. That is to say, resurrection was an event that would accompany the appearance of the Messiah (here identified as Michael), who would appear in a "time of trouble" when Israel would be vindicated after long years of humiliation, and when Israel's enemies would be vanquished in a show of God's retributive justice. I quote it here in full out of regard for its doctrinal importance among the Pharisees. "And at that time shall Michael stand up, the great prince which standeth for the children of thy people: and there shall be a time of trouble, such as never was since there was a nation even to that same time: and at that time thy people shall be delivered, every one that shall be found written in the book. And many of them that sleep in the dust of the earth shall awake, some to everlasting life, and some to shame and everlasting contempt. And they that be wise shall shine as the brightness of the firmament; and they that turn many to righteousness, as the stars for ever and ever. But thou, O Daniel, shut up the words, and seal the book, even to the time of the end."[1]

Resurrection thus formed part of a broader doctrine about the end times and responded to a theological question that was particularly Jewish: if the Jews were the Chosen of God, how could so many generations of Jews have died in vain under the heel of the Assyrians, the Babylonians, the Greeks, and the Romans? How could God be unjust with His very own Hebrew children for nearly six hundred years? Resurrection responded to this question: the many generations of Jews who had been wronged would arise and receive their recompense when the Messiah appeared. The appearance of the Messiah would bring as well the kingdom of God, and so the resurrected beings could also participate in the kingdom. The expectations for the kingdom were of course political in nature, and in a sense the resurrection was part of the same political theory for the Jews. Note that this concept of afterlife continues to be this worldly.

When Jesus appeared and brought the doctrine of the spiritual soul, this doctrine had vast implications for the afterlife. The existence of a spiritual reality implies an indestructible entity with an eternal existence. Rather than looking to the resurrection to reconstitute a material reality that has decomposed in the grave, in the doctrine of Jesus the soul never ceases to exist and so needs no reconstitution, no recovery from non-existence. Thus, the Jewish concept of resurrection was displaced in Christian doctrine by the concept of eternal spiritual (non-material) life, and resurrection was no longer a necessary concept. Furthermore, when placed into the Jewish context of ethics, the eternal nature of the soul also opened the possibility of reward and punishment in a future life, according to one's fulfillment of those moral and ethical principles.

The Christians were not necessarily alone in teaching the eternal existence of the soul. Threads in the writings of the rabbis in the Talmud apparently reflect a belief in an eternal soul, and Jewish thinkers were weaving these threads together with the concept of resurrection. Scholars think that ideas about eternal life may have filtered into Judaism as influences from neighboring races. The Greek philosopher Plato developed a concept of eternal soul four hundred years before Christ, and Alexander the Great had conquered the Middle East three centuries before Christ initiated His Mission. The Jews were intimately familiarized with Greek culture for most of that period, and the Jews were likewise familiar with the Platonic concept of the immortal soul. When the Jewish rabbis set down the Talmud as the standard of Jewish belief, this element of Platonic thought seems to have found credence among some of the rabbis.

However, there is a certain ambiguity in the Talmud about eternal life. It is referred to as the "world to come" (*olam ha-ba*), but this term is also applied to the material world that would result at the advent of the Messiah. Were the rabbis still working through this ambiguity and coming to terms with the concept of eternal life? Perhaps. The fact is that the Talmud is not a dogmatic set of doctrines, but a compilation of varied and sometimes conflicting interpretations, preserved as it were as a transcript of a many-faceted and ongoing debate, so we need not expect finality on all points. Regarding eternal life, the continuing existence of the soul was not a traditional Jewish concept in the first century, and it probably needed some adaptation and massaging to work into the rabbinic doctrine. It is difficult to fully reconcile a spiritual afterlife with the Jewish view of soul as a life force that animates the body and that dissipates upon death, so one suspects that the rabbis were indeed still struggling with these ideas and integrating them with the concept of physical resurrection, which seems to have had a firmer place in the Pharisaic doctrine.

In any case, it is likely that both the Christians and the Pharisees (and later the rabbis) were attempting to establish their own doctrine about the afterlife, in opposition to traditional Jewish thought—and in competition with each other! Josephus says that the teachings of the Pharisees about eternal life made their doctrine attractive to many Jews, and there is little doubt that the same applied to Christianity. But both Christians and Pharisees represented minority movements that were swimming against the current of Jewish orthodoxy, and seeking to establish a following. Perhaps the similarities in their respective messages made them especially fierce competitors. We will soon see evidence of their competition on this point in the pages of the Gospels. Much of what is said about the resurrection in the New Testament may well be viewed as a Christian response to the Pharisaic position, and an attempt to counter the Pharisaic-rabbinic view on the afterlife.

Although Jesus spoke explicitly of the afterlife, He seldom did so as if to argue for its existence and to convince anyone of its reality, but rather as if its existence were an established fact among His listeners. The Gospels do not contain a direct statement of Jesus saying anything comparable to this: "After this life there is another one much more glorious, everlasting, in a world invisible to us where your eternal and indestructible souls shall gather in the presence of God." Jesus simply encouraged His listeners to seek eternal life and delineated the requirements of its attainment, and those present either believed and accepted His statements, or not. To give examples: "Verily I say unto you, There is no man that hath left house, or brethren, or sisters, or father, or mother, or wife, or children, or lands, for my sake, and the gospel's, but he shall receive an hundredfold now in this time, houses, and brethren, and sisters, and mothers, and children, and lands, with persecutions; and in the world to come eternal life."[2] And: "A certain lawyer stood up, and tempted him, saying, Master, what shall I do to inherit eternal life? He said unto him, What is written in the law? how readest thou? And he answering said, Thou shalt love the Lord thy God with all thy heart, and with all thy soul, and with all thy strength, and with all thy mind; and thy neighbour as thyself. And he said unto him, Thou hast answered right: this do, and thou shalt live."[3]

However, in other cases when the Gospels argue in favor of the existence of the eternal soul, the presentation of Christian doctrine is much more subtle. As in the case of the kingdom, we find several in which the doctrine of Jesus is presented by contrasting it with that of the Jews, and in those contrasts we find implicit the eternal existence of the soul. In one such vignette, we observe the Jewish inability to conceive of life after death. Jesus is recorded as saying: "Verily, verily, I say unto you, If a man keep my saying, he shall never see death. Then said the Jews unto him, Now we know that thou hast a devil. Abraham is dead, and the prophets; and thou sayest, If a man keep my saying, he shall never taste of death. Art thou greater than our father Abraham, which is dead? and the prophets are dead: whom makest thou thyself?"[4] In other words, the Jews are voicing their belief that Abraham and all the prophets are dead and gone and have no more existence. This is in accord with their view that there is no continuing spiritual existence, only the grave. John has constructed this scene to contrast this belief with that of Jesus which is of eternal life.

Another scene implicitly pits Christian teaching against two different Jewish doctrines. The Sadducees pose a hypothetical situation to Jesus concerning a widow who married seven brothers successively as each one died. They ask to whom the widow will belong when all seven husbands resuscitate in the resurrection. The Sadducees did not believe in the resurrection, and in Mark's account they apparently think that they can trip up Jesus with this riddle. Perhaps they have heard Jesus refer to the resurrection, and their purpose is to discredit both the doctrine of resurrection and Jesus Himself, by entangling Him in an absurd hypothetical marital problem.

In this vignette, the doctrine of Jesus is placed in contraposition both to that of the Pharisees who believe in resurrection, and to that of the Sadducees who pose the question. Jesus does not respond to the Sadducees' question per se, but simply debunks the question as ill founded in its underlying assumptions. First He deals with the Sadducees, who disbelieve in the resurrection, by establishing the reality of the resurrection in a spiritual sense, since the resurrected ones are like "the angels in heaven": "For when they shall rise from the dead, they neither marry, nor are given in marriage; but are as the angels which are in heaven." Then Jesus implicitly turns His attention to the Pharisees who believe in the physical resurrection. "And as touching the dead, that they rise: have ye not read in the book of Moses, how in the bush God spake unto him, saying, I am the God of Abraham, and the God of Isaac, and the God of Jacob? He is not the God of the dead, but the God of the living: ye therefore do greatly err."[5] Now, we have to take Jesus at His word that God is the "God of the living," but as a corollary to that premise, Jesus implies that Abraham, Isaac, and Jacob are therefore very much alive, although physically they died long before God spoke those words to Moses. And since the patriarchs are living, they have no need to rise from the dead, and the doctrine of physical resurrection is debunked. In other words, the bodily resurrection is not even an issue, and thus Jesus rejects the Pharisee's belief in physical resurrection. In a broader sense, Mark's vignette is an argument in favor of the continuing existence of the soul after death, in opposition to the orthodoxy of the Sadducees who did not recognize any eternal spiritual existence at all, saying: "ye therefore do greatly err."

The Jews were not alone in their misunderstanding of eternal life, and even the disciples had difficulty grasping the idea of an afterlife, as we understand it today. The concept of an afterlife is one aspect of our modern culture that we take for granted, and it is inculcated by all sorts of media. We see television commercials depicting angels floating around on clouds, we share jokes about Saint Peter at the pearly gates, and even animated cartoons show the characters drifting away to heaven after some fatal calamity, with a pair of wings that sprout spontaneously from their shoulder blades. These images may be childish and naïve, but they are meaningful to us because we have a shared consciousness and a common set of symbols and assumptions about life after death.

These images testify to a cultural mindset about an afterlife. But in the first century there was still no such common mental framework about what today we call heaven, and if the disciples in the days of Jesus could have seen our modern images they would have found them totally incomprehensible, just as they were slow to assimilate the teaching of Jesus about life after death. Even though Jesus had referred continually to eternal life, the concept was still essentially foreign to His followers within their Jewish context, and had not yet taken form in their consciousness. This is reflected in the puzzlement that the disciples expressed as Jesus spoke of His departure from them, for example: "Thomas saith unto him, Lord, we know not whither thou goest; and how can we know the way?"[6] This incapacity to grasp fully the implications of life after death would plague the disciples as they faced the crucifixion with horror, until they realized that physical death only affected the outward semblance of human existence, and that the inner spiritual essence of which Jesus had taught them would continue eternally and would overcome even the greatest of all tragedies as manifested on the cross.

Having replaced the Jewish concept of physical resurrection of the body with the concept of an eternal afterlife, the term "resurrection" was freed up within the Christian lexicon to be applied to other concepts. One of these is found in the Gospel of Mark, where again the disciples are made the vehicle through which to voice the concerns of a Jewish or Jewish-Christian point of view, for here we find the disciples "questioning one with another what the rising from the dead should mean. And they asked him, saying, Why say the scribes that Elijah must first come?" In other words, the disciples are raising questions about the reappearance of the long-dead Prophet Elijah, who in Jewish traditions should usher in the Messiah. This is a doubt about the resurrection that would have come from Mark's Jewish-Christian audience. Jesus responds saying, "Elijah verily cometh first, and restoreth all things . . . But I say unto you, that Elijah is indeed come, and they have done unto him whatsoever they listed, as it is written of him."[7] Matthew in turn adds the note that "then the disciples understood that he spake unto them of John the Baptist,"[8] a fact that Mark leaves as implicit. The implication is that Elijah has "risen from the dead" and has reappeared in the person of John the Baptist, which we understand to mean that John took the role of Elijah and therefore was the resurrected Elijah in a figurative sort of way—a novel and creative application of the concept of resurrection!

Furthermore, Christians appropriated the Jewish vocabulary of "resurrection" in still another sense, in which it interacts with the vocabulary of "eternal life." There is no doubt that belief in the afterlife plays a central role in the Message of Jesus, but we would be shortchanging the doctrine of Jesus if we suggest that "eternal life" was merely continued existence in a spiritual realm. This is the quantitative dimension of eternal life—long life—and while the fact of an afterlife was an important innovation that Jesus brought to the Jewish tradition, it is perhaps not as important as the qualitative dimension of eternal life. For Jesus brought a "quality of life," which was born of knowing Him and loving Him.

"Verily, verily, I say unto you, He that believeth on me hath everlasting life."[9] Until the soul attains to this state of faith, the soul is not much different from an animal, or a plant, or a rock. The soul without faith is like a babe that is born into this world deaf, blind, and mute. Unable to see, hear, or communicate, the existence of such a child is as if dead. Real life is not material and does not begin until one can "see" God through faith, "for a man's life consisteth not in the abundance of the things which he possesseth."[10] Thus, in the Christian vocabulary, one who had attained to "eternal life" through faith in Jesus was counted among those who had been "resurrected" to a new consciousness and a new quality of life.

The Christian vocabulary about the soul and its eternal existence and its transformation contrasts markedly with the standard Jewish concept, and on this topic we find the Jews in the New Testament simply unable to relate to what Jesus was telling them. This is illustrated nowhere better than in the story of Nicodemus, as told by John. Nicodemus is portrayed as essentially a good man. He keeps the Law, he does what is right, and above all, he seeks out Jesus with an open heart and mind. Yet in spite of bearing a very serious message, the story of Nicodemus has a comical quality about it. Nicodemus asks what he must do to attain eternal life and Jesus tells him he must be born again. This response leaves Nicodemus nonplussed, as he asks the question that John here makes the mirror of the Jewish mentality. "How can a man be born when he is old? can he enter the second time into his mother's womb, and be born?" he exclaims in disbelief.[11] He simply cannot visualize himself becoming tiny and crawling back into his mother's womb, and what is more (and this is the point of the story), he is equally incapable of visualizing the sort of spiritual rebirth to which Jesus refers.

If this scenario actually happened, the apostles must have chuckled about Nicodemus' confused and bumbling naivety for many years to come ("Do you remember the look on the face of old Nicodemus when he said . . ."), but it is likely that John has doctored the situation to portray the incapacity of the Jews in general to capture the essence of the Message and Mission of Jesus. John has made Nicodemus to be the archetypical educated Jew who cannot, for the life of him, find within his experience or his knowledge of all the sacred Scriptures and the Law, any clue as to what Jesus is saying. Thus Jesus reproaches him, "Art thou a master of Israel, and knowest not these things?"[12] Nicodemus recognizes that Jesus is a great teacher, that His wonders must originate in God, and he is drawn to Jesus and poses his questions with a ready mind—yet he just cannot figure it out. Nicodemus can only scratch his head as to what this Nazarene is talking about, because it is all Greek to him, beyond his concepts and mindset.

The story of Nicodemus illustrates better than any other the clash of worldviews between Jesus and Jewish orthodoxy—spirit versus this world. Nicodemus is about as good as a Jew can get, yet with his Jewish education, he still cannot understand the Message of Jesus, and so, sadly enough, cannot participate in the eternal life that Jesus is offering. Rebirth and resurrection—these are the spiritual transformation of the Christian's life that initiates in this world and continues on to the next, and makes it irrelevant in which world one finds oneself. This is life that transcends time and space. Thus could Jesus speak of eternal life as initiating in the here and now: "He that heareth my word, and believeth on him that sent me, hath everlasting life, and shall not come into condemnation; but is passed from death unto life."[13] This is the dimension of existence that continues eternally.

In brief, everything that I said about the kingdom in the previous chapter applies to the present topic of eternal life. Both have a dimension that is here and now, and that is born in the soul, and at this level the kingdom and eternal life are synonymous. Both also have a dimension that extends into the future. And just as Jesus appropriated the Jewish vocabulary of the kingdom and gave it a spiritual meaning, so did Jesus take the words "life" and "resurrection," and give them an entirely different dimension. Life, eternal life, and resurrection, in the Christian context, took on a new, independent meaning—spiritual transformation and revitalization. LIFE! Quality of life! Without this transformation of the soul, one could breathe, walk, talk, eat, laugh, cry, sleep, and procreate—and still be dead. However, the Jews who did not accept the soul in all its implications could not understand Jesus as He spoke of "eternal life" in a totally new context. Like Nicodemus, they could only scratch their heads and walk away.

John subtly contrasts the Jewish and Christian concepts of life and resurrection in the story that is the centerpiece of Christian thought on the resurrection—the story of Lazarus. Jesus has been called to heal Lazarus, but delays in His arrival, and meanwhile Lazarus dies. His sister Martha expresses the hope, rooted in her Jewish traditions, that her brother will rise from the dead in the physical resurrection: "I know that he shall rise again in the resurrection at the last day."[14] Now, this is the perfect opportunity for Jesus to confirm the physical resurrection of the dead if that were His intention. This is the opportunity for Him to say, "Yes, Martha, keep the faith. Just be patient and wait a little longer, and before you know it, Lazarus will return just as you knew him." But that is not what Jesus says at all. Quite the contrary. Jesus gently corrects Martha, reminding her that she should not look to a long distant future for the resurrection. His words are a dramatic declaration of His own reality: "I am the resurrection, and the life: he that believeth in me, though he were dead, yet shall he live."[15] In other words, the resurrection that Martha waits for and expects to be material and futuristic, in reality is here and now (again, exactly like the kingdom—here and now), and is personified in Jesus Himself for those who will believe in Him and accept to be transformed by His love. In the next phrase, Jesus emphasizes that He is not referring to physical resurrection and existence when He says, "whosoever liveth and believeth in me shall never die."[16] It is obvious that all who believed in Jesus in that first century and ever since have indeed died in a material sense. By the time John penned these very words toward the end of the first century, many had already passed on, perhaps even Lazarus himself, hence physical life and physical resurrection are not the object of this teaching.

John has left still another clue of far less theological significance to suggest that the story of Lazarus is not to be taken literally. John states that when Lazarus comes out of the tomb, he was "bound hand and foot with graveclothes," which is to say, wrapped head to foot in his funeral shroud, making it virtually impossible for him to move. So how do we imagine that he emerged from his mausoleum? He would have had to come hopping out of his tomb with his feet tied together in a rather undignified display! Rather, might not those bindings that held him prisoner be some worldly attachments—perhaps even the Jewish traditions represented by the doctrine of resurrection that is the central theme of the story?

John has so crafted these two stories, that of Nicodemus and that of Lazarus, to put the doctrine of Jesus into stark contrast with Jewish doctrine, especially that of the Pharisees. Remember that John is speaking to an audience that probably still has many Jewish-Christians in it, and like Jesus correcting Martha, John is gently nudging his audience toward a realization that Jesus has used the Jewish vocabulary in a totally new sense. John continues to speak of resurrection, but he is attempting to open the eyes of his audience to a very different meaning than the Pharisaic interpretation that is circulating widely at the end of the first century.

This is the case when we refer to the resurrection as applied to the believer. When we turn to the resurrection of Jesus Himself, we find the same vocabulary applied in still another but related manner. What is more, we find a serious logical contradiction in the Gospel record, a contradiction that appears in two of the Gospels (Matthew and John) and is implied in the others. To illustrate this contradiction, let me reconstruct a New Testament episode that is one of the most fascinating from a spiritual standpoint, which is the calling of the disciples.

Galilee is a part of Palestine that is especially blessed by God. The soft winter rains turn its rocky hills green for several months of the year, and the warmth of early spring draws forth an explosion of color that lasts a few brief weeks. Ample patches of red and blue wild flowers dot the landscape, and wild cyclamen sprout among the beige limestone rocks. The spring breezes make the wild flowers bend and flow like ocean waves, creating new hues that add still more variety in color and giving the impression that the very hills are inhaling and exhaling. The colors of spring are brief, but vibrant, symbolic perhaps of the New Life that is about to break upon the land of the Jews after centuries of spiritual drought and famine.

Here in Galilee, life is simple. No one looks to Galilee for intellectual brilliance! The schools of Jewish learning are in Jerusalem. Neither are there riches in the villages of Galilee. Trade routes pass not far to the west, but the caravans leave none of their riches in Galilee. The well-to-do congregate in the cities of Sepphoris and Tiberias, but the countryside of Galilee is a land quite forgotten by the rich and powerful. No matter, here God takes care of His own. Shepherds feed their flocks on the green hills; farmers cultivate barley and lentils with the winter rains. To the north, the snows are still visible on the peaks of Mount Hermon, and these will melt over the next months and replenish the jewel of Galilee—its large freshwater lake, known to many as the Sea of Galilee. In a region that struggles for water during much of the year, such a large freshwater body is a special blessing of God. Here the local fishermen reap God's bounty on a daily basis, casting their nets and drawing their own sustenance from its depths. So have the Galileans learned to trust in God's providence and live from the harvests that He provides, little suspecting that soon the Lord will initiate His own harvest in their midst! For it is in Galilee that Jesus initiates His Mission. Just as the breeze makes the wild flowers bow and roll like ocean waves, so is the gentle wind of the Spirit about to blow over Galilee and stir the hearts of men to life.

Jesus stands on a hill over the lake for a few minutes and surveys its view. Is He calling to those receptive hearts from His vantage point? His gaze is steady and penetrating, and He knows what He seeks—the treasures destined by God to be revealed by His hand, the pure souls that God would convert into bastions of His love and champions of His cause. After a few moments of silent reflection, He descends toward the lake with a purposeful gait, as One who knows where He is going and why.

He approaches the fishermen in silence, but they pay Him no heed until He is standing over them. Does He wish to purchase some of the fishermen's catch? Simon and his brother Andrew raise their eyes expecting to find a buyer for their wares, but it is not a buyer that they see. Their eyes meet those of the stranger and the two youths experience a sensation that they have never known before. Their hearts move within them, their very being is shaken, and they are transported momentarily to a state unknown to them. A mystical communication has occurred, and the brothers feel as if this stranger is looking within them, through them, into their past and their future, as if Jesus and no one else truly knows them. Their response is determined even before the command is uttered: "Follow me," says Jesus. Without hesitation, Simon and Andrew leap to their feet in obedience to their hearts and to their Lord, to follow Him wherever fate may lead them.

Philip likewise is called unexpectedly, and he runs to his brother Nathanael with the Good News: "We have found him of whom Moses in the Law and also the prophets wrote, Jesus of Nazareth, the son of Joseph."

I have combined here the story in Matthew 4 of Simon and Andrew, who were called while they were fishing, and the story in John 1 of Philip, because jointly they illustrate a remarkable phenomenon. The point is, that the Gospels of both Matthew and John represent the response of the disciples as immediate, automatic, and heartfelt. There is no hesitation, no vacillation, no theological web weaving, and no questioning as to who this stranger is. Philip is even represented in this first brief encounter as recognizing Jesus as the Messiah promised by Moses and the Prophets. This spontaneous response may be passed off by some as mythologizing, but I see here something much more profound. This is the pure and receptive heart, untarnished by worldly attachments and human ego that often accompany intellectual achievement and learning—the pure heart brought face to face with the light of the sun. It does not ask, is this really the sun? Or, what should I do? Or, what about this or that theological point? It responds as if by instinct, as when a plant turns to the light or when a babe seeks its mother's milk. It traverses all limitations in a second and is ready to circle moth-like around the candle until it is drawn into the self-immolation of sacrifice. This is a mystery of the spiritual world that, if not rational or lending itself to reductionist analysis, is as much a reality as Jesus Himself.

So, returning to our theme, what is the contradiction with regard to the resurrection of Jesus? When we turn to the story of the resurrection, what do we find? Mark reports doubt and reticence on the part of the believers to accept the news of the risen Christ. Matthew says that the disciples sought out a spot where Jesus directed them to await Him: "Then the eleven disciples went away into Galilee, into a mountain where Jesus had appointed them. And when they saw him, they worshipped him: but some doubted."[17] Even seeing Jesus with their own eyes at the site that Jesus had appointed, not all the disciples believe! However, it is Luke and John who portray this doubt in terms that are truly remarkable.

Luke 24 tells the story of two believers who leave Jerusalem on foot to a nearby village. "And, behold, two of them went that same day to a village called Emmaus, which was from Jerusalem about threescore furlongs. And they talked together of all these things which had happened. And it came to pass, that, while they communed together and reasoned, Jesus himself drew near, and went with them. But their eyes were holden that they should not know him."[18] The two relate to their new-found travel companion what had transpired in the past week in Jerusalem, how they had placed their hopes on Jesus as the Messiah, and how some of the women had reported that He had risen from the dead. At this, Jesus upbraids them saying, "O fools, and slow of heart to believe all that the prophets have spoken: Ought not Christ to have suffered these things, and to enter into his glory? And beginning at Moses and all the prophets, he expounded unto them in all the Scriptures the things concerning himself . . . And it came to pass, as he sat at meat with them, he took bread, and blessed it, and brake, and gave to them. And their eyes were opened, and they knew him; and he vanished out of their sight."[19]

The version of John 20 is equally remarkable in portraying the doubts of the companions of Jesus and their inability to recognize Him: "Mary (Magdalene) stood without at the sepulchre weeping: and as she wept, she stooped down, and looked into the sepulchre, And seeth two angels in white sitting, . . . And they say unto her, Woman, why weepest thou? She saith unto them, Because they have taken away my Lord, and I know not where they have laid him. And when she had thus said, she turned herself back, and saw Jesus standing, and knew not that it was Jesus. Jesus saith unto her, Woman, why weepest thou? whom seekest thou? She, supposing him to be the gardener, saith unto him, Sir, if thou have borne him hence, tell me where thou hast laid him, and I will take him away."[20]

Of all such recorded instances, the case of Peter according to John is the most remarkable of all.

"After these things Jesus showed himself again to the disciples at the sea of Tiberias; and on this wise showed he himself. There were together Simon Peter, and Thomas called Didymus, and Nathanael of Cana in Galilee, and the sons of Zebedee, and two other of his disciples. Simon Peter saith unto them, I go a fishing. They say unto him, We also go with thee. They went forth, and entered into a ship immediately; and that night they caught nothing.

But when the morning was now come, Jesus stood on the shore: but the disciples knew not that it was Jesus. Then Jesus saith unto them, Children, have ye any meat? They answered him, No. And he said unto them, Cast the net on the right side of the ship, and ye shall find. They cast therefore, and now they were not able to draw it for the multitude of fishes. Therefore that disciple whom Jesus loved saith unto Peter, It is the Lord. Now when Simon Peter heard that it was the Lord, he girt his fisher's coat unto him, (for he was naked,) and did cast himself into the sea . . .

This is now the third time that Jesus showed himself to his disciples, after that he was risen from the dead."[21]

In all of these accounts we see that the disciples are incapable of recognizing Jesus, despite having spent three years in the warmth of His love; despite having heard His voice every day and having hung on His every word; despite having heard from His lips the promise to arise and meet them in a designated place where they subsequently gathered. And in the case of Peter and the others who were fishing in Galilee, they had already witnessed the risen Christ on *two* occasions. It should not have been at all difficult to recognize the glorified Christ after *two* encounters. (Note, too, that the morning sun would have illumined Jesus quite plainly standing on the western shore of the sea near Tiberias.) And all this blindness and incapacity and forgetfulness, despite having recognized Christ spontaneously three years earlier without ever having laid eyes on Him before! I repeat that this is a contradiction that at least two of the Gospel writers have very consciously incorporated into their narratives! This is especially incomprehensible in the case of John, who was the subtlest of all the Gospel writers, who crafted his accounts with great care to communicate the finest of theological points. One cannot imagine that such a glaring contradiction in his own written account would have escaped the attention of John. Impossible! This would be comparable to an author as meticulous as Conan Doyle neglecting so obvious a clue as a corpse stretched across the bed of Sherlock Holmes.

How can we explain the vivid and evident contrast between the first encounters when the disciples recognized Him immediately, and the subsequent encounters when they seemed totally incapable of recognition, even after three years of intimate communion with Him and multiple resurrection experiences? One must assume that one or other of these extremes is not to be taken literally; one simply cannot accept both at face value! I submit that it is in the resurrection that we must look for deeper significance; that the resurrection of Jesus has subtle and symbolic meanings that still have a profound message for us today, two thousand years after the fact.

One need not look too far for those meanings. They are explicit in the text of the Gospel, in verses that describe one of those occasions when Jesus referred to His resurrection in the presence of the disciples. Jesus promises to His loved ones His constant companionship in the days to come: "I will not leave you comfortless: I will come to you. Yet a little while, and the world seeth me no more; but ye see me: because I live, ye shall live also. At that day ye shall know that I am in my Father, and ye in me, and I in you. He that hath my commandments, and keepeth them, he it is that loveth me: and he that loveth me shall be loved of my Father, and I will love him, and will manifest myself to him."[22]

This is a warm and tender farewell to the disciples, and a promise of protection and companionship that continues to kindle faith and gratitude in millions of hearts even today. But in the moment that Jesus speaks, one of the disciples picks up on a detail that puzzles him. "Judas saith unto him, not Iscariot, Lord, how is it that thou wilt manifest thyself unto us, and not unto the world?"[23]

This is not a trivial question by any means. It is an unusual state of affairs that only His followers will be able to see Jesus risen from the dead. Did not everyone see Him as He sojourned in Palestine, in the synagogues and in the Temple? Did not Jews and Romans alike testify to His presence? Will He not have the same body when He resurrects, that will be visible to everyone? We can note again that in the formulation of this question, Judas is representing the Jewish point of view on physical resurrection (just as Martha did in the story of Lazarus), and that John has put this question into his mouth to contrast with the answer that Jesus will give. John has flagged this query for our own benefit and that of his first century audience, and we need to pay careful attention to the reply that Jesus gives to the query of Judas. "Jesus answered and said unto him, If a man love me, he will keep my words: and my Father will love him, and we will come unto him, and make our abode with him. He that loveth me not keepeth not my sayings: and the word which ye hear is not mine, but the Father's which sent me. These things have I spoken unto you, being yet present with you."[24]

In the first part of His discourse, Jesus emphasizes the love that the believers bear Him, and that He will manifest Himself to those that love Him. This is not sufficient for Judas, who expects to see Jesus with his physical eyes, and he cannot understand in this context how others will not see Him as well. Jesus, in His response, repeats the theme of love, saying that He and the Father will make their "abode" with all that love Him. In other words, Jesus is stating that He will manifest Himself in the love that His disciples and followers bear for Him. Here again, John contrasts the conventional Jewish material expectation of the resurrection, in the query put by Judas, with the spiritual reality that is posed by Jesus—that the resurrection has its reality in the love that lives in the hearts of the believers and is shared by them.

In this light we are reminded of other passages of the New Testament that equate the love among the believers with the very presence of Christ, for example: "For where two or three are gathered together in my name, there am I in the midst of them."[25] And in its simplest possible formulation of all, "God is love."[26]

Compare these reflections above with another commentary on the resurrection drawn from the Bahá'í Writings:

> "Therefore, we say that the meaning of Christ's resurrection is as follows: the disciples were troubled and agitated after the martyrdom of Christ. The Reality of Christ, which signifies His teachings, His bounties, His perfections and His spiritual power, was hidden and concealed for two or three days after His martyrdom, and was not resplendent and manifest. No, rather it was lost, for the believers were few in number and were troubled and agitated. The Cause of Christ was like a lifeless body; and when after three days the disciples became assured and steadfast, and began to serve the Cause of Christ, and resolved to spread the divine teachings, putting His counsels into practice, and arising to serve Him, the Reality of Christ became resplendent and His bounty appeared; His religion found life; His teachings and His admonitions became evident and visible. In other words, the Cause of Christ was like a lifeless body until the life and the bounty of the Holy Spirit surrounded it.
>
> Such is the meaning of the resurrection of Christ, and this was a true resurrection."[27]

It goes without saying that Jesus lives and reigns in that spiritual kingdom beyond our physical sight and senses. He lives, just as He Himself testified that Abraham, Isaac, and Jacob live. His existence is eternal and unending. Unquestionably, *Jesus lives*. Ironically, that fact is not the central reality of the resurrection of Jesus. And just as the resurrection of the believer is realized in his individual spiritual transformation, so is the resurrection of Jesus symbolic of the collective spiritual transformation of the body of His followers (which is to say, the church) after His martyrdom. And it initiated two or three days after the crucifixion, when the disciples gathered and, reviewing their experience and remembering the blessings of their Lord, they regained their faith and rekindled their love for Christ and for one another.

Now, you may take issue with this explanation of the resurrection. You may find this explanation to be lackluster and not worthy of an event so earthshaking as the resurrection of Christ. You may feel that the resurrection, which so moved the early Christians as to galvanize them even to martyrdom, must have been a reality far beyond something as common and ordinary as love.

Or *is* that love in fact so common and ordinary?

However we understand the resurrection, the fact remains that Jesus equated the love among Christians to His very presence. And by any measure, this is a stark challenge to every religion, every congregation, and every believer. Can you say that your experience with Christian love has been so vibrant, so vivid, that it lives up to this comparison? Perhaps you are fortunate and find a positive response to this question on a local level, in churches and chapels where the light of Christian fellowship burns bright among the brethren gathered together, but can we say that it is generally true? And does that Christian love reach beyond the immediate precincts of the individual congregation? Does it extend to the street, the office, the place of work? Does it embrace Catholic and Protestant, Jehovah's Witness and Adventist, Mormon and Orthodox? This is the real crisis in the church—we need not look for crises of theological questions or existential doubt. We can look at our own feet and to our right and left. Where is the Christian love that measures up to this criterion? And if we have difficulty in finding it, or if we must look for it in exceptional individuals instead of in the church as a whole, then we can well doubt that Christ has risen from the dead.

No, that love is not common and ordinary. It transcends practically all of the expressions of that emotion that we have come to designate by the name of love. And it certainly transcends the physical resurrection that was drawn from Jewish vocabulary to represent it.

The Gospels were written not to confirm the Jewish concept of resurrection, but to wean the Jewish-Christian believers from the Jewish concept of the dead who rise physically on the Day of Judgment. However, with the passage of time, the church sought to maintain both a Jewish concept of physical resurrection and a Christian concept of spiritual afterlife, formulating a doctrine something like the following. At the moment of death, the spirit passes to the spiritual heaven until some future time when the Lord returns, at which time the resurrection occurs and bodies return to life accompanied by their respective souls. This cobbling together of Jewish and Christian ideas gives rise to questions with no good answers. If a spirit world exists, why does the spirit need to come back to a material world? Is this not going backwards? Who would want to return to a flimsy and sickly material existence after once having tasted the delights of the spirit? Why is the spiritual afterlife not sufficient? One avoids these questions if one accepts that, indeed, the spiritual afterlife is the only one to which we need look forward.

When I wrote of the kingdom in the previous chapter, I referred to a backsliding of Christian doctrine to Jewish concepts of the material kingdom. Exactly the same phenomenon occurred in the case of the resurrection, as Christians adopted a Jewish concept of afterlife. This return to a Jewish concept of resurrection is more than analogous to what happened in the case of the kingdom, it was actually part and parcel of the same dialogue, since the resurrection formed part of the kingdom doctrine of the rabbis. As in the case of the kingdom, the fact of using a similar vocabulary of resurrection as derived from the Jewish tradition permitted backsliding into a Jewish point of view that was essentially this worldly. This situation continues to exist even today in the interpretation generally given to the resurrection.

Christianity, as it matured and started to flex its muscles, as it sought to displace Judaism as the legitimate heir of God's grace and as His true Israel in the earthly plane, eventually adopted the doctrine of its mother religion that it purported to replace. As Christians flailed the Jews with one hand and rebuked their refusal to accept Jesus as Messiah, they were unwittingly adopting the doctrine of the Jews and propagating it with the other, to the neglect of the doctrine of Jesus. This is one of the great ironies of history.

CHAPTER 9

HOLY SPIRIT: A GLIMPSE INTO THE SOUL OF THE PROPHETS

The Mission of Jesus in spiritualizing mankind within the Jewish ethical tradition focused on the human soul as its point of departure. The Jews had a concept of spirit, diffuse and different from our own concept, as the breath of God that animated all things, but not as a resident part of the human being. Whereas Jesus taught that soul was associated with, and was the very essence of, each and every individual. In other words, Jesus taught us about our own selves, our own reality, our own being, more than any other Messenger of God before Him. Thus did Jesus introduce innovations in the understanding of what it meant to be human. Therefore it is not surprising that another part of the Revelation of Jesus was concerned with His own spiritual nature, that is to say, His own Spirit. And He gave a special designation to that inner essence that He manifested, which He called the Holy Spirit (or the Holy Ghost in the King James translation).

The manner in which the Gospels presented the Holy Spirit was a new twist on the idea of spirit compared to the Old Testament. The Jews were witness through their own Scriptures to the intervention of God in history through His Spirit. Similar to the situation with the human soul, it is not clear in the Old Testament that the Spirit of God was an entity with an integral being. It is not even clear what distinction, if any, was made between the Spirit of God that inspired Scripture through His Chosen Ones, and the spirit that God breathed into the human form and that would return to God at death. There are only three references to "Holy Spirit" (*Ruah Ha-Qoddesh*) in the Old Testament, and they are not distinguished from other references to spirit. For example, "Cast me not away from thy presence; and take not thy Holy Spirit from me."[1] This passage could just as well refer to "sanctified spirit" or "immaculate spirit" as to "Holy Spirit." In other words, references to the "Holy Spirit" in the Old Testament should not be equated to similar references in the New Testament solely on the basis of the choice of words.

So what is different about the New Testament? Just as Jesus introduced a subtle but important difference in the concept of what the human spirit represented, He also refined the concept of the Holy Spirit. Regarding the spirit that animated the human being, in the doctrine of Jesus this was viewed as an integral entity with a continuing existence, rather than the passing Breath of God. Similarly, Jesus and the Gospels refer to the Spirit of God that inspired the Prophets as the "Holy Spirit," in the sense of a unique, integral entity that has a continuing existence. The integrity of the Holy Spirit is represented visually in all four Gospels where It is compared corporally to a dove that descends upon Jesus, and in the Book of Acts the references to Holy Spirit continually convey the sense of a specific spiritual entity that accompanies the disciples.

Jesus (or the Gospel writers if you will) broadened the scope of those Old Testament references to the inspiring Spirit, giving that Spirit an identity and a new sense of permanence. This sense of permanence is reflected in the great number of references to the Holy Ghost in the New Testament (89) versus 40 references to the "Spirit of God" or "the Spirit of the LORD" in the Old Testament, even though the Old Testament is three times as long! Nonetheless, this sense of a permanent abiding spirit does have a parallel in Judaism. When the rabbis set down the Talmud, they spoke of the *Shekinah*, or the continuing presence of God among the Hebrews, for example, by dwelling in the Tabernacle. So what is the difference? Permanence by itself did not distinguish the Christian concept of Holy Spirit from that of *Shekinah*, but permanence was a necessary characteristic to conceive of the Holy Spirit as it is viewed in the New Testament, as a unique spiritual entity. Thus, God can send His Holy Spirit, but in contrast He does not send His *Shekinah*. The New Testament presentation of this spiritual entity that mediates between man and God, and that reveals itself in Jesus, would eventually lead Christians to view Jesus as the very personification of the Holy Spirit. Jesus was not only accompanied by the Spirit of God, He manifested the Spirit of God in His very Self. This contrasts with the Jewish view of the Old Testament Prophets who, as human beings, were at most inspired by the Spirit, but in any case continued to be human beings.

In the Gospels, this sense of the eternal permanence of the Holy Spirit is nowhere expressed so eloquently, in such elegantly sweeping terms and all embracing simplicity, as in the first verses of John, where that spiritual entity is made to be the companion of God at the very dawn of existence. "In the beginning was the Word, and the Word was with God, and the Word was God. The same was in the beginning with God. All things were made by him; and without him was not any thing made that was made. In him was life; and the life was the light of men."[2] The similarity in tone to Genesis is obvious, and essentially John is rewriting the creation story that is found there, where creation is brought into being in the presence of the Spirit of God: "In the beginning God created the heaven and the earth. And the earth was without form, and void; and darkness was upon the face of the deep. And the Spirit of God moved upon the face of the waters. And God said, Let there be light."[3] John highlights the preexistence of that Spirit of God, declaring it eternal in its essence and God's instrument in the creation of the world, and he gives it a new name—the Word, or Logos. And the doctrine that declared the existence of this Spirit of God as a continuing, integral entity was an innovation of Jesus in amplifying upon the Jewish tradition. Jesus did not invent the Holy Spirit, but He did give us to understand that it is a reality that is essential and not casual, eternal and not passing—just as He gave us to understand that the human soul is essential and eternal.

Indeed, the Bahá'í Writings lead us to appreciate that some sort of intermediary between God and man is necessary, given the need to mediate between the infinite and the finite, the Perfect and the potential, the Exalted-above-all-attributes and the being who is only just awakening to the attributes within himself: " . . . there can be no tie of direct intercourse to bind the one true God with His creation, and no resemblance whatever can exist between the transient and the Eternal, the contingent and the Absolute . . ."[4] This implies the need for an intermediary, and Jesus gave this intermediary the name of Holy Spirit, for which He Himself was the channel to humanity. The same concept of an intermediary comes through explicitly in the Book of Hebrews where Jesus is identified as the "mediator of the new covenant"[5] and is compared to the high priest who served as intermediary between God and the Israelites. The Trinity likewise expresses the reality of an intermediate level of existence between God and man, as referred to in Matthew: "Go ye therefore, and teach all nations, baptizing them in the name of the Father, and of the Son, and of the Holy Ghost."[6]

However, the Jews were not receptive to the idea of an intermediary between God and man, and this concept was destined to be a sore point in Christian-Jewish relations. When the Jews sought to stone Jesus, their motivation was "because that thou, being a man, makest thyself God."[7] What stimulated this violent reaction was the statement of Jesus that He was "the Son of God," and even this sounded far too uppity to His Jewish audience. If the Jews had trouble agreeing amongst themselves on many things, at least they agreed on one God, and their interpretation allowed little flexibility. They had been the repositories of monotheism since the days of Abraham and this was an inheritance that was especially Jewish. They had laid down their lives in the name of monotheism against the Seleucids only two hundred years before, and so were sensitive to what they saw as incursions on this doctrine. Indeed, monotheism was at the center of their national identity. They were Jews because they were the children of Abraham, and their inheritance from Father Abraham was monotheism. In the days of the Roman occupation, monotheism was a continuing issue for the Jews, as they carefully avoided acts of worship toward the emperor who was the head of the state religion.

The Jewish resistance to attributing a transcendent station to Christ was undoubtedly an important issue that the church fathers had to deal with in relation to their Jewish-Christian flock, and a point that needed some careful defense to maintain the loyalty of their followers. Indeed, the relation of Christ to monotheism was an even broader issue in the early years of the church. For example, a sizable sect called the Arians clung to a strict monotheism, and was declared as heretical in the time of Constantine. We can well imagine that, in the first century, among first or second generation converts from Judaism, ideas of the absolute and exclusive oneness of God must have been a common barrier to accepting Christ as someone far above His contemporaries. We see these clashes in the text of the New Testament, as well as the arguments that the Gospel writers brought to the Jewish-Christians to assuage their concerns.

One very interesting and telling vignette is found in the Gospel of Mark, when Jesus is visiting the Temple, and what makes it most revealing is its atypical characteristic of expressing an essential harmony between Jesus and the Jewish scribe with whom He is conversing. The scribe asks Him, "Which is the first commandment of all?" to which Jesus replies by quoting the Shema from the Book of Deuteronomy where monotheism is proclaimed dramatically: "Hear, O Israel; The Lord our God is one Lord: and thou shalt love the Lord thy God with all thy heart, and with all thy soul, and with all thy mind, and with all thy strength: this is the first commandment. And the second is like, namely this, Thou shalt love thy neighbour as thyself." The scribe seems to be well satisfied with this response, saying, "Well, Master, thou hast said the truth: for there is one God; and there is none other but he: and to love him with all the heart, and with all the understanding, and with all the soul, and with all the strength, and to love his neighbour as himself, is more than all whole burnt offerings and sacrifices."[8]

It is interesting that the scribe starts by asking about the commandments, and then himself highlights monotheism as the focus of the question, above all "burnt offerings and sacrifices," which in fact are part of the commandments. The scribe seems to be espousing a Christian-like view of the Law, relativizing the law of sacrifice and making it inferior to the underlying spirit in a way that was not really called for by the context of his own question. While there might not be any particular problem with this from a Christian point of view, one wonders if Mark might be putting words in the mouth of the scribe that would not otherwise have been voiced. Beyond this, I think that the important point here is that the Jewish scribe finds the monotheism of Jesus to be perfectly acceptable and orthodox. "Well, Master, thou hast said the truth: for there is one God." It is as if Mark were using this vignette to highlight the monotheism of Jesus, which is confirmed by a Jew who normally would have been an opponent of Jesus. I suggest that having a learned Jew give his stamp of approval to the monotheism of Jesus is meant to calm the nerves of the Jewish-Christians who are wondering if they really embrace the doctrine about Christ that they have been hearing.

The intention of Mark in this interchange with the scribe seems to be confirmed by the scene that immediately follows, a scene that might appear unconnected, but in fact is a continuation of the previous theme. Jesus continues to teach in the Temple precincts, and asks His audience about the meaning of a passage from Psalms 110. Since the Psalms are attributed to David, Jesus cites David as the speaker in the verse that He quotes: "How say the scribes that Christ is the son of David? For David himself said by the Holy Ghost, The LORD said to my Lord, Sit thou on my right hand, till I make thine enemies thy footstool. David therefore himself calleth him Lord; and whence is he then his son?"[9]

Remember that, in the English translation of the Old Testament, the name LORD (capitalized as such) in fact is a substitute for YHWH, in accord with an ancient Jewish custom of not enunciating the Most Holy Name of God when the text was read aloud, but rather replacing it with "LORD." So we can also read this passage in Psalms as "YHWH said to my Lord." In other words, in quoting Psalms, Jesus is hinting that besides God (YHWH) there is another (that is, the Christ) who is also worthy to be called Lord, one who is above David and the other prophets and before whom all others will be made His footstool. In light of the previous interchange with the Jewish scribe, in which the monotheism of Jesus was confirmed, this passage is as if Mark is saying to his Jewish-Christian audience, "Yes, there is only one God, *but* . . ." Mark is introducing his audience to the idea that traditional Jewish monotheism does admit another level of Spirit, below God, but above other prophets and certainly above mankind.

It is highly significant that reference to this same verse of Psalms is maintained in Matthew and Luke, is repeated in Acts, and also appears in Hebrews, that book of the New Testament that is directed to a Jewish-Christian audience and that struggles against apostasy in the primitive church. The fact that so many authors cite this passage of Psalms suggests that it was a mainstay of the early church in the defense of Christian doctrine about the station of Jesus. In particular, Hebrews draws upon Psalms 110 at length to defend the superiority of Jesus among the prophets, as holding a position just below that of God and sitting at His right hand. "But to which of the angels said he at any time, Sit on my right hand, until I make thine enemies thy footstool?"[10] Here, Jesus is represented in the same light as in the opening of John's Gospel, as the very instrument of creation, insomuch as He is the "Son, whom he hath appointed heir of all things, by whom also he made the worlds." One suspects that in Mark's reference to Psalms, many of the same arguments of Hebrews are implicit—again making Mark's use of Psalms an important doctrinal sequel to the declaration by a Jewish scribe that Jesus "hast said the truth, for there is only one God."

A second vignette of Jesus and the Jews that is relative to His position appears in John, although this is no longer conciliatory, but rather very conflictive. Jesus has just declared that, "I and my Father are one." The Jews take offense at this statement and pick up stones to throw at Him. Jesus responds to their reaction, asking "Many good works have I shewed you from my Father; for which of those works do ye stone me? The Jews answered him, saying, For a good work we stone thee not; but for blasphemy; and because that thou, being a man, makest thyself God."[11] In a later verse, John implies that being one with the Father refers not to their essence, but to their relationship, for in praying for the unity of His followers, Jesus asks that, "they may be one, even as we are."[12] In the present scene, the monotheistic sensitivities of the Jews are explicit, and Jesus resorts to the Book of Psalms to defend His statement. "Jesus answered them, Is it not written in your law, I said, Ye are gods? If he called them gods, unto whom the word of God came, and the Scripture cannot be broken; say ye of him, whom the Father hath sanctified, and sent into the world, Thou blasphemest; because I said, I am the Son of God?"[13]

When we view this verse in the context of an argument directed toward the Jewish-Christians, we see that John is trying to highlight the subservience of Jesus to God, since Jesus emphasizes that He is the *Son* of God, even when the Psalms admit the existence of "gods." Furthermore, we see certain similarities with the vignette that we found in Mark. Although the relationship with the Jews is now portrayed as antagonistic, the response and the strategy to calm the fears of the Jewish-Christian audience is the same. That is, both Mark and John draw upon the Old Testament books (indeed, the same Book of Psalms) and find verses that qualify the Jewish understanding of monotheism and that permit another level of Spirit or existence. Mark and others found that argument in the verse, "the LORD said to my Lord" and John comes to a similar conclusion in quoting Psalms ("Ye are gods") and adding an interpretation that this refers to those "unto whom the word of God came," which we would gather refers to the Prophets of God. In both cases, the Gospel writers are responding to the same concerns of their audiences by citing Hebrew Scripture. In the latter case, in the Gospel of John, the argument is made within the context of Jewish accusations that Jesus has violated the sacrosanct principle of monotheism, demonstrating what a sensitive issue this was at the time.

The difficulty of understanding the subtleties of the relationship between Christ and God would plague the early church far beyond the life of the Jewish-Christian branch of Christianity. These were questions that arose as a direct result of those intimations of Jesus about His own spiritual nature, intimations

---

113

that were new to the Jewish tradition and that met with fierce opposition. This was a subject that was destined to be confusing and polemical, because in its essence this is a topic that is simply beyond our own realm of being and our capacity of conception. This is like a painting attempting to understand the relationship between the painter and the paintbrush that is his instrument in creating the painting, or a chair trying to fathom how the carpenter's hands serve the purpose of the carpenter. Being beyond our capacity and imagination, the relationship between Christ and God can only be represented by metaphors. Thus Jesus referred to that relationship as one of Father and Son. The Bahá'í Writings provide an illustration that serves to reflect over the relationship of God, Holy Spirit, and Jesus, which in its simplicity reveals much about the profound questions that have plagued Christianity ever since the appearance of Jesus. The illustration is the following.

Let us compare God with the sun. This is not all that far-fetched in some cultural traditions; the ancient Egyptians, the Romans, and more recently the Incas, could understand this image readily, if not literally. For our purposes, we use the sun to represent the glory of the Godhead, exalted in its incomparable power among all other astral bodies—at least from our standpoint—and unequalled in its indisputable role as source of all life on our planet. We on earth can contribute nothing to the sun, we can only circle moth-like around it and receive its bounty. Yet despite its central and incomparable role in sustaining life, the sun is unapproachable and would destroy any creature that drew near it, through the very power that sustains life when maintained at the proper distance.

Unable to approach the sun directly, we benefit from the sun through the intermediation of its rays that are born of the sun, and emanate from the sun. Thus the rays manifest the light, the heat, and the energy of the sun in a degree that is beneficial to life, without either destroying it or leaving it without nourishment. The rays are in a sense the sun, which is to say, they transmit the qualities of the sun, yet in another sense the rays are not the sun, since they have not the mass and substance that a body like the sun possesses. The rays have no existence of their own without the sun, but the existence of the sun implies the existence of the rays, and the rays are inherent in the sun. If we hold a mirror up to the sun, we will see the sun reflected. Now, is it the sun? "Yes," you might say, "there it is, I see it. That is the sun." Yet in reality we know that the sun is in the heavens some eighty million miles away. What we mean to say is that we see the image of the sun. Again, it *is* the sun if we refer to an image (what we *see*), but it is *not* the sun with regard to its essential reality, which is a material, distant globe. What is more, it is the rays that transmit that image from the material reality of the sun to the mirror where we visualize it. Sun, rays, and image—we see them as one reality and seldom stop to discriminate between them. In a sense, they *are* one reality from the perspective of the way we see them. In their essence, they are not.

In this example, the sun is symbolic of God—infinite, incomparable, and unattainable. The rays represent the Holy Spirit, the existence of which is inherent in the existence of God and which is diffused throughout creation bestowing life and consciousness. The mirror is the Person of Jesus, who in the Bahá'í Writings is referred to as a Manifestation of God, signifying that He manifests the very Spirit and perfections of God. Jesus, the mirror, reflects the perfections of the Creator that appear in His being as the Holy Spirit: "the Father, the Word, and the Holy Ghost: and these three are one."[14] From our standpoint, we see no difference; we see only one reality: "he that hath seen me hath seen the Father."[15] The existence of God implies the existence of the Holy Spirit, like the sun and the rays, and these are inseparable. Thus, "the Word was with God, and the Word was God."[16]

This example contains many lessons, and the early church would have benefited greatly from this simple illustration. The burning debate within the church in those first centuries was the nature of Christ. How many different natures did He have—one, two, or three? Monophysites said one; dyophysites said two. Eventually the church settled on three and adopted the doctrine of the Trinity at the Council of Nicaea in 325 CE. The Bahá'í Writings see all reality summed up in three levels of existence: God, creation including man, and the Holy Spirit as an intermediary between God and creation. Jesus as Manifestation of God spans these levels of existence and occupies two of them, as man and as Holy Spirit.

This ancient discussion can be viewed in the context of the following commentary from the Writings of Bahá'u'lláh in which He elaborates upon the nature of the Manifestation of God:

> "(God) hath ordained that in every age and dispensation a pure and stainless Soul be made manifest in the kingdoms of earth and heaven . . . He hath, moreover, conferred upon Him a double station. The first station, which is related to His innermost reality, representeth Him as One Whose voice is the voice of God Himself. To this testifieth the tradition: "Manifold and mysterious is My relationship with God. I am He, Himself, and He is I, Myself, except that I am that I am, and He is that He is." And in like manner, the words: "Arise, O Muhammad, for lo, the Lover and the Beloved are joined together and made one in Thee." He similarly saith: "There is no distinction whatsoever between Thee and Them, except that They are Thy Servants." The second station is the human station, exemplified by the following verses: "I am but a man like you." "Say, praise be to my Lord! Am I more than a man, an apostle?"[17]

The above passage of Bahá'u'lláh describing the double station of the Manifestation, divine and human, can be compared with the words of Christ as recorded by John. In these words we see both stations expressed—the eternal that speaks as God, and the human station with its limitations. In the first set of quotations, Jesus emphasizes His eternal, God-like reality that is born of the Holy Spirit. "Jesus saith unto him, Have I been so long time with you, and yet hast thou not known me, Philip? he that hath seen me hath seen the Father; and how sayest thou then, Show us the Father?"[18] "I and my Father are one."[19] "If ye had known me, ye should have known my Father also: and from henceforth ye know him, and have seen him."[20] "Jesus said unto them, Verily, verily, I say unto you, Before Abraham was, I am."[21]

And in the following verses, He speaks from His second station, as a man sent by God: "Verily, verily, I say unto you, The Son can do nothing of himself, but what he seeth the Father do: for what things soever he doeth, these also doeth the Son likewise."[22] "Believest thou not that I am in the Father, and the Father in me? the words that I speak unto you I speak not of myself: but the Father that dwelleth in me, he doeth the works."[23] "If I honor myself, my honor is nothing: it is my Father that honoreth me; of whom ye say, that he is your God."[24] "for my Father is greater than I."[25]

These statements of Jesus, on the surface contradictory, reflect that dual nature of the Manifestation of which we read in the passage from Bahá'u'lláh. I think that John has recorded these contrasting passages precisely to clarify to the Jewish-Christians that on the one hand, Jesus is indeed transcendent above His fellows, and that on the other, He is still subservient to the one God Almighty, thereby respecting the principle of monotheism. These statements and others like them are an integral part of the nature and spiritual reality of Christ that Jesus sought to reveal to His disciples.

Jesus presented His followers with the doctrine that His own inner essence was eternal and He called it the Holy Spirit. Furthermore, as we review the references in the New Testament to the Holy Spirit, it is apparent that the early Christian authors had assimilated the doctrine of an eternal Holy Spirit as the eternal intermediary between God and man. The advent of Jesus was not a unique intervention of the Holy Spirit, but was the most recent. It was likely the most profound up to that moment, but certainly not the only one. The Christians saw the Holy Spirit mediating between God and man for all time and through the medium of all the Prophets. Both 1 Peter and 2 Peter contain general references to the Holy Spirit or Spirit of Christ as the inspiration of the prophets: "For the prophecy came not in old time by the will of man: but holy men of God spake as they were moved by the Holy Ghost."[26] Mark quotes Jesus as saying, "For David himself said by the Holy Ghost . . ."[27] Paul referred to "that spiritual Rock that followed" the Israelites in the desert "and that Rock was Christ."[28] Similar statements are found in Acts regarding David, Isaiah, and the prophets in general; and in Hebrews regarding the revelation of the Pentateuch. These references span the time from Paul's letters (the first sections of the New Testament to be written), the Book of Hebrews, and the Book of Mark (the first Gospel to be set down) and extend through the time of Acts, and finally are articulated in the Gospel of John: "In the beginning was the Word . . ."[29]

Christians appropriated the Hebrew Bible and made their understanding of the Holy Spirit retrospective to the Old Testament prophets. The fact that so many of the New Testament authors referred to the Holy Spirit (or the Christ Spirit, in the case of Paul) as the inspiration of the Old Testament prophets, demonstrates that this concept had gained wide credence in the early Christian community. Although these references are brief, one must assume that much more was here than meets the eye. Where there is a common vocabulary, there is also some common understanding of the vocabulary, which in this case has profound doctrinal implications. When the Christian authors refer to the "Holy Spirit," they are assuming elements of a Christian doctrine that accompany that term. John is often credited by scholars as having raised the profile of the divine nature of Christ, and it may have fallen to John to articulate this doctrine more explicitly and elegantly ("In the beginning was the Word, and the Word was with God, and the Word was God."), in the very first verses of his Gospel and throughout his text. However, the essential understanding of Christ's station was already widespread.

Of course, the writers of the New Testament did not put much emphasis on the retrospective aspect of the Holy Spirit. It was simply not their purpose at that moment in history, rather they were announcing the advent of Jesus as yet a new revelation of that Spirit. Instead of dwelling on implications of the Holy Spirit in the distant past, their references to the inspiration of the Holy Spirit through prophets of the Old Testament were more or less casual. Still, might this not be part of that presentation to the Jewish-Christian community whereby church fathers sought to make their doctrine familiar and palatable to their Jewish-Christian audience? Might not the idea of the Holy Spirit as an intermediary between man and God have been more acceptable if the Jewish prophets were credited to have also been inspired of, and served as channels for, that Holy Spirit?

With this doctrine in mind, let us return to the example of the sun, the rays, and the mirror, and add a dimension of time. If the rays of the Holy Spirit fall on one mirror in one epoch, and another mirror in a later period, it is in any case the very same sun that is reflected in the mirror. So if the perfections of God appeared in Abraham, and later in Moses, and still later in Jesus, it is the expression of one and the same spiritual power and reality. Moreover, whatever differences in their messages that appear to make one Manifestation superior to another cannot be attributed to their inner spiritual state, which is one and the same, but rather to the capacity of humankind in distinct periods to benefit and partake of the spiritual blessings that are offered. "I have yet many things to say unto you, but ye cannot bear them now."[30] God speaks to mankind according to its capacity to "bear" His Message, not according to His own capacity to reveal truth.

The Bahá'í teaching of progressive revelation views all Prophets and Founders of religions as channels for the same eternal Spirit, and places them in the context of a progressive, expanding process of spiritual growth and advancing civilization. In this sense, the Christian doctrine of the Holy Spirit as inspiration of the Prophets is reaffirmed, and its scope is expanded to include the social progress of mankind. The Bahá'í Writings not only recognize Jesus, Moses, Abraham, and Noah as Manifestations of God, but also those Founders of religions outside of the Judeo-Christian tradition such as Buddha, Krishna, and Muhammad. Bahá'u'lláh Himself is likewise counted as a Manifestation whose Revelation is inspired of God.

In this same context of progressive revelation, and considering the evolving relationship of God and man, what was the impact of the doctrine of the Holy Spirit? What difference did it make that the Holy Spirit represents an eternal spiritual entity that occupies a level of existence between God and man, in contrast to the conventional Jewish view that the Spirit of God moves across the world as the breath of God, and animates all men and even nature more or less equally, recognizing that the role of the Prophet is superior to that of other humans? Do not both views place the ultimate authority and creative impulse in God? Does it matter whether we view this spiritual power as diffused from God or channeled through a preexistent spiritual entity that is manifested in a Chosen One? In other words, does this Christian viewpoint have any impact on our thinking? *Did it change anything?* The differences are perhaps subtle and by no means absolute, but they do influence greatly the way we look at the Manifestations and therefore the way we react to them.

Here we must refer to the manner in which the Jews viewed Moses. Their understanding of the station of Moses, as best we can visualize it, was that of another human being, chosen of God admittedly, and the greatest of all the Old Testament Prophets, but in the final analysis, still a man, fallible and mortal. While His revelation was considered perfect, the Messenger was just that—a messenger bearing a message, but Himself with no inherent rank above His fellows outside of His role as a channel. Christians, however, looked at Jesus in quite a different light, and their perspective of Jesus is a result of the teachings about His eternal, spiritual nature.

When viewed as unique expressions of this eternal, preexistent Spirit within their epoch, the Manifestations take on a greater importance for us. It raises their profile in our mindset and makes them the Central Figure and focus of our relationship with God: "If ye had known me, ye should have known my Father."[31] They give our devotion to God a focal point. They become the image of God for us, the expression of God's infinite perfections: "he that hath seen me hath seen the Father."[32] Furthermore, our knowledge of their spiritual reality highlights their authority in repealing old norms and establishing new ones: "Ye have heard that it hath been said, Thou shalt love thy neighbor, and hate thine enemy. But I say unto you, Love your enemies . . ."[33] As a Manifestation of God and channel of the Holy Spirit, the Manifestation is not merely a man who hears and repeats, but is a Being above His fellow men, commissioned by God to establish laws and ordinances, a King of the spirit and Sovereign of the hearts, who in His own being makes the Unknowable Essence just a little bit more knowable, and a bit more familiar and approachable. This implies a special duty for all humankind. "The first duty prescribed by God for His servants is the recognition of Him Who is the Dayspring of His Revelation and the Fountain of His laws, Who representeth the Godhead in both the Kingdom of His Cause and the world of creation."[34] When viewed as a whole, the Manifestations of God become the thread that gives continuity and integrity to human history, and that permits us to appreciate it as one vast evolutionary process.

Jesus first brought this concept of the Holy Spirit as an eternal spiritual entity, as the link between God and man, as the animating power of the Manifestations. By highlighting the spiritual station of the Manifestations, Jesus molded our views about Them as the axis around which the world revolves, as the critical Figures in the process of progressive revelation. This does not mean that the concept of progressive growth could not exist in a Jewish viewpoint as well as it could in the succession of Old Testament revelations. However, focusing our attention on the Manifestation, and on His advent as a watershed in history, consolidates our thinking about the progress of humanity from age to age, as well as making Him an object of our love and adoration.

In scholarly writings, the teachings about the nature of Christ are called Christology. Apart from the truth that it enshrines, what is the immediate relevance for our purpose of understanding the New Testament in the context of the historical setting in which it developed? In other words, what was its role in the Christian-Jewish dialogue in the age of the Gospel writing? We can only read between the lines in the context of other evidence that we have cited about the general milieu of the early church. The dialogue of Christians and Jews was lively and getting more heated as the first century drew to a close. The church was losing some converts to Judaism (reflected in concern about apostasy and proselytes to Judaism). Jewish nationalism was building to a head again, soon to flare up in the rebellion of Bar Kochba, and it was likely tempting to Jewish-Christians to adhere to the movement. Many Jewish-Christians were still under the influence of the synagogue, and rabbinic Judaism was becoming more aggressive and undoubtedly sought to denigrate Jesus in His role as Messiah, and by declaring that He claimed to be God.

In this environment, what would have been the role of Christology? And in particular, what would have been the role of the Gospel of John, which is the Gospel where the position of Christ is given far greater profile? The reader may have noted that, in previous chapters, John is the source of many of the arguments contradicting the Jewish point of view, for example, with regard to the resurrection and life after death. Yet the uniqueness of John's Gospel is nowhere so clear as in the explicitness of its Christology, in its emphasis on the position of Christ. Why? Was John moved to set down these truths in a desire to make them available to posterity as his own life drew to an end? Perhaps. But scholars are especially impressed with what they see as anti-Jewish feeling in John. I prefer to view it as a concern to avoid the danger of backsliding into Jewish orthodoxy and losing what was distinctive about the Message of Christ. In the particular case of Christology, the danger was that Jewish-Christians could yield to Jewish jibes that Jesus was at best a well-meaning rabbi who failed to bring about the expected kingdom, and at worst a fraud.

This particular attack on Jesus, being directly linked to frustrations about the non-fulfillment of the kingdom, was especially dangerous at that point in history, as it could have drawn Jewish-Christians into the maelstrom of Jewish revolt against Rome. In this increasingly confrontational environment, I see John as writing his Gospel to set the record straight about Jesus and about many points of His doctrine, and thereby protect the nascent Christian community from the crush of events that was embroiling the Jewish community in rebellion and certain disaster. The Christology of John was not the only element of this defense of Christianity, but it was one of the most important and was highlighted in the Gospel of John. In the final analysis, it gave us the most explicit doctrine about the nature of Christ that has come down to us, and has shaped our thinking about God and His Manifestations.

CHAPTER 10

SIN, SACRIFICE, AND REDEMPTION: GO AND SIN NO MORE

Jesus redeemed the world of sin. On this we all agree. But I suggest that there is far more to this statement than meets the eye, and that to appreciate the Mission and Message of Christ more fully, it is particularly important to understand this aspect of the Gospel. This dimension of the New Testament receives the most attention and has become the central theme in the presentation of the church, so that most Christian clergy would put first priority on the redeeming value of the sacrifice of Jesus in their presentation of the Gospel. Yet there is a certain danger precisely in our familiarity with the topic, that we can skate over important spiritual teachings and realities and miss their significance, assuming that we understand them through lifelong exposure to church doctrine and teaching.

Redemption is generally understood in the context of obtaining God's forgiveness of sin, and Christian doctrine has adopted the stance that only through the sacrifice of Jesus was God's forgiveness offered to the world. Sin came to the world through Adam and Eve in the episode of the serpent in Eden (i.e., original sin) and the world was under its yoke until Jesus appeared and took the sins of humanity upon His shoulders for all time. Until such time that Jesus made His supreme sacrifice, no soul had any option to attain salvation, every soul was separated from God by the weight of sin inherited from Adam and accumulated along the way ever since. However, the church recognized at least one of the difficulties implicit in this doctrine of one-time salvation—the question of souls that lived before Christ appeared. These souls, good or bad and including the Prophets of God, would be condemned simply because they came into being before the advent of Christ and had no opportunity of accepting Him. Thus the church had to invent a world of limbo where those souls would sit and wait for the advent of Christ, a sort of halfway house where they were neither condemned to hellfire nor had they yet made it to heaven.

The doctrine that God withheld forgiveness for some numberless millennia is not without other theological difficulties. Does not the changeless, eternal essence of God imply that He has always been the Most Compassionate, the Most Loving, the Most Exalted, the Ever-Forgiving? Does not the existence of these perfections of God imply that they must be expressed, like rays of light that cannot be bottled up inside the sun, but have to emanate throughout the universe? And how could the changeless, eternal God manifest all other attributes such as love, munificence, generosity, forbearance, and patience throughout all time and history, and withhold only one—forgiveness—reserving this for a single moment in history! Does not God's unchanging perfection imply that all His perfections find expression at all times? Jesus continually compared God to a loving Father: "what man is there of you, whom if his son ask bread, will he give him a stone? Or if he ask a fish, will he give him a serpent? If ye then, being evil, know how to give good gifts unto your children, how much more shall your Father which is in heaven give good things to them that ask him?"[1] The religious record of humankind testifies that God has vindicated this promise of Christ amply and in all ages.

The biblical solution to the theological problem is simple. God did *not* postpone forgiveness until the advent of Jesus. God did *not* withhold mercy from countless generations. On the contrary, the Old Testament testifies explicitly to multiple acts of forgiveness by God prior to the advent of Jesus, to His patience and forbearance with the Israelites in their most intransigent moments, such as when they turned their backs on Moses and forged the golden calf, or in their rebellion against Moses when He proposed to lead them into Canaan. Moses interceded and God acceded to His plea: "Pardon, I beseech thee, the iniquity of this people according unto the greatness of thy mercy, and as thou hast forgiven this people, from Egypt even until now. And the LORD said, I have pardoned according to thy word."[2] "For all this they sinned still, and believed not for his wondrous works . . . they did flatter him with their mouth, and they lied unto him with their tongues . . . But he, being full of compassion, forgave their iniquity, and destroyed them not: yea, many a time turned he his anger away, and did not stir up all his wrath."[3] Indeed, if the sacrifice of Jesus on the cross is the condition *sine qua non* for forgiveness, then even those acts of forgiveness that Jesus performed prior to His own martyrdom would be invalid!

Now, is it difficult for us to believe that God can be so forgiving? Is it theologically too simple to state that God forgives those who humbly seek His forgiveness? Do we feel that something is missing, that we need some formula to obtain God's pardon? If we need a formula, then how about this one: "Forgive and ye shall be forgiven,"[4] or in a slightly different but often repeated formulation in the Lord's Prayer: "And forgive us our sins; for we also forgive every one that is indebted to us."[5]

Jesus redeemed the world of sin. What does that mean? To understand redemption and how it overcomes sin, we need to take a step backward and reflect on the question of sin per se. This is not a trivial question, and I refer not to whether this or that action constitutes a sin, or how this or that action can be classified as a sin of commission or omission, or a greater or lesser sin. Rather, in its essence, what *is* sin? What makes a sin a sin? This question is not as simple as it might appear and, in fact, there are some important contrasts between the concept of sin as understood by the Jews and that presented in the New Testament. To investigate sin, we must, as it were, sneak in the back door of the church and see just what sin is made of. Western reductionism has delved into sexual behavior, criminology, and all the diverse manifestations of sin, but what do all these expressions of sin have in common that make them sinful?

For the Jews, sin was simple enough. Sin was any transgression against the Law, and the Law was the last word. Although the rabbis had classified transgressions into greater and lesser categories, their essential attitude toward sin came back to what the letter of the Law dictated. Thus, the Law was the yardstick of sin, and while the application of the Law and its derivatives might not have been so simple, the concept remained essentially the same—that a sin was an infraction of the Law and disobedience to God.

For the Jews, the Law was supposedly immobile. The Law had been given once and for all through Moses; it stood and could not be changed—at least in theory. In fact, the Law was subject to ample interpretation in its application, especially by the Pharisees whose traditions would eventually be formalized in the Talmud, and interpretation invariably threatens to lead to some manner of alteration. Yet even the rabbis felt obliged to justify their interpretation of the Torah by insisting that the oral traditions that became Talmud also had their origin in Moses, so legitimizing them and giving them an authority similar to the written Law. Implicitly, the rabbis were respecting the principle that the Law had to originate in Moses, and that man-made modifications were suspect.

The attitude of Jesus towards the Law that comes through the New Testament is rather liberal. Jesus is represented as relativizing the Law, which is to say, making its application dependent on the situation, but insisting on its inner spirit instead of its letter. For example, regarding the Law of the Sabbath, Jesus says, "What man shall there be among you, that shall have one sheep, and if it fall into a pit on the sabbath day, will he not lay hold on it, and lift it out? How much then is a man better than a sheep? Wherefore it is lawful to do well on the sabbath days."[6] Jesus does not care so much about the letter of the Law of the Sabbath, but rather the essence of the Law which is to do honor to God, and that permits—rather, *is served by*—doing good deeds on the Sabbath. To insist on the letter at the expense of the spirit is to miss the whole point of the Law. The contrast between the orthodox Jewish view of the Law and that of Jesus is probably familiar to Christians, but it is revealing to look at the structure of the verses that present this attitude toward the Law, in light of these verses being a teaching tool directed to Jewish-Christians.

If we turn to the Gospel of Matthew, we find a point-blank statement of Jesus regarding the Law: "For verily I say unto you till heaven and earth pass, one jot or one tittle shall in no wise pass from the law, till all be fulfilled."[7] This appears to be a firm commitment to the Law in a pretty orthodox manner. "Not one jot or one tittle." That is absolute and does not leave much maneuvering room for relativization. Matthew continues quoting Jesus: "Whosoever therefore shall break one of these least commandments, and shall teach men so, he shall be called the least in the kingdom of heaven: but whosoever shall do and teach them, the same shall be called great in the kingdom of heaven."[8] These verses, together with others, have led some Bible scholars to suggest that Matthew represents some of the more conservative elements in the Jewish-Christian community. Matthew was supposedly the most Jewish of all the Gospel writers, with a traditional commitment to the Law. However, this point of view does not hold up when one reads the verses that follow immediately, because the Jesus of Matthew proceeds to contradict Himself, relativizing and modifying one law after another. The typical structure of His teaching, repeated again and again, is: "Ye have heard that it was said of them of old time . . . But I say unto you . . ." And when we reach verse 5:31, we find that Jesus abrogates the law of divorce almost entirely: "whosoever shall put away his wife, saving for the cause of fornication, causeth her to commit adultery: and whosoever shall marry her that is divorced committeth adultery." It is not one jot and one tittle of the Law that is changed, but many jots and tittles!

So why does Matthew bother to record that statement that, "one jot or one tittle shall in no wise pass from the law?" I suspect that it is to soothe the fears of Jewish-Christians, and prepare them for what is to come next—a whole string of modifications on the Law. Implicit of course is the insistence that it is the spirit of the Law that counts, and that Jesus is in fact propagating the true, inner essence of the Law, but this point is made indirectly by declaring His commitment to the Law per se, in deference to Matthew's audience. The apparently conservative nature of this declaration does not so much reflect the stance of Matthew as it does the orientation of his audience, whom he is attempting to educate in the attitude towards the Law that Jesus has evinced.

In relation to the question of sin, relativization of the Law creates certain problems, because it is no longer so easy to determine what constitutes a sin. It now depends on such subtle intangibles as the purity of one's intention, the thoughts that one guards in one's heart, etc. In other words, sin is now made subjective instead of objective, and it is much more difficult to make judgments on another person's standing before God. In this context, the Law is much less useful to determine just exactly what a sin is and exactly who is sinning! The solution that Jesus offered for this situation seems to have been, "Judge not, that ye be not judged."[9]

And what of forgiveness in the Old Testament? We have cited examples of forgiveness drawn from the Old Testament, but beyond these, the Old Testament gave many acts of atonement in Numbers and Leviticus to attain God's forgiveness. These involved the offering of animals as sacrifices to God, specifically at the altar of the Temple (or prior to the Temple, in the tabernacle). Although the rabbis, in their reading of the Old Testament, found the need for sincere repentance to obtain forgiveness, in broad terms redemption from sin in the Torah is a question of Law and sacrificial rites of atonement. The greatest act of atonement for sin was the function and unique prerogative of the high priest of the Temple, who would sacrifice a bullock and then enter into the inner sanctuary, the Holy of Holies, once a year on Yom Kippur. With regard to animal sacrifice, Judaism was in no way unique in the ancient world. Animal sacrifice was standard practice among nearly all cultures in antiquity, with variations such as the reading of omens in the liver extracted from the sacrificial beast.

Another very important means of dealing with "sin" in Judaism was purification by water. Purification rites with water were an explicit prescription of the Mosaic Law for certain specific states of impurity, and were carried out scrupulously by Jews of varying inclinations. Excavations of Jewish archaeological sites in Palestine often unearth baths, or *mikvah*, that served for ritual cleansing through immersion. Bathing was used to make one ritually pure and fit to be in the company of the community or, in the case of priests, to officiate ceremonies. Although washing or sprinkling with water is referred to as "purification of sin," in many cases such bathing has apparent hygienic motivations, and in others is essentially symbolic. The idea of ritual purity was intricately bound up with the idea of sin, but did not necessarily derive from acts that we would consider sin today.

I have referred to one curious interpretation derived from the water purification rite, whereby the act of pouring water from a ritually correct vessel into one that was considered unfit would cause the water in the first vessel to be considered impure. This reflects not only attention to minute detail in observance of the Law in general, but great concern (or obsession?) with the very concept of purity. Such an obsession with purity might not have been the rule among Jews, but neither were the Jews immune to such behavior, nor even were Christians. Writings of the church fathers have left fragmentary evidence of baptismal sects in the first century, both Jewish and Jewish-Christian. Like sects in our own times, these extracted from a broad, rich, and balanced religious tradition one small fraction, and made it the all-absorbing fact of their existence. Bathing frequently, they would seem to have had little time for anything else.

This emphasis on purification is likewise evidenced in the text of the Gospels, where the Pharisees leveled criticism against Jesus and the disciples because they did not wash properly before eating. More than a question of personal hygiene, this reflects the Pharisees' concern with meeting the demands of the Torah. How was it possible, they asked, that a great teacher like Jesus did not fulfill even the most rudimentary of the purification rites of the Law? Here again, Jesus is portrayed as being indifferent to the details of purification, rather placing priority on inner purity as fit His spiritualizing Mission: "there is nothing from without a man, that entering into him can defile him: but the things which come out of him, those are they that defile the man."[10]

Jewish purification rites are the background of baptism in the New Testament, which was inherited through the example of John the Baptist. This is still another example of the role of Jesus in spiritualizing the Jewish tradition. The words of John, "he shall baptize you with the Holy Ghost, and with fire,"[11] illustrate the spiritual dimension of Jesus' Mission in this regard. The emphasis on a spiritual dimension of baptism including repentance did not prevent Christians from materializing Christian baptism, as occurred with some of the sects referred to above. And an excessive emphasis on baptism is in fact similar to the Jewish emphasis on ritual purity. Yet, even today, baptism is given a material interpretation, not unlike that of Jews and Jewish-Christians in the first century, although the baptism of children as currently practiced was neither a Jewish nor a Christian practice in that period.

Concern with ritual purity represented a mental milieu with its own criteria to determine whether or not one was right with God, and it was this mindset that Jesus addressed. Just as significant as a changing concept of purity in the teachings of Jesus, was an evolving concept of what constituted sin per se. While the Jewish concept of sin was focused on the Law, and was defined as a transgression against the Law, the concept of sin that emerges in the New Testament goes beneath the surface and identifies the root causes of sin. And the cause of sin is essentially to be found when man ceases to act like man and behaves like an animal, which is to say, when he abandons his high calling as a spiritual being and follows the animal instincts that are part and parcel of his physical existence.

The duality of the physical and spiritual sides of man is made explicit in the writings of Paul who saw the flesh at war with the spirit, thus implying a certain incompatibility of man's spiritual and physical natures. "For the flesh lusteth against the Spirit, and the Spirit against the flesh: and these are contrary the one to the other."[12] In speaking of two natures, Paul assumes the existence of an explicit spiritual entity, the soul, which was a novel teaching of Jesus within the Jewish tradition. In the verses immediately following this reference to man's dual nature, Paul gives a long list of sins that are born of the flesh: "adultery, fornication, uncleanness, lasciviousness, idolatry, witchcraft, hatred, variance, emulations, wrath, strife, seditions, heresies, envyings, murders, drunkenness, revellings, and such like."[13] James, too, at the other end of the early Christian spectrum from Paul, also attributes sin to the physical nature of man: "but every man is tempted, when he is drawn away of his own lust, and enticed. Then when lust hath conceived, it bringeth forth sin: and sin, when it is finished, bringeth forth death."[14]

The Bahá'í Writings expand upon this idea and refer explicitly to the world of nature in the sense of the animal existence from which man has emerged. "The body of man is a captive of nature; it will act in accordance with whatever nature orders. It is, therefore, certain that sins such as anger, jealousy, dispute, covetousness, avarice, ignorance, prejudice, hatred, pride and tyranny exist in the physical world. All these brutal qualities exist in the nature of man. A man who has not had a spiritual education is a brute."[15] One can see, in this distinction of spirit and flesh, the complement to a future scientific doctrine called "evolution," for the flesh arises from an inferior world through a process of biological change and adaptation of species, and the soul that defines the true identity of man has its origins in the world of the spirit that is beyond the changes and chances of material existence.

This viewpoint should not be confused with an attack on sexuality per se. When we equate man's physical nature with sexuality, we are missing the point. Sexuality is only one aspect of physical existence, while the references that I have cited are far broader than an abuse of the sexual instinct and include such negative character traits as "wrath, strife, seditions, heresies, envyings," "prejudice, hatred, pride," etc. When we manifest these characteristics, we are behaving like two dogs fighting over a bone, expressing traits that are inherited from the struggle for animal survival. As for sexuality, I do not think that either Paul or the Bahá'í Writings see the body and human reproduction as inherently evil. Human survival on this planet would be well served by eliminating "prejudice, hatred, pride," etc., but that very survival depends on sexuality.

In his letter to the Romans, Paul attributes the sinfulness of the flesh (which, again, is in a much wider sense than sexuality) not to an inherent evil in the flesh itself, but more specifically in one's own absorption in the flesh: "For they that are after the flesh do mind the things of the flesh; but they that are after the Spirit the things of the Spirit. For to be carnally minded is death; but to be spiritually minded is life and peace. Because the carnal mind is enmity against God: for it is not subject to the law of God, neither indeed can be. So then they that are in the flesh cannot please God."[16] The flesh, the body, is not in itself sinful although it is subject to the whims of nature. Sin emerges when one is "carnally minded," when the body dominates and absorbs the attention of the spirit. Being "spiritually minded" does not preclude living in this world, eating and drinking, and procreating. After all, if we have a dual nature, it is because God has created us with these potential contradictions that we are challenged to resolve. But the spiritual imperative inherent in our human condition does imply that the spirit ought to be free of attachments that make physical existence a higher priority than God.

The Bahá'í Writings refine this doctrine about the nature of sin adding that: "The animal is the source of imperfections, such as anger, sensuality, jealousy, avarice, cruelty, pride: all these defects are found in animals but do not constitute sins. But in man they are sins."[17] Thus, in a broader sense, sin is relative. Compared to animals, man is called to a higher level, and what was natural for the animal is simply no longer acceptable for us. And if we insist on limiting ourselves to the heritage that Darwin bequeathed to us and behaving like our simian ancestors or worse, we simply are not living up to our potential. We are like the adolescent who is faced with new challenges of intellectual discovery and social responsibility, but remains attached to childhood pastimes of cartoons and Nintendo games. ". . . attachment to the earthly world, in relation to attachment to the spiritual world, is considered as a sin. The good deeds of the righteous are the sins of the Near Ones . . . So bodily power is not only defective in relation to spiritual power; it is weakness in comparison."[18]

The duality expressed by Christ—"That which is born of the flesh is flesh; and that which is born of the Spirit is spirit."[19]—and expounded by Paul was a corollary of the recognition of the soul, and led to conclusions that went beyond the Jewish concepts of sin. This is not to denigrate the Jewish moral standard, which was and is extremely high and widely respected, and which recognizes many sins of the flesh as unacceptable behavior. To fail to recognize this would be a grave injustice. The point is rather that Paul's argument that sin arises when man is carnally minded, and that the spirit and the flesh are at odds with each other, would have had much less meaning from a Jewish standpoint in which the spirit was a life force, animating and giving life to the body, which itself was viewed as the identity of man. In Judaism, the concept of the dual nature within man would be somewhat foreign. The emphasis was on the human physical frame as the reality of man, and the spirit made possible its existence. From a Jewish viewpoint, to say that the flesh was at war with the spirit would be almost tantamount to saying that human existence was at war with itself.

Paul's doctrine may not be especially novel to us, and probably sounds like a routine Sunday sermon, but in fact it is a stance that could only be developed fully as a result of the teaching of Jesus about the nature of the human soul. Furthermore, this doctrine represents an important evolution in the concept of sin, since it dealt not only with the symptoms of sin (i.e., the actions that violate laws or religious commandments), but also the root causes. It identified the physical frame and the absorption of man in its appetites as the cause of man's rebelliousness and his multiple defects. Sin is thus no longer arbitrarily defined according to the Law, but is the result of man's animal instincts left to run their course without control or discipline. Having identified the root cause of sin, it is then possible to address sin at a more fundamental level, to "conquer" sin once and for all. It was in this sense that Jesus conquered sin—by educating His followers in a degree of spirituality that raised them above their animal appetites. And from what we have of the historical record of those early Christian communities, they did indeed manifest an active, involved mode of spirituality, expressed as caring, sharing communities with a high moral standard, disdainful of physical gratification, and admired as "true philosophers" by those who took the trouble to observe carefully. They conquered sin not by flagellating themselves, nor through rites of purification, but by purifying their hearts and thereby empowering themselves to fulfill a simple counsel that Jesus gave to one poor captive of the baser instincts with whom He dealt with exemplary mercy: "go, and sin no more."[20] We do not know to what spiritual heights that prostitute rose, if any, but she served humanity well by being the vehicle for the simplest of formulae to deal with a complex theological quagmire.

In light of the above, we derive a new understanding about sin, and the means to overcome sin, and the very meaning of salvation. 'Abdu'l-Bahá, son of Bahá'u'lláh and His appointed Successor, summed this up:

> "When the sanctified breezes of Christ and the holy light of the Greatest Luminary were spread abroad, the human realities—that is to say, those who turned toward the Word of God and received the profusion of His bounties—were saved from this attachment and sin, obtained everlasting life, were delivered from the chains of bondage, and attained to the world of liberty. They were freed from the vices of the human world, and were blessed by the virtues of the Kingdom. This is the meaning of the words of Christ, "I gave My blood for the life of the world" that is to say, I have chosen all these troubles, these sufferings, calamities, and even the greatest martyrdom, to attain this object, the remission of sins (that is, the detachment of spirits from the human world, and their attraction to the divine world) in order that souls may arise who will be the very essence of the guidance of mankind, and the manifestations of the perfections of the Supreme Kingdom."[21]

Note that 'Abdu'l-Bahá equates "the remission of sins" with "the detachment of spirits from the human world, and their attraction to the divine world." In other words, Christ conquered sin by teaching His followers to overcome its very source. He overcame sin through detachment from the animal nature: "It is the spirit that quickeneth; the flesh profiteth nothing."[22] "For to be carnally minded is death; but to be spiritually minded is life and peace."[16]

Now, let us return to the doctrine of the church and see where we stand. Early in this chapter, I referred to the doctrine of expiation—that all humanity was denied salvation until Jesus appeared and sacrificed Himself to cleanse humanity of its transgressions. When dealing with the question of sin and the theology of the modern church, the Book of Hebrews has been one of the most critical texts in defining the Christian understanding of the expiation of sin. Hebrews is interpreted as setting forth the role of Christ as the expiatory sacrifice, replacing the animal sacrifice as practiced in the Temple at Jerusalem. However, we need to look at Hebrews through a broader lens that permits us to see it in its historical setting.

Beyond the context of the expiation of sin, the Book of Hebrews is the New Testament text that most explicitly and clearly demonstrates the issues of the first century and the concern of the church with the fate of the Jewish-Christians, being written to fortify the faith of these young believers. "For when for the time ye ought to be teachers, ye have need that one teach you again which be the first principles of the oracles of God."[23] Hebrews is the example *par excellence* of the New Testament Scripture that seeks to respond to the opposition of the Jewish establishment, attending to Jewish concerns and written in Jewish vocabulary about Jewish concepts—all with the object of protecting the still immature believers in Christ from backsliding into a Jewish milieu that was putting heavy demands on them.

The text of Hebrews suggests firmly that the intended audience is composed of Jewish-Christians. On the one hand, it deals with an intricate interpretation of the Jewish temple rites that could only be appreciated by a Jewish audience: Hence its title (applied long after it was written)—Letter to the Hebrews. On the other hand, these Hebrews are not Jews who have rejected Christ, but rather are brethren of the writer who "have ministered to the saints, and do minister."[24]

Furthermore, these Jewish-Christians have already suffered persecution for their faith: " . . . call to remembrance the former days, in which, after ye were illuminated, ye endured a great fight of afflictions; partly, whilst ye were made a gazingstock both by reproaches and afflictions; and partly, whilst ye became companions of them that were so used."[25] There is a them-and-us context that implies antagonism: "For unto us was the gospel preached, as well as unto them: but the word preached did not profit them, not being mixed with faith in them that heard it."[26]

Within this context of antagonism and persecution, the Book of Hebrews makes explicit reference to the dangers of apostasy, and is a response to this danger.

The author warns that "it is impossible for those who were once enlightened, and have tasted of the heavenly gift, and were made partakers of the Holy Ghost, and have tasted the good word of God, and the powers of the world to come, if they shall fall away, to renew them again unto repentance; seeing they crucify to themselves the Son of God afresh, and put him to an open shame."[27] And another warning for backsliders, "if any man draw back, my soul shall have no pleasure in him."[28]

Specific references to sufferings of the church and to apostasy bring to mind visions of the Jewish-Christians being harassed by the Jewish majority in their surroundings, within the general milieu of Jewish nationalism that I described previously. Where was the Messiah who was to liberate the Jewish nation? How could Jesus of Nazareth be the Messiah if He had done nothing to establish the sovereignty of the Davidic throne, and rather had proposed submission to Roman power? A few weak souls had yielded to this logic, some were firm, and others still needed to be protected. It is in this atmosphere that the Book of Hebrews was written and the primary purpose of the author was to establish once again in the minds of the Jewish-Christians, the authority of Jesus as the Messiah. Hebrews cites numerous quotations from Psalms, Numbers, and other books that are applied to Jesus, to demonstrate His divine Sonship and His excellence among the Prophets and superiority over the angels. The text opens with the following verses, reminding the Christians of the Christology that would soon be articulated in the Gospel of John, in which Christ was present at the very creation of the world. "God, who at sundry times and in divers manners spake in time past unto the fathers by the prophets, hath in these last days spoken unto us by his Son, whom he hath appointed heir of all things, by whom also he made the worlds; who being the brightness of his glory, and the express image of his person, and upholding all things by the word of his power, when he had by himself purged our sins, sat down on the right hand of the Majesty on high."[29]

Given the Jewish background of his audience, the author employs the Jewish tradition of the high priest to convey a Christian concept, which is the Christology of the church—the concept of the role of Christ as intermediary between God and man. "Wherefore, holy brethren, partakers of the heavenly calling, consider the Apostle and High Priest of our profession, Christ Jesus; who was faithful to him that appointed him, as also Moses was faithful in all his house."[30] In the previous chapter, we saw that the concept of a divine intermediary was a sore point for some Jewish-Christians and one that the church fathers needed to reinforce. Thus, the Book of Hebrews uses the role of the high priest to illustrate the eternal spiritual role of the Christ Spirit. Once a year the high priest would enter the inner sanctuary of the Temple and sprinkle it with the blood of animals, in hopes of attaining the forgiveness of God for Israel. The high priest was thus the intermediary that interceded on behalf of the Jews. Christ, being that eternal

Spirit that mediates between God and His creation, has approached God in the inner precincts of heaven, where He intercedes for His loved ones.

The Book of Hebrews poses the sacrifice of Christ in the context of ancient Judaism, and the writer of Hebrews refers extensively to blood, saying that the blood of animals could never expiate sin, but only the blood of Christ. These references have a special significance for a Jewish audience, since blood was synonymous with life itself, as in Leviticus[31], "the blood is life." Hence the Jews were forbidden from eating the blood of an animal, as this would be tantamount to consuming the living animal, which would be inhumane. To say that Jesus gave His blood was another form of saying that He gave His life, as was expressed in the Gospels as well. In one sense, the references to blood reaffirm the willingness of Jesus to sacrifice His life, and the extensive reference to blood in the Book of Hebrews puts this fact within the context of the Jewish understanding of atonement of sins. Again, we must return to the concept of sin and redemption as presented in the quote from 'Abdu'l-Bahá in which He paraphrases the words of Christ, to appreciate the message that is contained in Hebrews: "I gave My blood for the life of the world"(that) is to say, I have chosen all these troubles, these sufferings, calamities, and even the greatest martyrdom, to attain this object, the remission of sins (that is, the detachment of spirits from the human world, and their attraction to the divine world)."

Although the immediate purpose of the author of Hebrews is to defend the young church, in the modern church the central theme of Hebrews is viewed as the expiation of sin. Church doctrine sees in the blood sacrifice of Jesus a substitute for ancient Jewish animal sacrifice, which was no more than a foreshadowing of His supreme sacrifice. Just as the Jews sought forgiveness in the sacrifice of a bullock, Jesus has purchased forgiveness through His own death and resurrection. Of course, the fact that the central issue of Hebrews in the first century was the defense of the church does not in itself contradict modern church doctrine. However, the defensive posture and the us-versus-them tone do serve as a coherent backdrop for the following reflections, and the analysis that follows fits well into the antagonistic environment that surrounded the composition of Hebrews.

When we look closely at the topic of expiation of sin in the Book of Hebrews, we find exactly the same pattern that we have seen with other topics—the use of a traditional Jewish vocabulary, the application of Christian spiritual content to that vocabulary, and the presentation of a contrast between conflicting Jewish and Christian concepts that is meant to instruct the reader and awaken him to the Christian viewpoint. In other words, the conflictive environment within which the Book of Hebrews was written carries over into the clash of ideas. Of course, in Hebrews we do not find Jesus presenting His own views as we do in the Gospels, and in direct conflict with the Jews. The contrast of ideas is present nonetheless.

The following passage is the climactic, watershed verse with regard to the contrast of Christian and Jewish doctrine. Let us pick it apart phrase by phrase and concentrate on what is actually being said, being careful for a moment not to slip into our long-ingrained mental framework about the expiation of sin. Here again we find the dichotomy of flesh and spirit (here referred to as "conscience"), which Paul presented in his letters. "For if the blood of bulls and of goats, and the ashes of a heifer sprinkling the unclean, sanctifieth to the purifying of the flesh: how much more shall the blood of Christ, who through the eternal Spirit offered himself without spot to God, purge your conscience from dead works to serve the living God?"[32] The Jewish concept of expiation of sin is represented in the "blood of bulls and goats," but its effect cannot go beyond the "purifying of the flesh," as the author puts it. Note that this purification of flesh is reminiscent of the Jewish tradition of ritual purity that was maintained by repeated acts of bathing, washing of hands, etc., as referred to previously. In the Gospels, Jesus opposed the concept of ritual purity or "purifying of the flesh" when He insisted that man is not made unfit by any physical impurity that enters his body, but by what comes out of his heart. Hebrews implies that this ritual purity is not sufficient to satisfy the believer in Christ.

The effect of the sacrifice of Christ, in contrast, is a change in "conscience" or mentality. It is a change at the level of the spiritual essence of the human soul that is inspired by the love of Jesus as expressed so sublimely on the cross, when the believer permits himself to be transformed by that image of selfless love. What is to be won through the sacrifice of Christ—to purge the "conscience from dead works"—addresses human behavior (and therefore sin) at its very roots. The central theme of this verse is an inner transformation that results in saintly behavior "to serve the living God." Note in particular that the objective of Christ's sacrifice in this passage is described in terms of service, works, and ethical behavior—not salvation from a mythical hell. And this behavior is born from a purified "conscience," which is to say, a new mindset focused on the spiritual. This is not the purchase of salvation that the church has depicted, but rather a model of inner transformation and outward behavior.

In the very next chapter of Hebrews, the theme of transformation and behavior continues and is extended to divine forgiveness. It is in this context that Hebrews quotes the Old Testament Prophet, Jeremiah, to make a point about exactly what was new in the New Covenant that Jesus had brought: "This is the covenant that I will make with them after those days, saith the Lord, I will put my laws into their hearts, and in their minds will I write them; and their sins and iniquities will I remember no more."[33] Here the author of Hebrews draws upon Jeremiah to make the point that God forgets the "sins and iniquities" when the "laws" are embedded in the "hearts" and "minds"—which is to say, when man attains to a new conscience and thereby learns not to sin. This is a very different formula for the forgiveness of sins than expiation—a formula that goes to the heart of the transforming Message of Jesus. The author of Hebrews carries the discussion of sin and forgiveness to a higher level, to its essential level of transformation of the heart and mind, beyond the superficial level of blood payment for justification as practiced in the Jerusalem Temple. This is the real message of forgiveness that is enshrined in the Book of Hebrews.

In summary, the author of Hebrews addressed the Jewish-Christian church to strengthen its faith in time of trials. The author uses terms drawn from the Jewish traditions in which the Jewish-Christians are still immersed, to remind them of the fact that Jesus was their true intermediary, their true High Priest. Some of their brethren have succumbed to pressure to return to those Jewish traditions, but the Christians should no longer look to the temple sacrifice. Rather they should permit themselves to be inspired by the supreme sacrifice of Jesus, which would purge their minds and hearts of worldly attachments and thereby free them from sin and dead works.

The Jewish rite of atonement as mediated by the high priest served the author of Hebrews as a vehicle through which to represent the intercession of Christ between God and man, and His spiritual station as intermediary, and His unlimited selflessness in sacrificing Himself. With the passage of time, the medium has become the message. This Jewish rite of atonement has become the essence of the Christian doctrine of salvation and, contrary to both biblical text and logic, the only way forgiveness can be attained by humanity. Thus has church doctrine gone full circle on this point, as it has on many others, to return to a Jewish understanding of atonement of sins, as opposed to a purification of conscience and an uplifting of morals as was originally the Mission of Christianity.

Nevertheless, there remains the question of the very sacrifice of Christ and its effects on the world. Is there no particular significance to this supreme sacrifice? Does the martyrdom of the promised Messiah have no more ultimate impact than if He had lived out His life in peace and tranquility, in honor and comfort? Is it merely an expression—later symbolized in the crucifix—of His unbounded good will, and His readiness to give His all?

First, if we take this question outside of the context of religion, martyrs have an influence that extends far beyond their own sphere and lifetime. The fact of their martyrdom raises them to a level in the consciousness of humanity that they could not have attained otherwise, and even prolongs their active contribution to the cause that they espoused. Martin Luther King fueled the civil rights movement long after his death, until his cause had achieved all its objectives. The tragic death of Gandhi punctuates his philosophy almost as much as his life did. This certainly applies to Christ as well, and the image of the crucified Christ is one of the most powerful that the world has ever witnessed, and has moved hearts and inspired minds in all cultures and climes for two thousand years. Yet on this point I cannot remain silent and refrain from interjecting a point of faith. The martyrdom of a Manifestation of God embraces this level of reality and much more, and cannot be compared to that of any other martyr. Regarding the sacrifice of Christ, Bahá'u'lláh says the following, which amplifies the effects of His martyrdom and raises it to a much higher level.

> "Know thou that when the Son of Man yielded up His breath to God, the whole creation wept with a great weeping. By sacrificing Himself, however, a fresh capacity was infused into all created things. Its evidences, as witnessed in all the peoples of the earth, are now manifest before thee. The deepest wisdom which the sages have uttered, the profoundest learning which any mind hath unfolded, the arts which the ablest hands have produced, the influence exerted by the most potent of rulers, are but manifestations of the quickening power released by His transcendent, His all-pervasive, and resplendent Spirit.
>
> We testify that when He came into the world, He shed the splendor of His glory upon all created things. Through Him the leper recovered from the leprosy of perversity and ignorance. Through Him, the unchaste and wayward were healed. Through His power, born of Almighty God, the eyes of the blind were opened, and the soul of the sinner sanctified.
>
> Leprosy may be interpreted as any veil that interveneth between man and the recognition of the Lord, his God. Whoso alloweth himself to be shut out from Him is indeed a leper, who shall not be remembered in the Kingdom of God, the Mighty, the All-Praised. We bear witness that through the power of the Word of God every leper was cleansed, every sickness was healed, every human infirmity was banished. He it is Who purified the world. Blessed is the man who, with a face beaming with light, hath turned towards Him."[34]

In this passage, Bahá'u'lláh places the sacrifice of Christ into a broader perspective, beyond the simple forgiveness of this or that sin, beyond even the inspiration of which we are consciously aware, and into the mystical context of raising humanity to a higher level wherein the imperfections of the past are overcome by spiritual growth. Furthermore, the "wisdom" of the "sages," "the profoundest learning which any mind hath unfolded," and "the arts" all result from this invisible influence that Christ brought to the world. This is a doctrine that, like the doctrine of expiation, is only valid through faith, yet it is a vision that permits us to view all God's plan in a broader and more profound perspective. For, while the sacrifice of Jesus in the act of offering up His life may have been unique among Manifestations of God up to that time, suffering and sacrifice are an integral part of the life of every Manifestation. Bahá'u'lláh expounds further on the effect of these multiple acts of sacrifice, referring to the intention of Abraham to offer up His own son in obedience to God's command,

> " . . . so that His steadfastness in the faith of God and His detachment from all else but Him may be demonstrated unto men. The purpose of God, moreover, was to sacrifice him as a ransom for the sins and iniquities of all the peoples of the earth. This same honor, Jesus, the Son of Mary, besought the one true God, exalted be His name and glory, to confer upon Him. For the same reason was Husayn offered up as a sacrifice by Muhammad, the Apostle of God.
>
> No man can ever claim to have comprehended the nature of the hidden and manifold grace of God; none can fathom His all-embracing mercy. Such hath been the perversity of men and their transgressions, so grievous have been the trials that have afflicted the Prophets of God and their chosen ones, that all mankind deserveth to be tormented and to perish. God's hidden and most loving providence, however, hath, through both visible and invisible agencies, protected and will continue to protect it from the penalty of its wickedness. Ponder this in thine heart, that the truth may be revealed unto thee, and be thou steadfast in His path."[35]

Abraham, Moses, Joseph—all bore severe trials in the course of carrying out their respective missions. This is natural if the Manifestation is to bring change and progress by uprooting past traditions and long-standing dogmas, and it is a part of His Mission that each Manifestation accepts with acquiescence in His desire to please God and to serve Him: "O my Father, if it be possible, let this cup pass from me."[36] This sacrifice from age to age has been the spiritual leaven that raises the mass of humanity. In other words, if we look at the sacrifice of the Manifestations in the context of progressive revelation, and remember that each One represents a step in the spiritual, social, and intellectual progress of humanity, then we can see that in this mystical world of the Manifestation, the successive sacrifices throughout the ages have fueled the progress of the world and its spiritual advancement. For example, the Bahá'í Writings refer to the far-reaching impact of the trials that overcame Abraham:

> "Abraham then came into the region of the Holy Land. His enemies considered that His exile would lead to His destruction and ruin, as it seemed impossible that a man banished from His native land, deprived of His rights and oppressed on all sides—even though He were a king—could escape extermination. But Abraham stood fast

and showed forth extraordinary firmness—and God made this exile to be to His eternal honor—until He established the Unity of God in the midst of a polytheistic generation. This exile became the cause of the progress of the descendants of Abraham, and the Holy Land was given to them. As a result the teachings of Abraham were spread abroad, a Jacob appeared among His posterity, and a Joseph who became ruler in Egypt. In consequence of His exile a Moses and a being like Christ were manifested from His posterity, and Hagar was found from whom Ishmael was born, one of whose descendants was Muhammad. In consequence of His exile the Báb appeared from His posterity, and the Prophets of Israel were numbered among the descendants of Abraham. And so it will continue for ever and ever. Finally, in consequence of His exile the whole of Europe and most of Asia came under the protecting shadow of the God of Israel. See what a power it is that enabled a Man Who was a fugitive from His country to found such a family, to establish such a faith, and to promulgate such teachings."[37]

Regarding the impact of pure deeds and selfless sacrifice upon the world, I am reminded of Abraham's rather whimsical conversation with God about the destruction of Sodom. Abraham asks if God would spare Sodom if there were fifty righteous men in the city.[38] God appears to humor Abraham and says, "If I find in Sodom fifty righteous within the city, then I will spare all the place for their sakes." In true Mid-Eastern fashion, Abraham sets about to bargain and asks if God would spare the city for the sake of forty-five righteous. Yes, for forty-five righteous God would spare the city. "And for thirty? And twenty? And ten?" Having thus bargained on behalf of humanity, the text concludes saying "the LORD went his way . . . and Abraham returned unto his place," as if Abraham had worn the Lord down and the Lord gave up in desperation, unable to argue with Abraham in His commitment to protect humanity. Whimsy aside, I think that the gist of the story is that God is ready and willing to reward any and all sanctified acts and righteousness that He finds in the world, even in the midst of sinful Sodom. And if these sanctified acts originate in the most unselfish acts of sacrifice of His very own Messengers—might He not be disposed to satisfy the longing that those Holy Souls bear in Their inmost heart, that God forgive that same humanity for which those Manifestations sacrifice themselves, and raise humanity to a level whereby they will no longer sin? "Go, and sin no more."

Thus, the Manifestations of God have all sacrificed Themselves in their desire to purge humanity of its sins. Their purpose has been to raise humanity to new heights of purity in each age, inspiring the children of men with their words, their lives, and their selfless love. Beyond seeking forgiveness for humanity, They have sought to conquer sin by teaching us new patterns of behavior that spring from the heart and that originate in detachment from worldly desires. Some of the effects of their sacrifices are evident and visible to us, for example, the patience of Moses in dealing with the rebellious Hebrew tribes and His intercession that gained God's forgiveness. Other effects are more subtle and occur in the mystical plane, wherein the Manifestation nurtures humanity toward those greater heights of spirituality—a nurturing of which we are scarcely aware, except through faith.

CHAPTER 11

CRISIS IN THE CHURCH:
CAUGHT BETWEEN TWO EXTREMES

It is common today to talk about crisis in the church, and has been as long as I can remember. This is nothing new and has been the story of the church for two thousand years. In its first century, the early church was denied its foremost leaders when most of these were martyred. It was plagued with internal conflicts of gentile Christian versus Jewish-Christian. It was beset with persecution, apostasy, and theological disputes about the nature of Christ. As the church moved into the Middle Ages, former crises faded and those of power, politics, and corruption came to the fore. Luther's revolt presented a new phase of sectarian dissension that rent the church forever, yet the church continued, wounded and divided, but there it was. As the Age of Reason dawned, a new sort of doctrine opposed the church, that of modern science. One crisis followed another as in each successive area of intellectual endeavor, human genius knocked down the shibboleths accumulated over centuries. Copernicus and Galileo, Newton, eventually Darwin, and finally Freud made inroads into truths that the church had defended as indispensable corollaries of religious faith. The church was forced to cede intellectual leadership to science.

So what is new? Is there any particular danger today that the church has not weathered in the past? Is there any special reason to worry? I think that what is happening is perhaps more subtle, but unprecedented, insomuch as the church is rapidly ceding intellectual leadership in one last field of study—in the field of religion! In the past one hundred and fifty years, and more rapidly in the past fifty, the study of religion has moved from seminary to university, from chapel to classroom, from cleric's study to professor's library and archaeologist's dig. This brings a new dimension to religion that can be healthy and enlightening if it is properly assimilated, but likewise can represent a threat to the very foundation of faith.

The church is dealing with the intellectual examination of the historical context of Jesus, an exercise drawing on the tools and skills of several branches of scholarly inquiry, such as archaeology and linguistics. This now legendary quest for the historical Jesus originally aimed at validating once and for all the truth of the Gospel versions, but it took a different turn, and with results that were unexpected at the outset of the quest. Along the way, the common ground of Judaism and early Christianity has come to the forefront, to such a degree that many in the scholarly community agree that Christianity in its first decades was a sect of Judaism, no more and no less. The first Christians thought of themselves as Jews and they thought of the church as the restoration of the true Israel.

So what exactly is the danger? In many circles, this line of investigation is changing the way people think not only about the early church and the first Christians, but also about Jesus Himself. Many scholars now classify Jesus as a typical apocalyptic prophet that roamed Palestine in those years, one who expected the end of the world at any moment, and called upon humanity to prepare itself accordingly. In other words, the early Christians had a very Jewish perspective about the movement to which they subscribed. In this view, Jesus Himself considered His Mission and His own person within the same limited context, and was calling Palestine to the kingdom of God, which He thought was just around the corner, and would dawn as soon as God destroyed the old order and called the dead to the resurrection.

This scholarly view is not a new phenomenon and has been developing for part of the nineteenth century and all of the twentieth. The scholarly standard of this approach, given its goal of revealing the real life of the historical Jesus, is historical objectivity, which as a matter of principle must set aside questions of faith as subjective. Likewise, historical objectivity as presently practiced demands ignoring doctrine about Jesus as a transcendent Being who is a channel for God's intervention in history, since such transcendence is only valid as an article of faith. In any case, a doctrine of transcendence should have no bearing on objective efforts to unravel the chain of events that represent His life and actions.

However, once the transcendence of Jesus is set aside as irrelevant to this approach, a vacuum is created that surrounds Jesus Himself. If Jesus did not understand Himself as transcendent, then how did He see Himself? At this point, other options are entertained to explain His motives, His self-understanding, and His view of His own Mission. Having barred the way to transcendental answers to these questions, no other responses can remain except this-worldly answers. Under the lens of historical objectivity, Jesus is quickly reduced to a product of the first century. His Mission is circumscribed to the context of first century Judaism. His vision and His own spirituality are similarly reduced to the context of a renewal of Israel. As a result, many now view Jesus as a reforming rabbi whose Mission was to restore Israel to a state of purity. He tried to push the issue by confronting the Jewish authorities and by cleansing the Temple. His plan backfired and He was crucified. Under this scenario, Jesus is reduced to a victim of circumstances, and Jesus Himself becomes circumstantial.

In this view of the circumstantial Jesus, even if Jesus *did* resurrect physically from the dead, so what? What does the resurrection represent if Jesus was a victim of circumstances and His death was an accident of the times? The resurrection would be just one more circumstance of His sad, event-driven existence.

The reduction of Jesus to the status of apocalyptic prophet is one serious challenge to Christianity, and while it was not my purpose to address that challenge in my own personal reflections, it became inevitable to do so at some moment. I started this book stating that I had come to terms with Jesus precisely through a study of Judaism, and that is true. I can now see Jesus within the context of the first century and yet transcending it. And I could only see that transcendence clearly by understanding better what first century Judaism represented, and in what ways Jesus reflected Judaism, and in what ways He contrasted with it and transcended it. And that is why I say that Judaism led me to Jesus. However, along the way I have come to the conclusion that the irony of ironies has occurred in Christianity.

First, I see that Jesus sought to spiritualize the Jewish ethical tradition. This was the essence of His Mission and is expressed nowhere more succinctly as in the belief of the eternal human soul. The early church fathers struggled to establish this message, employing a Jewish vocabulary, but seeking to inject new spiritual content into that vocabulary. With the passage of time, the church gained the upper hand, but meanwhile, having adopted Jewish content of the symbols that Jesus used, the church unconsciously reverted to Jewish doctrine.

The church raised physical resurrection, which in Judaism was a secondary doctrine that not even all Jews accepted, to a central position in the church. Physical resurrection was employed as symbolic imagery, on the one hand for spiritual rebirth of the individual, and on the other hand, the collective rebirth of the followers of Jesus after His death. With time, the symbolism was lost in favor of a literal interpretation, reverting to the understanding of the Pharisees.

As to the Jewish doctrine of expiation of sins by blood sacrifice, this was certainly more important to Judaism than was resurrection, and was undeniably a part of normative Judaism. This ceremony was carried out in the Temple on Yom Kippur when Jews would gather from all over Palestine. Even so, the expiation of sins was *not* the one central overbearing issue of the Jewish Covenant, over and above the practice of the Law. And when the Temple no longer existed, Judaism adjusted and learned to live without the ceremony of expiation, focusing on Torah and Talmud. The church, on the other hand, having at one time symbolized the spiritual role of Christ as that of the high priest who offered the blood sacrifice in the Temple, established the Jewish expiatory doctrine as central to Christianity, eventually overshadowing spiritual renovation as the central issue of the Mission of Jesus. While the Jewish doctrine of expiation died out in Judaism after the loss of the Temple, it survived in the doctrine of the church.

And these two doctrines of Judaism came to dominate Christianity.

As these two symbols were melded into one doctrine of the resurrected Christ having paid for mankind's sins, they also were interjected into the rites and celebrations of the church. The Eucharist, beyond a symbol of participation in the Covenant of Jesus and a sharing in the spirit and teachings of His church, became a materialization of the risen Christ embodying a mystical saving grace, eventually being formulated as transubstantiation. Rite displaced simple, heartfelt prayer, and implicitly, it also took priority over the practice of that spirit in acts of service, which became an afterthought in the doctrine of theologians such as Luther, who emphasized salvation by faith alone.

Perhaps even more damaging in the long run is the effect of this on Christianity's self-understanding. As the event of the physical resurrection came to be seen as unprecedented in religious history, and the sacrifice of Jesus as the unique vehicle of God's salvation, this combination has led to claims of exclusivity among the world's religions. Too often, orthodox Christians view their faith as inherently superior to other religions, based largely on these two aspects of its doctrine that have been misconstrued once they were disengaged from the context in which they were originally used, as tools to nurture Christian doctrine in a Jewish-Christian audience.

In the battle for the early church, although the Christians eventually gained ascendancy in the political realm and outnumbered the Jews a thousandfold, in a sense the Jews won out in the end in the field of doctrine, for it was Jewish doctrine that finally stood the test of time. As the church took an increasingly aggressive attitude toward the Jews—an attitude that became ingrained culturally in the West—that very church was propagating the doctrine of its victims and making it the centerpiece of its faith. And this is its greatest irony.

I should add here that this scenario has no bearing on the way I feel about Judaism. If I am dismayed at the way Christianity reverted to Jewish doctrine, this does not imply that I view Judaism askance as the source of that doctrine. I have other reasons for respecting Judaism, both ancient and modern. And as I mentioned above, the Jewish doctrines that came to dominate Christianity were in fact not even so central to Judaism as was the Law and its commitment to Covenant, which are two of the most admirable and enduring aspects of Judaism, and which the rabbis highlighted in their renewal of the Jewish faith.

So how do I see the crisis in the church? At present, Christianity finds itself between two extremes. On the one hand is the view of much of academia that all too often has materialized Jesus through the mechanism of historical analysis. On the other hand is church orthodoxy, which upholds the doctrines of expiation and resurrection that have ill served the cause of Christ through the course of its two millennia of history, and that will scarcely meet the challenge of academia. I find neither to be satisfying, and I do not think that the future of Christianity lies in either.

I think that what is going on in intellectual circles is more threatening to the future of Christianity, and potentially more damaging than Galileo, Newton, and Freud all put together. The first-century, Jewish apocalyptic teacher-turned-savior—in other words, the academician's Jesus now stripped of transcendence—will not maintain the interest of the man in the street for long, and Jesus will soon be discarded altogether as irrelevant to modern society. Perhaps I am overly pessimistic about the power that academia might exercise over the faith of the faithful, but the promise of revealing the real, historical Jesus holds great power of attraction, as illustrated in the recent phenomenal popularity of the book and film, *The Da Vinci Code*. To the extent that academia can publicize their own materialized version of the historical Jesus, I fear that sooner or later they will find a receptive audience. And once convinced of that version of Jesus, then Jesus will be irrelevant.

On the other hand, the future of the church lies not in defending outmoded and questionable doctrines, any more than it lay in defending a universe with the earth at its center. Christians need both to believe in a transcendent Christ, and to come to grips with the intellectual challenges that are relativizing Jesus to the limits of the first century. And they need to do the latter not by denial or receding into fundamentalism, but by finding viable answers to those challenges. The obscuring dust of accumulated dogmas needs to be wiped off to revitalize the spiritualizing Mission of Jesus. The church must find an outlet for that spiritualizing influence of Jesus that was the essence of His Mission, and that outlet I suggest is in the one last horizon that Jesus left to His followers—the kingdom.

Might not we all find an answer in those aspirations that at one time united Christian and Jew, before these two traditions drifted apart like two alienated siblings, like Jacob and Esau, or Isaac and Ishmael? Might not Christianity and Judaism find renewed common ground, by taking common inspiration in the Old Testament vision? Might not Jewish and Christian expectations again converge and coalesce around the promises of the kingdom that animated the first century? Might not Christianity be refreshed by deriving a new vision from those expectations of the kingdom that were left pending when Christ left this world, when the apostles ceased to preach, when the church finally set down its roots, but without the heavenly aura that Jesus might have wished? Might not the church find its own salvation, its own resurrection, in seeking that kingdom that animated those first Christians? In a world that is crying out in need, should we not find our challenge in responding to it? Might not even Muslims join in such an effort to serve what is a common element of all three traditions? And if all three traditions insist that this is a future state that must await the advent of God's promised Messenger, might we not reply that that Messenger, in any case, would be no less pleased to find the world a little bit closer to that vision when He arrives?

Jews look to the same Old Testament prophecies that spurred their enthusiasm in the first century, and that in the intervening centuries have been elaborated in dozens of Messiah legends. Christians maintain the doctrine of two advents of the Messiah and set hopes on their own interpretations, now with certain legend-like qualities. All agree that the advent of the kingdom would be timely. All might see the kingdom as the culmination of the spiritual and material progress, the next step in the spiritual evolution of the planet, the next step in progressive revelation. If monotheism, the Law, and knowledge of the soul led us to fulfillment for the individual, there remains the step of extending faith to a world-embracing social organization.

In the context of the Old Testament, some of the most inspiring verses visualize a world in which all nations are united in a common purpose, a world in which war has been abolished by common consent. These verses have come to symbolize the longings of all humanity:

> "And it shall come to pass in the last days, that the mountain of the LORD's house shall be established in the top of the mountains, and shall be exalted above the hills; and all nations shall flow unto it.
>
> And many people shall go and say, Come ye, and let us go up to the mountain of the LORD, to the house of the God of Jacob; and he will teach us of his ways, and we will walk in his paths: for out of Zion shall go forth the law, and the word of the LORD from Jerusalem.
>
> And he shall judge among the nations, and shall rebuke many people: and they shall beat their swords into plowshares, and their spears into pruning hooks: nation shall not lift up sword against nation, neither shall they learn war any more."[1]

So far reaching is this state of peace that it is represented as harmonizing the most disparate elements of society, symbolized as natural enemies among animals. "The wolf also shall dwell with the lamb, and the leopard shall lie down with the kid; and the calf and the young lion and the fatling together; and a little child shall lead them. And the cow and the bear shall feed; their young ones shall lie down together: and the lion shall eat straw like the ox. And the sucking child shall play on the hole of the asp, and the weaned child shall put his hand on the cockatrice' den. They shall not hurt nor destroy in all my holy mountain: for the earth shall be full of the knowledge of the LORD, as the waters cover the sea."[2]

A common denominator of these visions, and a powerful symbol, is that of the holy mountain—a vision that exists in many of our religious traditions. Mountains convey something of transcendent power that originates in God. The Greeks turned to Olympus. Moses went to Sinai for His Revelation. Even the Samaritans worshipped at Gerizim, and in the days of Solomon, Mount Moriah came to be the focus of worship and sacrifice, symbolizing God's presence among the Jews. Christian Scripture picked up this tradition when Jesus delivered His Sermon on the Mount. Bahá'ís also look to a holy mountain, Mount Carmel, which is their World Center and which Isaiah saw to be a site blessed by God in those days of the future: " . . . the desert shall rejoice, and blossom as the rose. It shall blossom abundantly, and rejoice even with joy and singing: the glory of Lebanon shall be given unto it, the excellency of Carmel and Sharon; they shall see the glory of the LORD, and the excellency of our God."[3] In the image of a mountain is symbolized the transcendence of God's faith. In the lifetime of the Manifestation, it serves as a pedestal for God's Spokesperson, symbolically elevating Him above His contemporaries. After His passing, it is God's high place, in sight of all and offering hope for the future, while the rest of us seek to catch up to God's vision.

And what of the kingdom? Sometimes it seems as if it was never so near, but never so far.

We are now confident that it will not be the Marxist workers' paradise upon which millions in the twentieth century set their hopes, for which they shed their blood, killed, and died. And we sincerely hope that it will not be the kingdom of western consumerism that has reached the furthest corners of the earth and captured the admiration of the majority of its inhabitants.

What kingdom would *you* want? Should it not be built on the Judeo-Christian principles of ethics, rule by law, and love? But would we leave out the compassion and tranquility of the Buddhist? Would we forget the insight and meditation of the Hindu? Would we omit the communion with nature of the Native Americans? Would we sacrifice the Islamic sense of humility before God? Would we neglect the wisdom and healing arts of the Chinese? As we look around the world, we see these and many other elements that we would want to include in the kingdom, without which God's world would seem incomplete. Indeed, it seems as if we have all the elements of an earthly paradise here at hand, waiting only for the sharing.

These are not vague ideas. The kingdom is already beginning to occur. All religions have real opportunities to express their own dimension of spirituality—opportunities that should be viewed as responsibilities by the world's religious leaders. The world's greatest minds see a vast field of service waiting for religion to play its role. Indeed, as the twentieth century drew to a close, the world witnessed a series of events that previous ages would have been aghast to behold. Forward-looking leaders of divergent faiths joined hands to add their moral weight to causes such as the protection of the environment, human rights, and socio-economic development.

No event was so impressive and highlighted the potential role of the world's faiths as that convened by Kofi Annan, as a preliminary step leading to the Millennium World Peace Summit in the year 2000. The spirit of that conference and its foremost challenge were summed up succinctly in a message read on behalf of the Dalai Lama, in words that could be described as its overriding mission statement:

> "The world's religions can contribute to world peace, if there is peace and growing harmony between different faiths . . . It is also my belief that whereas the 20th century has been a century of war and untold suffering, the 21st century should be one of peace and dialogue . . . However, there can be no peace as long as there is grinding poverty, social injustice, inequality, oppression, environmental degradation, and as long as the weak and small continue to be trodden by the mighty and powerful. The world's spiritual and religious leaders need to address these real and pressing issues and find ways to contribute towards their elimination. These are the enemies of peace and true tyrannies of our times."[4]

Ironically, since that meeting in New York, the divisions among religions seem to have deepened rather than healed, as a result of tragic and earth-shaking events that brought religious fanaticism to the headlines as never before. In a document circulated to the world's religious leaders in May 2002, the Universal House of Justice, the governing body of the Bahá'í Faith, noted the progress made in overcoming prejudices of race, gender, and nationalism during the twentieth century. Religion, to the contrary, has not advanced at a similar pace in overcoming those ingrained prejudices of past ages. "Other segments of society embrace the implications of the oneness of humankind, not only as the inevitable next step in the advancement of civilization, but as the fulfilment of lesser identities of every kind that our race brings to this critical moment in our collective history. Yet, the greater part of organized religion stands paralyzed at the threshold of the future, gripped in those very dogmas and claims of privileged access to truth that have been responsible for creating some of the most bitter conflicts dividing the earth's inhabitants."[5]

The key to freeing itself from those "dogmas and claims of privileged access to truth" is to recognize the truth in other religions, as enunciated by Bahá'u'lláh in the following passage in which He describes the essential truths of progressive revelation: "There can be no doubt whatever that the peoples of the world, of whatever race or religion, derive their inspiration from one heavenly Source, and are the subjects of one God. The difference between the ordinances under which they abide should be attributed to the varying requirements and exigencies of the age in which they were revealed. All of them, except a few which are the outcome of human perversity, were ordained of God, and are a reflection of His Will and Purpose. Arise and, armed with the power of faith, shatter to pieces the gods of your vain imaginings, the sowers of dissension amongst you. Cleave unto that which draweth you together and uniteth you."[5]

These words imply the need for "renunciation of all those claims to exclusivity or finality that, in winding their roots around the life of the spirit, have been the greatest single factor in suffocating impulses to unity and in promoting hatred and violence."[5]

"It is to this historic challenge that we believe leaders of religion must respond if religious leadership is to have meaning in the global society emerging from the transformative experiences of the twentieth century. It is evident that growing numbers of people are coming to realize that the truth underlying all religions is in its essence one. This recognition arises not through a resolution of theological disputes, but as an intuitive awareness born from the ever widening experience of others and from a dawning acceptance of the oneness of the human family itself. Out of the welter of religious doctrines, rituals and legal codes inherited from vanished worlds, there is emerging a sense that spiritual life, like the oneness manifest in diverse nationalities, races and cultures, constitutes one unbounded reality equally accessible to everyone. In order for this diffuse and still tentative perception to consolidate itself and contribute effectively to the building of a peaceful world, it must have the wholehearted confirmation of those to whom, even at this late hour, masses of the earth's population look for guidance.

Because it is concerned with the ennobling of character and the harmonizing of relationships, religion has served throughout history as the ultimate authority in giving meaning to life. In every age, it has cultivated the good, reproved the wrong and held up, to the gaze of all those willing to see, a vision of potentialities as yet unrealized. From its counsels the rational soul has derived encouragement in overcoming limits imposed by the world and in fulfilling itself. As the name implies, religion has simultaneously been the chief force binding diverse peoples together in ever larger and more complex societies through which the individual capacities thus released can find expression. The great advantage of the present age is the perspective that makes it possible for the entire human race to see this civilizing process as a single phenomenon, the ever-recurring encounters of our world with the world of God."[5]

One way or the other, the vision described above is underway. Like it or not, we are well on the way to the kingdom. The world is shrinking and fusing, against all efforts to resist integration. Like it or not, Christian, Jew, Muslim, Buddhist, and Hindu are involved. But if they lag behind in their contribution or even resist participating, then everyone will suffer the consequences.

Meanwhile, the Bahá'ís are out to make a point—that it is possible for races, cultures, and nations to live and work together; that the integration of the world *can* be peaceful. Around their World Center on Mount Carmel, Bahá'ís are building a community, not only an international community, but also a supranational community, with its own culture—not a subculture but a supra-culture. With organized communities in more than one hundred and eighty countries, and among more than two thousand ethnic groups, the Bahá'í Faith is considered to be the second most widely diffused religion in the world, after Christianity. As a result, the most important contribution of the Bahá'ís to this process of the kingdom at this critical juncture in history is the very vision of world community, and the conviction that it is possible.

Shall we wait for a kingdom that comes down out of heaven? What comes out of heaven is God's Word and guidance. In this world we apply God's guidance.

Jews benefited from the divine intervention of God to free them from Pharaoh, but God did not build them their nation in the Promised Land, rather He gave them the ethics and laws to do so themselves. The Christians witnessed miracles at the hands of Jesus, but Jesus did not build their community and their church for them. Rather He gave them the teachings and inspired them with love to do it themselves. Do we expect God to do our work for us now? Or do we pick up the ball and play our role? If someone chooses to sit and wait for God to do it, so be it. That is his or her choice. But it has not been God's way in the past, and we have no reason that I can see to expect that He will do it any differently this time around.

In any game plan to improve this world, Christians ought to play an important role. Christianity continues to be the most populous religion on the face of the earth, and Christendom plays an important role in every dimension of day-to-day life, including trade, economics, and politics. The Christian West wields great power, for better or worse. Do Christians feel the weight of that responsibility? Are they morally prepared to assume their part? Many are, but more need to be so.

Or, are Christians in danger of losing their spiritual center of gravity, caught in a state of limbo between academia's vision of the apocalyptic prophet, and age-old church orthodoxy? If these two contrasting extremes were to set the limits on Christianity's horizons, then Christianity would lose its moral force altogether, and a vast segment of humankind would be left morally adrift, incapable of fulfilling its calling at a most challenging time in history.

I began this book on a personal note, relating my own difficulties with coming to terms with Jesus. I seem to have strayed far from that point of departure, yet a common thread runs from my own experience through to the state of Christianity and its present challenges. By looking at Jesus through the lens of the first century I was able to see Him both within a Jewish context and transcending it. This led me through a process that encouraged me to discount outworn church doctrines—the very doctrines that have contributed to an air of exclusivity within Christianity. Rather than destroying the foundation of the church, discounting those doctrines opens whole new vistas and fields of service for the church. In a social context, this suggests that the church could well direct its attention toward uniting with other religions in a concerted effort to further the well-being of humankind.

On a personal level, this same process of discarding dogmas also made Jesus more transparent and appealing. Stripped of those exclusive dogmas, Jesus stands with His own doctrine in hand, inviting His followers to eternal life that is to be found in loving Him and in serving His loved ones. For my part, as a Bahá'í, I finally feel comfortable with Jesus. I have found space for both a transcendental Jesus and for pursuits that seek to open new horizons of the spiritual.

Jesus gazes at the crowd. He seems at ease, even in the twenty first century—so much so that one might think that He is standing in His hometown of Nazareth. With a sense of penetrating calm His gaze surveys the faces that look back at Him. He reads these souls with the same intensely compassionate understanding as if He were looking at a crowd of fishermen, scribes, and tax collectors two thousand years ago.

The crowd gazes back at Jesus. Some swell with triumphant pride at the thought of "their" Savior walking amongst them, visibly convinced that He has finally appeared to confirm their victory over other churches and faiths. Others look at Him with neither loving adoration nor hostility in their faces, but rather with a heightened sense of curiosity, as if they are looking at an anachronism from a long dead age. Who is this apocalyptic prophet? What is He doing here? Does He not know that the world did not end two thousand years ago as He thought it would? Why did His cause not die long ago with the other apocalyptics?

For a brief moment, Jesus looks straight at me. Our eyes meet and I feel a thrill run through me—not of anxiety this time, but a moment of exaltation that is tempered by a sharing of the peaceful calm that Jesus Himself radiates and instills in others. It would be presumptuous of me to say that we understand each other, but let us say that we understand enough of each other to appreciate where each one stands, and for my part, I have been carried to the point that I can start to trust Him. At last, I can say that I feel comfortable with Jesus.

Notes

Chapter 2

1.   Exod. 4:12 Authorized (King James) Version, 2000, available at: http:www.bartleby.com/108/—used for all following Bible citations.
2.   Isa. 2:3-4.
3.   John 3:6.
4.   John 10:28.
5.   Matt. 16:26.
6.   John 17:21.
7.   Matt. 26:41.
8.   Deut. 18:10-12.
9.   The Talmud. Berakoth 60b, third paragraph. Available at: http//www.come-and-hear.com/berakoth/berakoth_60.html#PARTb.
10.   Gen. 1:1-3.
11.   Gen. 2:7.

Chapter 3

1.   Luke 23:34.
2.   Matt. 21:9.

Chapter 4

1.   Luke 4:16-20.
2.   Acts 13:15.
3.   Acts 17:1-3; 10-11.
4.   James 2:2.
5.   Matt. 24:2.

Chapter 5

1   John 16:2.
2   John 8:7.
3   Luke 20:25; see also Mark 12:17; Matt. 22:21.
4   Matt. 26:52.
5   Luke 14:26.
6   Deut. 21:23.
7   1 John 2:18-19.
8   1 John 2:22.
9   1 John 4:2-3.
10   Heb. 3:12; Heb. 6:4-6.

Chapter 6

1   Rom. 11:2; 11:4.
2   1 Cor. 15:3.
3   1 Pet. 1:10.
4   Zech. 9:9.
5   Matt. 21:5-7.
6   Mark 7:18.
7   Mark 8:17.
8   Mark 7:15.
9   Mark 7:18-20.

Chapter 7

1   Isa. 11:6-9.
2   Luke 20:25; see also Mark 12:17; Matt. 22:20.
3   Matt. 24:36.
4   Matt. 4:17.
5   Luke 17:20-21.
6   Matt. 11:12.
7   Matt. 12:28.
8   Luke 10:8-9.
9   Luke 16:16.
10   Matt. 25:34.
11   Mark 4:14. Other quotes in this paragraph are to be found in Mark 4:16-20.
12   Mark 4:13
13   Mark 4: 2-9, 14-20, 26-29, and 30-32.
14   Mark 4:11.

15 Matt. 6:31-33.
16 John 18:35-36.
17 John 3:5.
18 1 Cor. 15:50.
19 Rom. 14:17.
20 Matt. 5:3.
21 Matt. 18:4.
22 Luke 9:62.
23 Matt. 5:20.
24 The Kitáb-i-Aqdas, verse 83, page 49. Bahá'í Reference Library, available at: http://reference.bahai.org/en/t/b/KA/.
25 Matt. 7:21.
26 Matt. 16:18.
27 Matt. 16:19.
28 Matt. 16:28.
29 Matt. 6:10.
30 Luke 21:28-31.
31 Luke 17:20.
32 Mark 4:11.
33 Mark 4:15.

Chapter 8

1   Dan. 12:1-4.
2   Mark 10:29-30.
3   Luke 10:25-28.
4   John 8:51-53.
5   Mark 12:25-27.
6   John 14:5.
7   Mark 9:10-13.
8   Matt. 17:13.
9   John 6:47.
10 Luke 12:15.
11 John 3:4.
12 John 3:10.
13 John 5:24.
14 John 11:24.
15 John 11:25.
16 John 11:26.
17 Matt. 28:16-17.
18 Luke 24:13-16.

19 Luke 24:25-31.
20 John 20:14-15.
21 John 21:1-7, 14.
22 John 14:18-21.
23 John 14:22.
24 John 14:23-25.
25 Matt. 18:20.
26 1 John 4:8.
27 Some Answered Questions, page 104. Bahá'í Reference Library, available at: http://reference.bahai.org

Chapter 9

1 Ps. 51:11.
2 John 1:1-4.
3 Gen. 1:1-3.
4 Gleanings from the Writings of Bahá'u'lláh, selection XXVII, paragraph 4. Bahá'í Academics Resource Library, available at http://bahai-library.com
5 Heb. 12:24.
6 Matt. 28:19.
7 John 10:33.
8 Mark 12:29-33.
9 Mark 12:35-37.
10 Heb. 1:13.
11 John 10:32-33.
12 John 17:22.
13 John 10:34-36.
14 1 John 5:7.
15 John 14:9.
16 John 1:1.
17 Gleanings from the Writings of Bahá'u'lláh, selection XXVII, paragraph 4.
18 John 14:9.
19 John 10:30.
20 John 14:7.
21 John 8:58.
22 John 5:19.
23 John 14:10.
24 John 8:54.
25 John 14:28.
26 2 Pet. 1:21.
27 Mark 12:36.

28 1 Cor. 10:4.
29 John 1:1.
30 John 16:12.
31 John 14:7.
32 John 14:9.
33 Matt. 5:43-44.
34 Kitáb-i-Aqdas, paragraph 1, p. 19.

Chapter 10

1   Matt. 7:9-11.
2   Num. 14:19-20.
3   Ps. 78:32-38.
4   Luke 6:37.
5   Luke 11:4.
6   Matt. 12:11-12.
7   Matt. 5:18.
8   Matt. 5:19.
9   Matt. 7:1.
10 Mark 7:15.
11 Matt. 3:11.
12 Gal. 5:17.
13 Gal. 5:19-21.
14 James 1:14-15.
15 Some Answered Questions, page 119.
16 Rom. 8:5-8.
17 Some Answered Questions, page 119.
18 Some Answered Questions, page 126.
19 John 3:6.
20 John 8:11.
21 Some Answered Questions, p. 125.
22 John 6:63.
23 Heb. 5:12.
24 Heb. 6:10.
25 Heb. 10:32-33.
26 Heb. 4:2.
27 Heb. 6:4-6.
28 Heb. 10:38.
29 Heb. 1:1-3.
30 Heb. 3:1-2.
31 Lev. 17:11.

32   Heb. 9:13-14.
33   Heb. 10:16-17.
34   Gleanings from the Writings of Bahá'u'lláh, selection XXXVI, p. 85-86.
35   Gleanings from the Writings of Bahá'u'lláh, selection XXXII, p. 75-76.
36   Matt. 26:39.
37   Some Answered Questions, p. 12-13.
38   Gen. 18:23-33.

Chapter 11

1   Isa. 2:2-4.
2   Isa. 11:6-9.
3   Isa. 35:1-2.
4   Message read on behalf of the Dalai Lama at the Millennium World Peace Summit of Religious and Spiritual Leaders, August 31, 2000, quoted by permission of the World Tibet Network News. Available at http://www.tibet.ca/wtnarchive/2000/8/31_1.html.
5   To the World's Religious Leaders. The Universal House of Justice. 2002. Available at http://www.uga.edu/~bahai/wrldldrs.html.

INDEX

A

'Abdu'l-Bahá
  understanding of sin 129, 132
Abraham
  and story of Sodom 157
  Bahá'í Writings on trials of 136
  children of 71, 92
  historical context of 11, 25
  inheritance of 11
  introduction of monotheism by 11
  story of 13-24
Acts
  attitude of Paul portrayed in 63
  chapter 13
    Paul invited to speak in synagogue 45
  confirming role of Paul 52
  on Peter visiting Temple 52
  references to Holy Spirit 109
acts of aggression against
  Paul 55
  Peter 55
Adam and original sin 121
administration of Mosaic Law 25
adoption
  of doctrine of Trinity 115
  of Old Testament by Christians 49

adulteress
  and Jesus 55
advent of Jesus in Hebrew Bible 76
afterlife 107
  and doctrine of soul 93
  and Jewish concept of soul 94
  belief in 97
  Christian concept of 97
  Christian doctrine of 94
  Jesus speaking of 95
  Jewish view of 92
  media depiction of 96
  modern understanding of 96
  Old Testament references to 92
  Pharisaic doctrine of 94
  spiritual 107
  this worldly concept of 93
Alexander the Great 30, 94
Alexandria 7, 32, 41
Andrew
  calling of 101
animal sacrifice 14, 27, 34, 125, 130
  in Judaism 125
  Mosaic Law on 38
anointing 26
antichrist 60
Antiochus 30, 37

apocalyptic prophet
  Jesus as 140
apocalypticism 31
  Jewish 81
apostasy
  among Jewish-Christians 64
  dangers of 130
  in Book of Hebrews 61
  in early church 60
Aquila and Priscilla 53
archaeological dating of advent of
    Moses 14
archaeological site
  of Masada 31
  of Nuzu 10
Arians 111
Ark of Covenant 14, 19, 26, 27
association of the church with the
    kingdom 86
Assyrians 29, 93
atonement
  for sin through high priest 125
  Jewish rite of 134
attendance
  of Jewish-Christians at synagogue 46
authoritative Christian Scripture 66
authority
  of history 8
  of Jesus established in Book of
    Hebrews 131
authors of New Testament 69
autonomy of synagogue 45

B

Babylonia 29, 38
background of baptism 126
Bahá'í community 148
Bahá'í Faith 6
  governing body of 146
  holy mountain of 145

on integration 148
  Prophet-Founder of 86
  teaching of progressive revelation 118
  vision of world community 148
Bahá'í Writings 15
  commentary on resurrection 105
  illustration on relationship of Trinity 114
  Manifestation of God in 25, 118
  on intermediary 110
  on Jesus as Manifestation of God 115
  on man's physical nature 127
  on nature of sin 128
  on progressive revelation 23
  on three levels of existence 115
  on trials of Abraham 136
  Prophets in 25
Bahá'u'lláh
  concept of kingdom 86
  on nature of Manifestation of God 115
  on sacrifice of Manifestations 136
  on truth in religions 146
  perspective of sacrifice of Jesus 135
ban of Christianity from synagogue 46
baptism
  background of 126
  Christian 126
  in first century 125
Bar Kochba 56, 58, 119
  as Messiah 35, 57, 82
belief
  in afterlife 97
  in soul 18
Birkat-ha-Minim 46
blood
  reference to in Book of Hebrews 132
Book of Hebrews
  apostasy in 61
  concept of intermediary in 110
  expiation of sin in 130
  historical context 130
  on authority of Jesus 131

on expiation of sin 132
on forgiveness 134
on sacrifice of Jesus 132
reference
    to blood 132
    to dangers of apostasy 130
    response to Jewish opposition 130
brother of Jesus
    James 46, 52, 79
building of Temple 27
burning of Rome 58

C

calling of disciples 102
Canaan 11, 122
    Hebrew settlement in 25, 26
canon
    question of 67
    selection as 68
Capernaum 42
cause of sin 126
central issue of Mission of Jesus 142
challenges
    at present to Christianity 149
    faced by gentile Christians 53
    faced by Jewish-Christians 55
    of Jewish orthodoxy 55
    of liberality 54
characteristics of house church 53
children of Abraham 71, 92
Christian adoption of Old Testament 49
Christian authors
    citing of Hebrew Scripture 76
    reference to Holy Spirit 117
Christian baptism 126
Christian canon
    limits of 70
Christian civilization 21, 54
Christian concept
    of afterlife 97

of Holy Spirit 109
of kingdom 84, 85
of Scripture 49
Christian doctrine
    in contrast with Jewish 91, 133
    of afterlife 94
    of Holy Spirit 118
    of salvation 134
    on forgiveness 121
    spiritual life in 94
Christian literature
    late first century 64
    second century 65
Christian love 54, 105, 106
Christian response to kingdom 83
Christian Scripture 43, 49
    authoritative 66
    development of 66
    early years of 80
Christian theologians in second century 89
Christian view of destruction of Temple 46
Christian vocabulary about the soul 98
Christian worship in early years 53
Christianity
    and Hebrew Bible 50, 117
    and Roman oppression 58
    and situation in first century Palestine 64
    apostasy in early years of 60
    as minority 57, 71
    banned from synagogue 46
    church orthodoxy in 142
    common ground with Judaism 140, 143
    conversion to 52
    early years of 21, 34, 65
    early years of:intellectual
        leadership of 70
    Ebonite sect of 50
    future of 143
    gentile 52
        challenges faced by 53
    Greco-Roman 54

historical context of 23
Jewish heritage of early 50
mystical elements of 50
origins of 23, 43
pagan influence on early 54
persecution of 58
present challenges to 149
reversion to Jewish doctrine 142
role of 148
social pressure on in early years 58
split with Judaism 46
Christian-Jewish debate 47
Christology 72, 119, 120, 131
of Gospel of John 120
of John 120
church
and science 139
and state 27
association with kingdom 86
crisis in 106, 149
debate on nature of Jesus 115
end of Jewish-Christian 65
expansion of gentile 64
gentile 62, 63
in Corinth 50
in first century 86, 139
in Middle Ages 139
in Palestine 59, 62, 64
integration with other religions 149
Jewish-Christian 51, 52, 57, 61
Jewish heritage of early 50
of Jerusalem 52, 62, 69
orthodoxy of Christian 143
pagan influence in early years 54
problems facing Jewish-Christian 71
role of Peter in 86
circumcision 61, 63, 65
civilization
Christian 21, 54
clash between Jesus and Jewish
orthodoxy 98

coming to terms with Jesus 6
commentary on resurrection from Bahá'í
Writings 105
common ground between Judaism and
Christianity 143
concept
held by Christians
of afterlife 97
of Holy Spirit 109
of kingdom 84, 85
of Scripture 49
held by Jews
of expiation of sin 133, 141
of intermediary 110
of kingdom 82, 85, 88, 90
of resurrection 94, 106
of sin 123, 126
of soul 19, 92
of soul and its relation to afterlife 94
of spirit 20, 108
of state and religion 28
of the spiritual 19
of intermediary in Book of Hebrews 110
of soul introduced by Jesus 20
conformity to Mosaic Law 32
Constantine 21, 87, 111
context of Jesus 9
contradiction regarding resurrection of
Jesus 106
contrast
between Temple and synagogue 42
of Christian and Jewish
doctrine 91, 133
of Jewish-Christian and gentile
churches 62
contribution of Luke to gentile
Christianity 52
conversion to Christianity 52
Copernicus 139
Corinth
church in 50

Corinthians
First Epistle of Paul to 50
council of apostles 63
Council of Nicaea 115
creation story
rewriting by John 110
crisis in church 106, 149
Cyrus 29

D

daily life of Hebrews 15
Dalai Lama's message 146
dangers of apostasy 130
Darwin 2, 128, 139
David
aspiration to kingship 26
historical role of 27
kingdom of 28, 36, 81
monarchy of 35
Dead Sea Scrolls 7, 32
destruction
of Sodom 137
of Temple 29, 33, 73, 82
of Temple: Christian view of 46
development
of Christian Scripture 66
of Law 14
of synagogue 50
Dialogue with Trypho 47
Diaspora 29, 41, 45
disciples
calling of 102
portrayal by Mark 77
recognition of Jesus 103
divisions among religions 146
Docetists 61
doctrine
Christian reversion to Jewish 142
contrast of Christian and Jewish 91,
133

held by Christians
of afterlife 94
of Holy Spirit 118
of salvation 134
on forgiveness 121
Jewish 142
misunderstanding of
New Testament 90
of expiation of sin 130
of Holy Spirit according to Jesus 116
of Jesus on the soul 93
of sin according to Paul 128
of soul
implications for afterlife 93
of Trinity
adoption of 115
spiritual life in Christian 94
dual monarchy 28
dual status of Jerusalem 27

E

early Christianity 21, 34, 65
and kingdom 83
intellectual leadership of 70
Scripture of 66
social pressure on 58
use of Jewish vocabulary 141
worship 53
early diversity of Judaism 35
Ebonite sect of Christianity 50
Elijah 97
entry of Jesus into Jerusalem 77
Epistle
of Paul to Galatians 63
of Paul to Romans 127
of Peter 76
Epistles of Paul 68, 71
essence of Mission of Jesus 141
Essenes 31
passivity of 33

eternal life
  ambiguity in Talmud 94
  Old Testament concepts of 92
ethics 22
  in context of religion 15
Eucharist 21, 54, 88, 142
evolution of New Testament 66
expansion of gentile church 64
expiation of sin 76, 132
  doctrine of 130
  in Book of Hebrews 130, 132
  Jewish concept of 133, 141
Ezra 37

F

fall of Jerusalem 56
fanaticism
  modern religious 146
  of Zealots 56
Fertile Crescent 11
first century
  baptism in 125
  church in 86, 139
  context of New Testament in 81
  Palestine in 72
  situation in Palestine 64
First Epistle
  of John 60
  of Paul to Corinthians 50
forgiveness
  by God 122
  Christian doctrine on 121
  in Book of Hebrews 134
  in Old Testament 125
foundations of gentile Christianity 52
Founders of religions 6, 118
Fourth Philosophy
  Zealots 33
freedom from Jewish orthodoxy 66
Freud 21, 139

function
  of priestly class 41
  of synagogue 39
fund-raising by Paul 64
future of Christianity 143

G

Galatians
  Epistle of Paul to 63
Galileo 139
Gandhi 134
Gemarah 14
gentiles
  Paul's conversion of 52
  tension with Jewish-Christians 62
gentile Christianity 52
  challenges faced by 53
  foundations of 52
  Luke's contribution to 52
gentile church 62, 63
  contrast with Jewish-Christian
    church 62
God
  forgiveness of 122
  intervention in history 28, 140
Golden Age of Israel 27
Good Samaritan
  parable of 69
Gospel
  of John 74
    Christology of 120
    distinction of 75
    role of 120
  of Luke 69, 83, 88
    24th chapter of 102
    Jesus in synagogue in 40
  of Mark 73, 77, 91
    on resurrection 97
    visit of Jesus to Temple 111
  of Matthew 73

of Thomas 68
spread by Paul 45, 63
Gospels 65, 71, 80
 approach to 9
 on eternal soul 95
 on purification 126, 133
 on resurrection 106
 origins of 74
 political environment of 73
 presentation of Holy Spirit 108
 references to Old Testament in 76
 representation of kingdom 89
 timing of writing 63
 vision of kingdom in 87
governing body of Bahá'í Faith 146

H

Hanukkah 37
Hasmoneans 30, 37
 kingdom of 31
Hebrew Bible 39, 49, 68, 77
 and advent of Jesus 76
 and Christianity 50, 117
 as focus of synagogue service 41
 on monarchy 25
Hebrew Scripture
 citing by Christian authors 76
 Jewish attitude to 49
 uniqueness of 49
Hebrews
 daily life of 15
 settlement in Canaan 25, 26
 tribal structure of 14
Herod 31, 37, 55
high priest
 as intermediary 110, 131
 atonement for sin 125
 role of 131
historical context
 New Testament in 119

of Abraham 11, 25
of Book of Hebrews 130
of Christianity 23
of Jesus 6, 25, 140
of Moses 25
historical Jesus 78, 79, 143
historical role of David 27
history
 as authority 8
 intervention of God in 28, 140
 Jewish view of own 40
 of Jewish-Christians 22
holy mountain of Bahá'í Faith 145
Holy Spirit 120
 Christian concept of 109
 Christian doctrine of 118
 Jesus' doctrine of 116
 New Testament references to 109, 116
 permanence of 109
 presented
  in Gospels 108
  in Old Testament 108
 references
  in Acts to 109
  of Christian authors to 117
house church
 characteristics of 53

I

illustration on relationship of Trinity
 from Bahá'í Writings 114
importance of Temple 37
impurity
 Mosaic Law on 125
inheritance of Abraham 11
integration
 Bahá'í Faith on 148
 of religions 149
intellectual leadership of early
 Christianity 70

interaction of Christians and Jews
  recorded in New Testament 43
intercession by Moses 122
intermediary
  Bahá'í Writings on 110
  Book of Hebrews concept of 110
  high priest as 110, 131
  Jesus as 131
  Jewish concept of 110
internal divisions of Judaism 30
introduction of monotheism 13
Irenaeus 89
Israel
  Golden Age of 37
  lost tribes of 29

J

Jacob
  sons of 14
  stone pillow of 4
James, brother of Jesus 46, 52, 79
Jeremiah 133
Jerusalem 27
  as mother church 63, 69
  as spiritual center 27
  church of 52, 62, 69
  dual status of 27
  entry of Jesus into 77
  fall of 56
  Temple in 39
Jesus
  adoption of Jewish vocabulary 89, 99
  advent in Hebrew Bible 76
  and adulteress 55
  and Peter after resurrection 103
  as apocalyptic prophet 140
  as intermediary 131
  as Manifestation of God in Bahá'í
    Writings 115
  as Messiah 51, 60, 69, 83, 131

authority of established in Book of
  Hebrews 131
Bahá'u'lláh's perspective of sacrifice of 135
Book of Hebrews on sacrifice of 132
central issue of Mission of 90, 142
clash with Jewish orthodoxy 98
coming to terms with 6
concept of soul 20
confrontation with Pharisees 83, 85
context of 9
contradiction regarding resurrection of
  100-106
contrasted with Judaism 75
debate within church on nature of 115
doctrine
  of Holy Spirit 116
  of soul 93
entry into Jerusalem 77
essence of Mission of 141
historical 143
  and Paul 78
historical context of 6, 25, 140
in synagogue
  in Gospel of Luke 40
James, brother of 46, 52, 79
Jewish background of 8
kingdom of 90, 91
martyrdom of 134
Message of 23, 24, 74, 97
Mission of 21, 90, 108, 121, 126
monotheism of 111
oral traditions of 68
recognition by disciples 103
regarding Law 123
relation to monotheism 111
relationship to Judaism 23
resurrection of 100, 104, 106
role of 16, 19
sacrifice of 76, 121, 130, 134
  in Book of Hebrews 132
speaking of afterlife 95

spirituality of 24
station of 112
transcendence of 140
view of kingdom 87
vision of spirit 20
visit to Temple, according to Gospel of
    Mark 111
within Jewish context 69
Jewish apocalypticism 81
Jewish attitude to Hebrew Scripture 49
Jewish background of Jesus 8
Jewish concept
    of expiation of sin 133, 141
    of intermediary 110
    of kingdom 82, 85, 88, 90
    of resurrection 94, 106
    of sin 123, 126
    of soul 19, 92
    of soul and relation to afterlife 94
    of spirit 20, 108
    of spiritual 19
    of state and religion 28
Jewish context
    Jesus within 69
Jewish distrust of spiritual 21
Jewish doctrine 142
    Christian reversion to 142
    in contrast with Christian 91, 133
Jewish expectations of Messiah 55
Jewish heritage of early church 50
Jewish influence on Paul 69
Jewish insight of Luke 69
Jewish monarchy 25
Jewish monotheism 112
Jewish moral standard 128
Jewish nationalism 55, 59, 119
Jewish opposition
    Book of Hebrews response to 130
Jewish oppression
    by Romans 55
Jewish orthodoxy 61, 72, 79

challenges of 55
clash with Jesus 98
freedom from 66
view of Law 124
Jewish revolt
    against Rome 35, 55
    against Seleucids 30
Jewish rite of atonement 134
Jewish roots 36
Jewish Scripture 39
Jewish sects 32
Jewish sites
    archaeological excavations of, in Palestine
        125
Jewish view
    of afterlife 92
    of Messiah 26, 35, 79, 81
    of Moses 118
    of own history 40
    of parable of Good Samaritan 69
    of Prophets 72, 109
    of Samaritans 70
Jewish viewpoint of Matthew 69
Jewish vocabulary 72
    early church use of 141
    Jesus' adoption of 89, 99
    of kingdom 99
Jewish-Christian audience of the New
    Testament 77
Jewish-Christian church 51, 52, 57, 61
    contrast with gentile church 62
    end of 65
    problems facing 71
Jewish-Christian debate 47
Jewish-Christians 51
    addressed by Mark 78
    apostasy among 64
    as minority 57
    attendance at synagogue 45, 51
    challenges faced by 55
    history of 22

influence on New Testament 69
persecution of 64, 130
social pressure on 64
tension with gentiles 62
John
  as author 104
  Christology of 120
  distinction of Gospel of 75
  environment of 74
  First Epistle of 60
  Gospel of 74
  on resurrection 102, 105
  portrayal of Nicodemus 98
  rewriting of creation story 110
  role of Gospel of 120
  story of Lazarus 99
Josephus 7, 31, 33, 34, 52, 56, 94
Judaism
  animal sacrifice in 125
  common ground with Christianity 140,
    143
  contrasted with Jesus 75
  early diversity of 35
  focus
    on synagogue 42
    on Temple 42
  internal divisions of 30
  reasons for studying 8
  relationship
    to Jesus 23
    to origins of Christianity 23
  split with Christianity 46
judges 25
Justin Martyr 47, 89

K

kingdom
  and early Christianity 83
  association with church 86
  Bahá' u'lláh's concept of 86

Christian concept of 84, 85
Christian response to 83
common element of three traditions 143
critical questions relative to 82
Gospel vision of 87
Jesus' view of 87
Jewish concept of 82, 85, 88, 90
Jewish vocabulary of 99
material 81, 88, 89, 107
of David 28, 36, 81
of Hasmoneans 31
of Jesus 90, 91
of Solomon 28
Old Testament vision of 85
Paul's spiritual view of 85
representation in Gospels 89
spiritual 82, 84, 86, 90
universal 87
worldly 87
Kofi Annan 146

L

Law
  administration of Mosaic 25
  development of 14
  Jesus regarding 123
  Jewish orthodox view of 124
  Mosaic 15
  of Sabbath 123
  on sin 123
  Pharisaic view of 126
  revelation of 13
  stance of Matthew on 124
  study of 33, 41
  Tablets of 14, 19, 27
Lazarus
  John's story of 99
liberality
  challenges of 54
life after death. See afterlife

limbo 122
literature
  late first century Christian 64
  second century Christian 65
lost tribes of Israel 29
love
  Christian 54, 105, 106
Luke 69
  as historian of Paul 63
  contribution to gentile Christianity 52
  Gospel of 83, 88
    24th chapter 102
  Jewish insight of 69
  on Jesus in synagogue 40
  portayal of Paul 63
Luther 142

M

man's physical nature
  Bahá'í Writings on 127
Manifestation of God 119
  Bahá'u'lláh on sacrifice of 136
  in Bahá'í Writings 25, 118
  Jesus as 115
  Mission of 87
  nature of in Writings of Bahá'u'lláh 115
  sacrifice of 137
Mark 69
  addressing Jewish-Christians 78
  Gospel of 73, 77, 91
  on resurrection 97
  on visit of Jesus to Temple 111
  parable of sower 85
  portrayal of the disciples 77
Martin Luther King 134
martyrdom 134
  of Jesus 134
  of Stephen 55
Masada, archaeological site 31
material kingdom 81, 88, 89, 107

Mattathias 30
Matthew
  Gospel of 73
  Jewish viewpoint of 69
  on entry of Jesus into Jerusalem 77
  stance on Law 124
  version of calling of Simon and Andrew
    101
meaning of redemption 123
meaning of spiritual 18
meeting place
  synagogue as 43
message of Dalai Lama 146
Message of Jesus 23, 24, 74, 97
Messengers and Prophets 22
Messiah
  Bar Kochba as 35, 57, 82
  Jesus as 51, 60, 69, 83, 131
  Jewish expectations of 55
  Jewish view of 26, 35, 79, 81
  Pharisaic view of 93
Middle Ages
  church in 139
Midwest religion 2
Millennium World Peace Summit 146
minority
  Christianity as 57, 71
  Jewish-Christians as 57
Mishnah 14
Mission
  of Jesus 21, 90, 108, 121, 126
    central issue of 90, 142
    essence of 141
  of Manifestation of God 87
missionary journeys of Paul 52
misunderstanding of New Testament
    doctrine 90
modern religious fanaticism 146
modern understanding of afterlife 96
monarchy
  Davidic 35

dual 28
in Hebrew Bible 25
Jewish 25
Old Testament view of 26
monotheism 22, 110
importance of 13
introduction of 13
by Abraham 11
Jewish 112
of Jesus 111
relation of Jesus to 111
moral standard
Jewish 128
Mosaic Law 15
administration of 25
conformity to 32
on animal sacrifice 38
on impurity 125
on occult 19
on witchcraft 19
Moses
archaeological dating of advent of 14
historical context of 25
intercession by 122
Jewish view of 118
role of 13
mother church
Jerusalem as 63, 69
Mount Carmel 145
Mount Gerizim 29, 38
mystical elements of Christianity 50

N

nationalism
in twentieth century 146
Jewish 55, 59, 119
nature
of Jesus
debate within church on 115
of Manifestation of God

Bahá'u'lláh on 115
of sin in Bahá'í Writings 128
of spirit 18
Nazareth 42
Nebuchadnezzar 29
Nehemiah 37
Nero 58
Newton 139
New Testament
authors 69
evolution of 66
in first century context 81
in historical context 119
Jewish-Christian audience of 77
Jewish-Christian influence on 69
misunderstanding of doctrine of 90
on interaction of Christians and Jews 43
references
to Holy Spirit 109, 116
to synagogue 41
scholarly approach to 8
view of sin 121, 126
next step in progressive revelation 144
Nicodemus portrayed by John 98
Nuzu archaeological site 10

O

occult 21
Mosaic Law on 19
Old Testament
Christian adoption of 49
concepts of eternal life 92
forgiveness in 125
on soul 19
presentation of Holy Spirit 108
prophecies in 87, 144
references to
afterlife 92
in Gospels 76
resurrection 93

view of monarchy 26
vision of kingdom 85
oral traditions of Jesus 68
Origen 89
original sin 121
origins
  of Christianity 43
    and relationship to Judaism 23
  of Gospels 74
  of synagogue 38
  of Christianity 23
orthodoxy
  challenges of Jewish 55
  freedom from Jewish 66
  Jewish 61, 72, 79
    clash with Jesus 98
    view of Law 124
  of Christian church 143
  of Sadducees 96
overcoming prejudice
  progress made in 146

P

pagan influence on early Christianity 54
pagan religion 50
Palestine
  archaeological excavations of Jewish
    sites in 125
  church in 59, 62, 64
  in first century 64, 72
  return to 29, 38
Palm Sunday 77
parable
  of Good Samaritan 69
  of sower 84
    Mark's versions 85
Paul
  acts of aggression against 55
  and historical Jesus 78
  Epistles of 68, 71

Epistle to Galatians 63
Epistle to Romans 127
fund-raising by 64
his conversion of gentiles 52
invited to speak in synagogue 45
Jewish influence on 69
Luke as historian of 63
missionary journeys of 52
on sins of the flesh 127
raised as Pharisee 33
role confirmed in Acts 52
spiritual view of kingdom 85
spreading Gospel 45, 63
use of Hebrew Scripture 76
persecution
  of Christianity 58
  of Jewish-Christians 64, 130
Peter
  acts of agression against 55
  and Jesus after resurrection 103
  Epistle of 76
  use of Hebrew Scripture 76
  visiting Temple 52
Pharisaic Judaism 34
Pharisees 33
  belief in resurrection 92, 96
  confrontation with Jesus 83, 85
  doctrine of afterlife 94
  influence of 34
  view of Law 126
  view of Messiah 93
Philemon 53
Philip
  calling of 101
Philistines 26
Philo 7
physical nature of man
  Bahá'í Writings on 127
physical resurrection 33, 96, 104, 141
Plato's concept of the eternal soul 94
political environment of Gospels 73

polytheism
   limitations of 12
prejudice
   progress made in overcoming 146
present challenges to Christianity 149
priestly class 42
   function of 41
progressive revelation 23, 87, 90, 118,
      119, 136
   Bahá'í Faith's teaching of 118
   Bahá'í Writings on 23
   essential truths of 146
   next step in 144
   prophecies of Old Testament 87, 144
prophecy
   use of 77
Prophet-Founder of Bahá'í Faith 86
Prophets
   and Holy Spirit 120
   and Messengers 22
   in Bahá'í Writings on 25
   Jewish view of 72, 109
   role of 16
purification
   in Gospels 126, 133
   of sin 125
   of Temple 37
   rites of 32, 50, 78, 125, 126

Q

questions relative to kingdom 82
Qumran colony 31
Qumran sect 37
Qumran writings 92

R

rabbinic Judaism 33, 119
   early view of soul 19
rebuilding of Temple 29

recognition of Jesus by disciples 103
redemption 138
   from sin 125
   meaning of 123
relationship
   between Jesus and Judaism 23
   of Judaism to Christianity 23
relation of Christ to monotheism 111
religion
   and state
      Jewish concept of 28
   ethics in context of 15
   focus on rituals 15
   in Midwest 2
   pagan 50
   study of 139
religions
   Bahá'u'lláh on truth in other 146
   divisions among 146
   Founders of 6, 118
   integration of 149
   unity of 13
religious fanaticism
   modern 146
representation of the kingdom in the
      Gospels 89
response to Jewish opposition
   of Book of Hebrews 130
resurrection 92
   Bahá'í Writings' commentary on 105
   in Gospels 106
   in Gospel of Mark 97
   Jewish concept of 94, 106
   nonbelief of Sadducees in 96
   of Jesus 100, 104, 106
      contradiction regarding 106
      Peter after 103
   of Lazarus 99
   Old Testament references to 93
   Pharisaic belief in 92, 96
   physical 33, 96, 104, 141

writing of John on 102, 105
return to Palestine 29, 38
revelation
  of Law 13
  progressive 23, 87, 90, 118, 119, 136,
    144, 146
revolt
  Jewish against Rome 35, 55
  Jewish against Seleucids 30
rite of atonement 125
  Jewish 134
rites of purification 32, 50, 78, 125, 126
rituals
  in Temple 34, 38
  religious focus on 15
role
  of Christianity 148
  of Gospel of John 120
  of high priest 131
  of Jesus 16, 19
  of Moses 13
  of Paul confirmed in Acts 52
  of Peter in church 86
  of Prophets 16
Romans
  Epistle of Paul to 127
Roman oppression
  of Christianity 58
  of Jews 55
Rome
  burning of 58
  Jewish revolt against 35
roots of Judaism 36

S

Sabbath
  Law of 123
sacrifice 138
  in Temple 42
  of animals 14, 27, 34, 125, 130

stipulated by Mosaic Law 38
of Jesus 76, 121, 130, 134
  Bahá'u'lláh's perspective of 135
  in Book of Hebrews 132
of Manifestation of God 137
  Bahá'u'lláh on 136
Sadducees 33
  nonbelief in resurrection 96
  orthodoxy of 96
Saint Augustine 65, 89
salvation
  Christian doctrine of 134
  of soul 121
Samaritans 29, 38
  Jewish view of 70
Sanhedrin 37, 63
Saul 26
scholarly approach to New Testament 8
science and the church 139
Scripture
  authoritative Christian 66
  Christian 43, 49
  Christian authors citing Hebrew 76
  Christian concept of 49
  development of Christian 66
  early years of Christian 66
  Hebrew 49
  Jewish 39
second century
  Christian literature 65
  Christian theologians 89
sects of Jews 32
Seleucids
  Jewish revolt against 30
settlement of Hebrews in Canaan 25, 26
sexuality 127
Shekinah 109
Sheol 92
Simon
  calling of 101
sin 121-138

'Abdu'l-Bahá's understanding of 129, 132
atonement for through high priest 125
cause of 126
expiation of 76, 132
   in Book of Hebrews 130, 132
   Jewish concept of 133, 141
Jewish concept of 123, 126
Law on 123
meaning of 123
New Testament view of 121, 126
of flesh 127
original 121
purification of 125
redemption from 123, 125
social pressure
  on early Christians 58
  on Jewish-Christians 64
Sodom
  destruction of 137
Solomon 27
  kingdom of 28
  Temple of 37
sons of Jacob 14
soul
  afterlife and doctrine of 93
  belief in 18
  Christian vocabulary about 98
  concept of Plato of 94
  doctrine of Jesus on 93
  early rabbinic view of 19
  in Gospels 95
  in Old Testament 19
  in Talmud 94
  Jesus' concept of 20
  Jewish concept of 19, 92
  Jewish concept of
    and relation to afterlife 94
  salvation of 121
sower
  parable of 84

spirit 92
  Jesus' vision of 20
  Jewish concept of 20, 108
  nature of 18
spiritual
  Jewish concept of 19
  Jewish distrust of 21
  meaning of 18
spiritual afterlife 107
spiritual center
  Jerusalem as 27
spiritual kingdom 82, 84, 86, 90
  Paul's view of 85
spiritual life in Christian doctrine 94
spiritual transformation 106
spirituality 22
  of Jesus 24
split between Judaism and Christianity 46
state and religion 27
  Jewish concept of 28
station of Jesus 112
Stephen
  martyrdom of 55
stone pillow of Jacob 4
structure of Gospels 74
study
  of Judaism
    reasons for 8
  of Law 33, 41
  of religion 139
  of Torah 34, 40
  synagogue as center of 40
synagogue
  as center of study 40
  as meeting place 43
  as sole focus of Judaism 42
  autonomy of 45
  Christianity banned from 46
  contrast with Temple 42
  development of 50

function of 39
Hebrew Bible as focus of service 41
Jesus in 40
Jewish-Christian attendance at 45, 51
New Testament reference to 41
origins of 38
Paul invited to speak in 45
role in study of Torah 40
Torah in 49

T

tabernacle as a model for Temple 14
Tablets of Law 14, 19, 27
Talmud 14, 34
   ambiguity about eternal life 94
   eternal soul in 94
Temple
   as focus of Judaism 42
   building of 27
   Christian view of destruction of 46
   contrast with synagogue 42
   destruction of 29, 33, 46, 73, 82
   importance of 37
   in Jerusalem 39
   of Solomon 37
   Peter visiting 52
   purification of 37
   rebuilding of 29
   reestablished 37
   rituals in 34, 38
   sacrifice in 42
   tabernacle as a model for 14
   visit of Jesus to 111
Ten Commandments 14
tension between gentile and Jewish-
      Christians 62
this worldly concept of afterlife 93
Thomas
   Gospel of 68

Titus 39, 46, 56
Torah
   focus on 40
   in synagogue 49
   redemption from sin in 125
   study of 34, 40
transcendence of Jesus 140
transformation
   spiritual 106
trials of Abraham
   Bahá'í Writings on 136
tribal structure of Hebrews 14
Trinity
   adoption of doctrine of 115
   Bahá'í Writings illustration on
      relationship of 114
truth in religions
   Bahá'u'lláh on 146
twentieth century nationalism 146

U

uniqueness of Hebrew Scripture 49
unity of religions 13
Universal House of Justice
   governing body of Bahá'í Faith 146
universal kingdom 87
use of prophecy 77

V

Vespasian 56
view of sin in New Testament 121, 126
vision
   held by Bahá'í Faith of world
      community 148
   of kingdom in Gospels 87
vocabulary
   Christian about soul 98
   early church use of Jewish 141

Jesus' adoption of Jewish 89, 99
Jewish 72

W

witchcraft
  Mosaic Law on 19
worldly kingdom 87
world community
  Bahá'í Faith's vision of 148

Y

YHWH 112

Z

Zealots 56
  fanaticism of 56
  Fourth Philosophy 33